Formless Infinity

MW00775276

In contemporary psychoanalysis, a key concept and aim of clinical practice is to distinguish the boundaries of any mental state. Without this boundary-setting, the patient has nothing but the 'formless infinite' of primitive mental states. *Formless Infinity: Clinical Explorations of Matte Blanco and Bion* draws on the work of these two authors to explore how analysts can work with patients to reveal, understand and ultimately contain their primitive mental states.

Riccardo Lombardi discusses the core concepts of the unconscious, the role of the body in analysis, time and death. He displays the clinical implications of Matte Blanco's theoretical extension of Freud's theory of the unconscious, presenting numerous clinical examples of working with psychosis and other severe pathologies.

Formless Infinity, a stimulating teaching text for students, trainers and seasoned mental health practitioners, is essential reading for psychoanalysts and psychoanalytic psychotherapists. It is particularly recommended to analysts interested in widening the scope of the analytic practice by exploring the functioning of the deep unconscious, primitive mental states, psychosomatic pathologies and psychotic conditions.

Riccardo Lombardi is a psychoanalyst, psychiatrist and doctor of medicine. He has a full-time private practice in Rome and teaches at the Roman Psychoanalytic Institute of the International Psychoanalytic Association (IPA). He is a Training and Supervising Analyst at the Italian Psychoanalytic Society.

THE NEW LIBRARY OF PSYCHOANALYSIS
General Editor: Alessandra Lemma

The New Library of Psychoanalysis was launched in 1987 in association with the Institute of Psychoanalysis, London. It took over from the International Psychoanalytical Library which published many of the early translations of the works of Freud and the writings of most of the leading British and Continental psychoanalysts.

The purpose of the New Library of Psychoanalysis is to facilitate a greater and more widespread appreciation of psychoanalysis and to provide a forum for increasing mutual understanding between psychoanalysts and those working in other disciplines such as the social sciences, medicine, philosophy, history, linguistics, literature and the arts. It aims to represent different trends both in British psychoanalysis and in psychoanalysis generally. The New Library of Psychoanalysis is well placed to make available to the English-speaking world psychoanalytic writings from other European countries and to increase the interchange of ideas between British and American psychoanalysts. Through the *Teaching Series*, the New Library of Psychoanalysis now also publishes books that provide comprehensive, yet accessible, overviews of selected subject areas aimed at those studying psychoanalysis and related fields such as the social sciences, philosophy, literature and the arts.

The Institute, together with the British Psychoanalytical Society, runs a low-fee psychoanalytic clinic, organizes lectures and scientific events concerned with psychoanalysis and publishes the *International Journal of Psychoanalysis*. It runs the a training course in psychoanalysis which leads to membership of the International Psychoanalytical Association – the body which preserves internationally agreed standards of training, of professional entry, and of professional ethics and practice for psychoanalysis as initiated and developed by Sigmund Freud. Distinguished members of the Institute have included Michael Balint, Wilfred Bion, Ronald Fairbairn, Anna Freud, Ernest Jones, Melanie Klein, John Rickman and Donald Winnicott.

Previous general editors have included David Tuckett, who played a very active role in the establishment of the New Library. He was followed as general editor by Elizabeth Bott Spillius, who was in turn followed by Susan Budd and then by Dana Birksted-Breen.

TITLES IN THIS SERIES

TITLES IN THE NEW LIBRARY OF PSYCHOANALYSIS TEACHING SERIES

Formless Infinity

Clinical Explorations of Matte Blanco and Bion

Riccardo Lombardi

Translated by Karen Christenfeld, Gina Atkinson, Andrea Sabbadini and Philip Slotkin

Routledge
Taylor & Francis Group
LONDON AND NEW YORK

First published 2016
by Routledge
27 Church Road, Hove, East Sussex, BN3 2FA

And by Routledge
711 Third Avenue, New York, NY 10017

Routledge is an imprint of the Taylor & Francis Group, an informa business

British Library Cataloguing-in-Publication Data
A catalogue record for this book is available from the British Library

Library of Congress Cataloging in Publication Data
Lombardi, Riccardo (Psychoanalyst)
  Formless infinity : clinical explorations of Matte Blanco and Bion /
Riccardo Lombardi.
    pages cm. — (The new library of psychoanalysis)
  1. Medicine, Psychosomatic. 2. Mind and body. I. Title.
  RC49.L56 2016
  616.08—dc23   2015008191

ISBN: 978-1-138-01856-3 (hbk)
ISBN: 978-1-138-01858-7 (pbk)
ISBN: 978-1-315-67975-4 (ebk)

Typeset in Bembo
by Apex CoVantage, LLC

Contents

Permission acknowledgements

Chapter 1 was previously published as Bria, P., & Lombardi, R. (2008). The logic of turmoil: some epistemological and clinical considerations on emotional experience and the infinite. *International Journal of Psychoanalysis*, 89: 709–726. Reprinted by permission of Wiley-Blackwell.

Chapter 2 was previously published as Lombardi, R. (2009). Symmetric frenzy and catastrophic change: a consideration of primitive mental states in the wake of Bion and Matte Blanco. *International Journal of Psychoanalysis*, 90: 529–549. Reprinted by permission of Wiley-Blackwell.

Chapter 3 was previously published as Lombardi, R. (2009). Through the eye of the needle: the unfolding of the unconscious body. *Journal of the American Psychoanalytic Association*, 57: 61–94. Reprinted by permission of Sage.

Chapter 4 was previously published as Lombardi, R. (2010). The body emerging from the "neverland" of nothingness. *Psychoanalytic Quarterly*, 79: 879–909. Reprinted by permission of Wiley-Blackwell.

Chapter 5 was previously published as Lombardi, R., & Pola, M. (2010). The body, adolescence and psychosis. *International Journal of Psychoanalysis*, 91: 1419–1444. Reprinted by permission of Wiley-Blackwell.

Chapter 6 was previously published as Lombardi, R. (2003). Knowledge and experience of time in primitive mental states. *International Journal of Psychoanalysis*, 84: 1531–1549. Reprinted by permission of Wiley-Blackwell.

Eugenio Montale, Mottetti II, Le occasioni, 1928–39, reproduced with permission (© 1977 Arnoldo Mondadori Editore S.p.A., Milano I edizione novembre 1977 II edizione novembre 1979).

Chapter 7 was previously published as Lombardi, R. (2008). Time, music, and reverie. *Journal of the American Psychoanalytic Association*, 56: 1191–1211. Reprinted by permission of Sage.

Chapter 8 was previously published as Lombardi, R. (2010). Flexibility of the psychoanalytic approach in the treatment of a suicidal patient: stubborn silences as "playing dead". *Psychoanalytic Dialogues*, 20: 269–284. Reprinted by permission of Taylor & Francis.

Chapter 9 was previously published as Lombardi, R. (2013). Death, time and psychosis. *Journal of the American Psychoanalytic Association*, 57: 691–726. Reprinted by permission of Sage.

Preface

Riccardo Lombardi has written *Formless Infinity* in order to consider certain ideas of Bion's, to explicate and clarify concepts of Matte Blanco's that many colleagues have found difficult to understand – the *unrepressed Unconscious, symmetrical* and *asymmetrical* logic, the *generalization principle,* and *unfolding* – and to show how these can be usefully applied clinically. Lombardi's purpose is to use his discussion of Matte Blanco and Bion as a springboard for discussion of how effective psychoanalytic work with psychotic patients can be done, and to underline the richness of what is learned from an exploration of primitive mental states. He calls particular attention to the importance of bodily experience and the need for it to be addressed within the psychoanalytic encounter. He explores the utility of the concept of the infinite, and goes on to take up the recognition of life and of death as matters of importance in clinical psychoanalytic work. At every turn, Lombardi seeks to illustrate his theoretical discussion with vivid and compelling clinical examples.

In all of this, Lombardi is admirably successful. But his important contribution in this book goes even further.

Lombardi shows us how psychoanalytic theory, properly approached, is an open, constantly evolving project. Unhappily, psychoanalytic schools of thought have all too often congealed into closed systems, orthodoxies statically preserved in the name of maintaining standards. Lombardi, on the contrary, regards 'the psychoanalytic corpus as something one examines and questions, rather than the source of an organic system of answers'. This is a definition that should be posted in every psychoanalytic society.

Similarly, in his discussion of clinical topics, and in his evocative vignettes, Lombardi presents a model of personal flexibility, receptivity to the patient's contributions, and willingness to undertake reciprocal internal change – sometimes change requiring real courage on the analyst's part. Critics have indicted psychoanalysis as being not an authentic inquiry and an effective therapy, but rather a proselytizing effort in which the analyst invites the patient to find within himself or herself what the analyst already assumed a priori to exist. Lombardi provides the antidote.

From his experiences working with difficult to reach, sometimes catastrophically disturbed patients, Lombardi has drawn insights than can enliven every psychoanalytic treatment. He has recaptured the spirit of creative adventure that characterized psychoanalysis at its beginning, and which offers the only hope for its future.

By Owen Renik, M.D.

INTRODUCTION[1]

The infinite is the principle of all things . . . whence they have their origin, there too they pass away, as destiny will have it.

—Anaximander (c. 610–c. 546 BC)

This book brings together a variety of observations about the psychoanalysis of primitive mental states: it is primarily a clinical contribution derived from my own experience. As I continued to explore primitive mental states, I found myself wondering about a series of epistemological questions which led me to reflect on infinity and on the current need to expand our theoretical horizons in psychoanalysis.

The most important psychoanalytic contribution on Infinity was introduced by Ignacio Matte Blanco with his innovative studies on the unrepressed Unconscious. Wilfred Bion made also a relevant contribution to shift the psychoanalytic perspective from the repressed to the unrepressed Unconscious, but, since his theories are generally well know, I'll focus in this introduction mainly on Matte Blanco's. This perspective reformulates the discoveries of Sigmund Freud's repressed Unconscious in the light of the general logical functioning of the human mind: the emphasis shifts from the *contents* of the repressed Unconscious to the *form* that characterizes mental functioning, so that the Unconscious is seen in its unrepressed dimension as a mental structure. Psychic events thus reveal the contrast between *two different forms of logic*, the *asymmetrical* one that takes distinctions into account and the *symmetrical* one that obliterates them: this is the source of the definition of *bi-logic*. The consequences of this reformulation do not, obviously, concern logic alone, but also the analytic relationship and the way in which psychoanalytic technique is understood.

1

I am enduringly grateful for the time in which I studied with Matte Blanco at the Istituto di Psicoanalisi Romano, because of his ability to make one's experience of the Freudian heritage something creative, partly by highlighting the internal tensions and creative contradictions to be found in Freud's works: contradictions that Matte Blanco interpreted as an expression of the attempt to describe the multidimensionality that resists the restraints of logic and linear space-time. From his teaching I learned to regard the psychoanalytic corpus as something one examines and questions, rather than the source of an organic system of answers. In this sense Matte Blanco tended to foster individual thought, in contrast to a certain incorporative tendency (Searles 1951/1965) on the part of schools of psychoanalysis, whereby the psychoanalyst incorporates some part of the teaching of a school and becomes in his turn incorporated in it. Having encountered Freud's discoveries about the Unconscious and Melanie Klein's about the emotions of small children, Matte Blanco was attracted by the oscillation between the finite and the infinite to be found in descriptions by the great masters, which underscored the unceasing search for knowledge – together with the capacity to tolerate the unknown – that forms a part of the psychoanalytic exploration of one's inner world. Matte Blanco, like Winnicott, Bion and other original writers who have appeared throughout the history of psychoanalysis, are carriers of a strong spirit of independence in the face of knowledge, spurring the examination of new phenomena.

Since Matte Blanco's research has distinctly epistemological features and is essentially abstract, his contribution runs the risk of seeming undefined or even difficult to apply, particularly given the paucity of his clinical references.

My contribution does not pretend to be a systematic application of Matte Blanco's thinking, but is instead a study of my encounters with primitive mental states, which revealed an interesting correspondence with his perspective. For this reason, clinical experiences have the place of honour in this book.

Working with my patients, particularly the psychotic ones, has had a significant influence on me. After my training, clinical practice brought me up against patients who were 'difficult' to reach (Joseph 1975), and I had to learn to make ever greater room for the patients' contributions, so as to try to find the wavelength that was most useful for them, with the aim of constructing a dialogue and fostering analytic evolution. Clinical psychoanalysis today inevitably involves dealing with very complex cases: the analyst must have personal flexibility, great intersubjective sensitivity and an openness to constant change in levels of functioning. In our work we are continuously stimulated, on both the conscious and the unconscious levels, by the relationship with our analysands, and this spurs us to change internally, just as they accept change under the impact of their relationship with us. Thus I can say that this book benefits from the work of a certain number of implicit co-authors – as well as of the colleagues who collaborated with me in writing two of the chapters, Pietro Bria and Marisa Pola – to the extent that, particularly in the clinical sections, the contribution of my analysands was unquestionably a motive power.

As a clinical psychoanalyst I must admit to a certain apprehension with regard to what is known as 'Matteblancism' – not unlike my reaction to all the various approaches to psychoanalysis whose omni-comprehensive pretensions run the risk of transforming a theory into a Procrustean bed. Thus I do not consider an interest in Matte Blanco to be antagonistic towards or an alternative to contemporary psycho-analytic thinking: on the contrary, I believe his thinking is complementary to other theories, even as it proposes its own peculiar vantage point which turns out to be particularly original and stimulating.

Before launching upon the exploration, in the course of this volume, of a few clinical experiences that show an interesting complementarity with his thought, I shall attempt to familiarize the reader with some essential aspects of his approach.

The unrepressed Unconscious

I do not intend to offer a systematic presentation of Matte Blanco's thought (for which see Rayner & Tuckett 1988; Rayner 1995); hence I shall present in this introduction only a few of his essential ideas.

The existence of an unrepressed Unconscious was recognized by Freud in 1923 in 'The Ego and the Id', when he wrote: 'We recognize that the Ucs. does not coincide with the repressed; it is still true that all that is repressed is Ucs., but not all that is Ucs. is repressed. A part of the ego, too – and Heaven knows how important a part – may be Ucs., undoubtedly is Ucs' (p. 18).

Matte Blanco systematically develops the Freudian intuition of an unrepressed Unconscious. His investigations start from the logical qualities of the Unconscious described by Freud, which Matte Blanco considers the truly revolutionary core of psychoanalytic theory. Thus, his approach to knowledge of unconscious emotional life focuses on the logical aspect, whereas the Freudian tradition concentrates mostly on its energy. It is interesting to observe that Pine (2006) has recently stressed the importance of the mechanisms of condensation and displacement – precisely the principal logical mechanisms of the Unconscious – as a potentially significant link between the various approaches of today's pluralistic analytic world.

The essential characteristics of unconscious processes, from which secondary characteristics can be derived, were concisely stated by Freud, first in *The Interpretation of Dreams* (1900) and later in *The Unconscious* (1915), where they are said to be given as the absence of both mutual contradiction and negation, displacement, condensation, timelessness and the replacement of external by internal reality. Matte Blanco reduces the various characteristics of the Unconscious to two basic logical principles – the *generalization principle* and the *symmetry principle* – in order to make Freud's discovery more accessible and useful in terms of clinical technique. He further believes that the functioning of the Unconscious is similar to that of the mind in the presence of intense emotions, so his theory of the Unconscious is also a theory about the mental functioning of emotions, or what Freud considered the seething core of the id.

Thus the disorganizing pressure of the Unconscious and of emotional life in general is conceived as a continuously present component of the mind, existing also in the context of the psychoanalytic session. Similarly, Bion (1957) holds that the mind includes the pressure of the so-called psychotic area of the personality, rather like an 'amorphous mass of unconnected and undifferentiated elements' (Bion 1992, p. 46).

Matte Blanco views the mind as a classifier that functions with the kind of logic we find in set theory. For example, when a patient speaks of his father, his teacher, or his psychoanalyst, he is referring to an emotion to which that subject tends to give rise in him, so that he feels the subject belongs to a class we might, for instance, call the *class of fathers*. Thus a single subject undergoes *a logical process of generalization* (father – class of fathers, analyst – class of analysts/fathers, etc.). If the ability to make distinctions were to stop at this point, it would still be operative within the same class, so that there would continue to be a distinction between father, teacher and analyst.

The functioning of the unrepressed (or structural) Unconscious also implies, however, the operation of a second principle, the *principle of symmetry*, according to which every element becomes the symmetrical equivalent of another element. To state this more formally, *the Unconscious treats asymmetrical relationships, which are based on distinctness, as if they were symmetrical relationships.* Through the operation of the principle of symmetry, distinctions within a class vanish, so that the father, the teacher and the analyst are treated emotionally as if they were absolutely indistinguishable. We can find this sort of confusion when we treat more difficult patients, as in the case of the psychotic patient who, after some years of analysis, took his analyst to court to demand recognition as his adoptive son.

So a crucial distinction in Matte Blanco's thinking is that distinction between asymmetrical and symmetrical relations. Let us say that John and Archie are father and son. In the proposition 'John is the father of Archie,' there is an asymmetrical relation between subject and predicate. The converse of this proposition is not identical or even true: 'Archie is the father of John.' The first proposition is asymmetrical and logical; it is not a matter of chance that propositions of this kind are the foundation of all the functioning of the conscious mind. The second proposition, by contrast, is a symmetrical relation foreign to classical logic but consonant with the functioning of the Unconscious. Such relations are important for the psychoanalyst because they capture certain characteristics of profound emotions, not to mention the distinctive logic of the Unconscious altogether. It is hardly fortuitous that we are not surprised if, at the level of emotional exchange, a father can in certain circumstances feel as if he were the son of his own son. It should be stressed that *the symmetry principle is the real propulsive force of the unrepressed Unconscious* since, by doing away with distinctions, it leads to a truly devastating derangement of the spatio-temporal structures of our thought.

The absence of temporal awareness also seems closely correlated to with the dominance of symmetry (Fink 1993): it is no accident that Freud (1924) connects the appearance of time on the mental horizon with the functioning of the apparatus of perception–consciousness. Melanie Klein (1923) ascribes the origin of the idea of time to the passage from the intrauterine phase to birth. Time introduces a mental order within representable material, in contrast to the typically atemporal Unconscious: in the clinical material I am about to present in some chapters of this book, time is associated with the unfolding of the Unconscious toward conscious representations.

The utmost limit to which the operation of the principle of symmetry leads is *indivisibility*, as a result of which logical distinctions and spatio-temporal organization are nullified. A consequence of the formulation of this parameter is the clinical revaluation of all mental acts that involve differentiation and spatio-temporal distinction.

Normal and pathological symmetrizations

The operation of the principle of symmetry is particularly evident in the thinking of schizophrenics; it is very like what von Domarus (1944) and Arieti (1974) have described as *paleological thinking*. Let us consider a clinical example given by von Domarus: 'A schizophrenic patient of an Insane Asylum of the University in Bonn believed that Jesus, cigar boxes and sex were identical. How did he arrive at that strange belief? Investigation revealed that the missing link for the connection ... was supplied by the idea of being encircled. In the opinion of this patient the head of Jesus, as of a saint, is encircled by a halo, the package of cigars by the tax band, and the woman by the sex glance of the man' (quoted in Skelton 1990, p. 472). The three disparate categories have thus not only been generalized to the point where they belong to the same class, but they have become mutually indistinguishable. 'The principle of symmetry makes its appearance at certain points and, like a powerful acid, dissolves all logic within its reach, that is the territory where it is applied' (Matte Blanco 1975, p. 54).

The intertwining of asymmetrical logic (or normal logic) and symmetrical logic, which undermines and parasitizes Aristotelian thought order, is called *bi-logical structure*. The passage from the Unconscious to consciousness is mediated by a process Matte Blanco calls *unfolding*, a function that has the task of representing asymmetrically what, where symmetry is dominant, would be otherwise be unrepresentable.

It should be borne in mind that the operative principle of symmetry does not perform only a pathological and life-denying function: it can also have a useful and life-enhancing effect, for example in creating a sharing of experiences, such as happens in communicative projective identification (Bion 1962/1984). Thus, the bi-logical study of this mechanism makes it possible to keep the unipersonal functioning of the Freudian Unconscious – focused as it is on the logic of dreams and affects – connected with the specifically bi-personal or intersubjective point of view, according to which the analyst or the analysand 'feels that he is the other' (see Matte Blanco 1988, pp. 138–165; Grotstein 2000).

Hence a moderate dose of symmetry is, in fact, actually fundamental to phenomena generally described as 'empathy' (Kohut 1979; Bacal 1990; Goldberg 1988), a mechanism that appears to be rooted in our actual genetic structure itself, through mirror neurons (Gallese & Goldman 1998; Carr, Iacobini, Dubeau, Mazziott, & Lenzi 2003). The need to modulate one's empathic orientation, so that the analyst 'feels with' the patient without a resultant confusion of identities between the two, and at the same time 'thinks about' him or her without too much distancing, can be connected to a balanced participation, in the analytic relationship, of the two modes of being described by Matte Blanco (1988): the symmetric or indivisible mode, which relates to feeling, and the asymmetric and dividing mode, which relates to thinking. As Matte Blanco sees it, empathy turns out to be rooted in a logical (or rather bi-logical) concept that derives directly from the specific way the Unconscious functions.

The different proportions of symmetry and asymmetry that are present in various mental manifestations allow us to take account of the various levels of depth of involvement of the Unconscious.

The concept of level is generally used in psychoanalysis to distinguish between more superficial and deeper manifestations (see Roth 2001). Matte Blanco's contribution makes it possible to formulate this concept by interpreting the difference between more superficial and deeper levels in relation to the various components of symmetry and asymmetry: *the more symmetry increases, the deeper the level.* The superficial levels are those of the conscious; there people or objects are distinct and differentiated, in accordance with the systematized logical criteria of the Western intellectual tradition derived from Aristotle. At the deepest levels – the so-called basic matrix – symmetry, as we have noted, is dominant, to the point where differentiation between subject and object vanishes. This theory allows us to understand how it is possible for the analyst to 'feel like' the patient in a projective identification (Klein 1946; Bion 1962/1984) at a deep level without losing his or her identity, thanks to the analyst's capacity for asymmetric differentiation. *Thus analysis involves a continual need to fluctuate between the symmetric and the asymmetric, between deep and superficial levels.* It is generally the task of interpretation to recast asymmetrically the patient's profound emotions and confused experiences of a symmetrical nature, which are part and parcel of the analytic relationship and the transference, in keeping with Freud's assertion that 'where id was, there ego shall be' (1933, p. 80).

Thought, feeling and the infinite

Even when he confronts the most bizarre bi-logical characteristics that emerge from the unrepressed unconscious, Matte Blanco always uses a linear logic, since he considered such logic the only existing instrument for describing and indeed for understanding the mental world, even in its primitive areas – in which, as we have seen, the principle of symmetry introduces a devastating derangement of logical order. Thus Matte Blanco starts from an appreciation of the values of simplicity and clarity which are implicit in *bivalent logic* – or common logic based on the logical principle of non-contradiction – remaining consistent with what is the basis of any scientific procedure. Despite this linear logical underpinning, his original conceptualization may initially cause the reader some bewilderment because of its considerable novelty, the point of which is to simplify a few epistemological problems that are central to psychoanalysis, such as the contraposition of conscious and unconscious, and of thought and feeling.

The central role that Matte Blanco ascribes to the symmetry-asymmetry antithesis leads, in fact, to a reappraisal of the importance generally accorded to the conscious-unconscious and thought-feeling antitheses. From a bi-logical perspective, clinical manifestations are not considered in the light of their characterization as conscious or unconscious, rational or emotional, but rather in keeping with the proportions of symmetry and asymmetry that they contain. This conception has much in common with Rapaport's observation (1960, quoted by Matte Blanco 1975, p. 284 fn.) that every form of thought implies the participation, to differing degrees, of the *primary and secondary processes* (Freud 1900), with one or the other dominant. Matte Blanco's perspective focuses on the contrast between the two processes that Freud describes, since extensive symmetry involves a more radical dissolution of relations than is generally the case in the context of the primary process.

Matte Blanco's original conception of affects thus implies the inclusion of mental processes, so that 'there is thinking in feeling and feeling in thinking' (1975, p. 286). If *thought* is characterized by the domination of asymmetry and by accurate spatiotemporal organization, in *feeling* the spatiotemporal order of thought is disturbed because a member of the class occupies the entire space of the class to which it belongs (in other words, the single member of the class is emotionally perceived as the class in its entirety).

The continuity between the conscious and the unconscious and between thought and feeling in Matte Blanco is, in its clinical implications, comparable to Bion considering all the material of the session to be endowed with 'oneiric' potentialities for the purpose of extending receptiveness to unconscious communications, whereas, in classic analysis, the business of the unconscious tends to be mostly concerned with actual dreams. In addition, the analyst who is confronted with the explosive emotions of psychotic analysands builds on the feeling-thought continuity by fostering the components of thought that are present in feeling, even when the latter has the explosive and strongly symmetrical characteristics of an acute psychotic crisis. The exploitation of the components of thought to be found in extreme emotions allows the psychotic analysand to discover the reasons at the root of his or her own emotions, thus recognizing a first logical sense in his or her own affective experience. This perspective seems to be in line with what has been reported by those analysts of psychotic subjects, for whom accepting and assigning some meaning to the patient's unendurable affects make it possible to foster the organization of the emerging ego: 'For affect to become the well-spring of subjectivity, it must become imbued with a kind of psychic investment that gives motion to the emotion' (Garfield 2001, p. 116).

For Matte Blanco, the concept of feeling implies, in addition to symmetrical relations, the concept of *infinite sets*: emotional experience is, in fact, typified by its *engrossing and infinitizing nature*, as a result of which the object is invested with all the characteristics of the class to which it belongs. If the principle of symmetry governs the processes of the profound unconscious, then *the part is identical to the whole*: so if *a* is part of *B*, *B* is part of *a*; consequently *a* and *B* are identical. *The equivalence between the part and the whole is characteristic only of infinite sets.*

In keeping with such a principle, a schizophrenic patient may find that having blood taken from his arm becomes indistinguishable from having his arm removed. Or an analysand can feel that a separation from his analyst – who is, in his symmetrical view, himself – is an amputation of his own body. Thus we discover that the unconscious does not deal with parts or individuals, but with classes or sets, and the application of the principle of symmetry to different classes results in an infinite set. Whenever the part and the whole are treated as if they were identical, we are face to face with an infinite set. Matte Blanco quotes Cantor's acknowledgment of amazement when confronted with the conclusions of his research into infinite sets: *'Je le vois, mais je ne le crois pas'* (I see it, but I can't believe it) (Matte Blanco 1975, p. 147).

In point of fact, *the infinite occupies emotion!* On the contrary, from the logico-dividing point of view, 'the concept of the infinite is the expression of the desperate efforts of the heterogenic mode and its logic to try to understand the indivisible' (Matte Blanco 1988, p. 96).

Psychoanalytic research becomes entwined here, in multidisciplinary terms, not only with mathematics and logic, but also with philosophy: not by chance were thinkers like Parmenides, Zeno, Nicola Cusano, Giordano Bruno and even Galileo fascinated by the profoundly ontological dimension of investigations of the infinite.

'The realm of emotion in human beings is not the realm of *one* infinite set but of both several and many' (Matte Blanco 1975, 274): given the expansive and infinitizing nature of intense emotions, their involvement in the working through can give rise to unusual problems, such as transference psychosis, erotic transference, or homicidal transference. Dealing clinically with profound emotions is not without its difficulties and dangers, but it does have enormous potential for mental change and growth. Viewed from the perspective of infinite sets, emotion is in fact 'a reservoir of more than atomic energy' (1975, p. 392). One thinks perforce of Bion when he writes of 'an intense catastrophic emotional explosion' in which 'mental space being infinite, the fragments of the link are dispersed instantaneously over infinite space' (1970, p. 14).

Matte Blanco's concept of emotion underlines the value of the psychoanalytic exploration of psychoses and the so-called serious pathologies, revealing in them an extensive aspect of challenge, growth and knowledge: something more complex than treating a death instinct or the reappraisal of destructive impulses. Furthermore, dealing with explosive feelings trains the analyst to make the most of the precious contribution offered by profound emotions even in the analysis of neurotic patients.

Multidimensionality, pure sensation and sensation-sentiment

Applying the principle of symmetry to space implies the existence of multidimensional space: thanks to the exploitation of multidimensionality, according to Matte Blanco, phenomena which are inexplicable by means of the everyday logic of three-dimensional space can become comprehensible. In particular, dreams can become a means of approaching a multidimensional world in the eyes of a dreamer who is used to the three-dimensional world only. For example, when the ego is concealed behind the various characters in a dream (Freud 1900), the personality manages to represent itself in multidimensional terms, thus avoiding the limitations of three-dimensional space. The presence of emotion in the mind implies the existence of a multidimensionality, or even of an aspatio–atemporality. Matte Blanco has a decided affinity to the Bion who wrote, 'The mental realization of space is therefore felt as an immensity so great that it cannot be represented even by astronomical space because it cannot be represented at all' (1970, p. 12). If the principle of symmetry leads to the generation of multidimensional space, thought, which tends by its nature to be asymmetrical, corresponds to a space of fewer dimensions, since 'human molecular consciousness cannot "contain" or grasp more than a few relations at a given time' (Matte Blanco 1975, 376–377).

The existence of our bodily nature, which is structurally three-dimensional, leads to a conflict or at least confrontation with our multidimensional/adimensional nature – a theme which we shall encounter in some detail in the course of the present book, with regard to the unfolding of the unconscious body. Limiting ourselves, however, to more general parameters, we can say that Matte Blanco sees man as an expression of an aspatio–atemporality (resulting from the infinite sets of emotions) immersed in a determinate spatio-temporality in the form of his physical body. Our body, as an object of perception, is at first alien to us and we must make serious mental efforts if we are to approach it. Hence Matte Blanco stresses the role of *sensation-sentiment* as a bridge that connects the body with *thought* (for details, cf. my essay from 2009). Also, as, in general, sensation cannot have access to consciousness if it is not clad in thought, the primitive state in which sensation is still waiting to be clad in thought is what Matte Blanco calls *pure sensation*.

11

The area of *primary sensations* and of *sensation-sentiment* is under the sway of the principle of symmetry: 'around the obscure sensation-feelings, which, as we have seen, refer to or are the result of bodily processes, we build or develop a colossal halo of symmetrical relations' (Matte Blanco 1975, p. 263). If sensation is exposed to symmetrizations, this implies that sensations can become intense, extreme and unthinkable, like the sensations described by Tustin (1981) apropos of autistic children or autistic nuclei in neurotic patients.

Entering into the dark and 'inexpressible' (Wittgenstein) world of sensations becomes inevitable for the analyst who is faced with psychoses and other particularly serious cases: in this way he or she gains direct experience of the homogeneous and indivisible levels of Being of which Matte Blanco speaks. In fact, 'feeling' lays one open to containing objects characterized by infinite sets, which are taken up, in their entirety, by sentiment (cf. Matte Blanco 1975, p. 286). These are structurally unthinkable levels which are mysteriously experienced and contained – because of their explosive implications – in the depths of ourselves, but can in various ways be subject to 'unfolding' through the bi-logical structures of the unconscious, as if in a desperate attempt to think the unthinkable.

Emerging from formless infinity: limit as a key concept

As we saw before, a concept that accounts in large measure for the importance of Matte Blanco's contribution to psychoanalysis is that of the *infinite* (together with such related expressions as *infinite experiences* and *infinitization*): clinical practice generally confronts us with manifestations of the infinite through such experiences as omnipotence, impotence and omniscience. In addition, studying the logical functioning of the mind in the presence of emotions shows how any feeling contains elements of infinity: 'one feels that the intensity is frightening, and without formulating it explicitly, one also feels, though in an obscure manner, that it has no limit. In other words, it tends towards the infinite' (Matte Blanco 1988, p. 141). This idea is expressed figuratively by many writers and artists, including, for example, Lewis Carroll, when he describes how Alice, after shedding some tears soon finds herself in danger of drowning in them.

A cardinal aspect of the therapeutic action of psychoanalysis thus becomes divesting emotions of their infinite features and then placing them in a thinking context characterized by the recognition of limits. In this way the logic of the Unconscious, which itself tends symmetrically towards the infinite, can be reconciled with the differentiating logic of consciousness, and can thus become capable of responding more effectively to the subject's vital needs.

In clinical psychoanalysis the usefulness of the concept of the infinite is evident, for example, in the pathology of panic, in which extreme mental turmoil and the accompanying sense of helplessness result in the overwhelming re-emergence of infinite feelings. Analytic work in cases of panic involves the unfolding of the patient's infinite feelings, an unwinding into finite space–time of something that in itself shuns the limitations of space and time.

For example, a patient suffering from panic attacks reported that as a little girl she would shut herself up in a room and start counting when anxiety seemed to get the upper hand in her family. Thus she revealed a 'model' of her current mental functioning, both in sessions and elsewhere. In fact, by keeping herself 'shut up' and unconnected with her emotions through the constant employment of her capacity for calculation and abstraction, she disconnected her asymmetrical mental capacity – with its potential for containment – from her symmetrical sentiments.

The finite and the limit, or boundary, are the direct opposites of the infinite, as we see in the geometric representation of the point that transforms an infinite line into a half-line, or the two points that transform a line into a segment.

In terms of the perspective of this book, *the limit or boundary becomes the key concept of contemporary psychoanalysis to the extent that it dynamically opposes the formless infinite of primitive mental states.* Through adopting and elaborating the notion of boundaries, the subject can liberate himself or herself from the 'dark and formless infinite' – as Milton, cited by Bion (1967), put it – of the primitive condition, and then approach a differentiated mental dimension.

Being able to oscillate dynamically from infinite to finite, and vice versa, leads us directly to the choice of the title of this book, which gives prominence to the concept of the infinite and of primitive mental states. The internal movement that characterizes the analytic couple when it is facing the deepest levels involves continual oscillation: emerging from the formless infinite alternating with the opposite movement of falling into the formless infinite, submerged by the oceanic undertow of primitive emotions; a systolic and diastolic cycle of thought requiring constant openness to oscillation between non-thought and thought.

This is the mysterious generative dimension of 'mothers', at the border of the obliteration of space and time, described by Goethe:

Gestaltung, Umgestaltung, Des ewigen Sinnes ewige Unterhaltung.
(Formation, Transformation, Eternal Mind's eternal re-creation.)
Faust, II Part, 6287–6288

This is an 'infernal' area, about which Dante, among other poets, has increased our sensibility:

Io venni in loco d'ogne luce muto,
che mugghia come fa mar per tempesta,
se da contrari venti è combattuto.
La bufera infernal, che mai non resta.

[I came to a place deprived of every light,
And crashing like the tempest-tossèd sea
When assailèd by contrasting winds.
The hellish storm, the one that never rests.]
La Divina Commedia, Inferno V, 28–31

This germinative area of undifferentiated abysses and 'hellish' storms assails us personally as analysts called upon to face the experience of those of our analysands who live in this primordial condition, even when they show an interest in struggling – not without ambivalence – to emerge and become differentiated.

A brief outline of the book

The first two chapters of this book work out some of the implications of Matte Blanco's hypotheses in line with the personal affinity with which I reacted to his thinking in the light of my clinical experience. I make no particular claim to orthodoxy in my approach to Matte Blanco, if indeed such an orthodoxy could exist. I have particularly sought to discover the interaction between Matte Blanco's thought and that of Wilfred Bion.

In the third chapter I consider the subject of the body as a potential springboard for emerging from the formless infinite of the unrepressed Unconscious, with various sequences from the analysis of both adolescents and adults as illustrations. In the two subsequent chapters my intention is to stress the role of the body, as it fosters such an emergence when the formless infinite is that of psychosis.

I then tackle the subject of time as one of the main asymmetrical elements that make it possible to emerge from the formless infinite, with more general reflections about some specifically technical methods in which time is actively brought to the patient's attention in the context of the psychoanalytic dialogue. In the next chapter, this leads to a consideration of the role of the analyst's sensory reverie in accompanying important transformative phenomena that foster the acquisition of a personal temporality. In what I call the *musical reverie*, prominence is given to phenomena of deep symmetry in the analytic couple, which leads to experiences of emotional contact whence an inner and relational awareness of time can arise.

The last two chapters are devoted to the recognition of death and life, as well as to the unfolding of the symmetrization that cancels the difference between life and death in difficult patients – particularly those patients who are unable to feel emotionally alive. In the first of these two last chapters I explore the case of a patient at serious risk of suicide, and I describe the elaboration that led him to set in motion his first organizing asymmetries and to free himself from a paralysing symmetry. Finally, in the last chapter I explore the case of a psychotic analysand who shows us, during the course of many years of analysis that include various catastrophic phases, an interesting evolution: the culminating moment of this evolution centres on the confrontation with a delusion of the theft of time that erased all forms of temporal differentiation from her mind.

It is my hope that this investigation of mine may stimulate the further evolution of this perspective, but particularly that it may contribute to spurring greater interest in primitive mental states, or rather in the more complex and extreme forms that we can approach with our psychoanalytic instruments.

Note

1   Translated by Karen Christenfeld.

References

Arieti, S. (1974). *Interpretation of schizophrenia* (2nd ed.) New York: Basic Books.

Bacal, H. A. (1990). The elements of a corrective selfobject experience. *Psychoanalytic Inquiry*, 10: 347–372.

Bion, W.R. (1957). Differentiation of psychotic from the non-psychotic personalities. In *Second thoughts* (pp. 43–64). London: Karnac Books, 1967.

Bion, W. R. (1962). *Learning from experience*. London: Karnac Books, 1984.

Bion, W. R. (1967). *Second thoughts*. London: Karnac Books, 1984.

Bion, W. R. (1970). *Attention and interpretation*. London: Karnac Books.

Bion, W. R. (1992). *Cogitations* (F. Bion, Ed.). London: Karnac Books.

Carr, L., Iacobini, M., Dubeau, M.-C., Mazziott, J., & Lenzi, G. (2003). Neural mechanisms of empathy in humans: a relay from neural systems for imitation to limbic areas. *Science*, 100: 5497–5502.

Fink, K. (1993). The bi-logic perception of time. *International Journal of Psychoanalysis*, 74: 303–312.

Freud, S. (1900). The interpretation of dreams. *Standard Edition*, 4: 1–627.

Freud, S. (1915). The unconscious. *Standard Edition*, 14: 159–215.

Freud, S. (1923). The ego and the id. *Standard Edition*, 19: 1–66.

Freud, S. (1924). A note upon the 'mystic writing-pad'. *Standard Edition*, 19: 227–232.

Freud, S. (1933). New introductory lectures on psycho-analysis. *Standard Edition*, 22: 1–182.

Gallese, V., & Goldman, A. (1998). Mirror neurons and the simulation theory of mind-reading. *Trends in Cognitive Sciences*, 2: 493–501.

Garfield, D. A. (2001). The use of vitality affects in the coalescence of self in psychosis. *Progress in Self Psychology*, 17: 113–128.

Goldberg, A. (Ed.). (1988). *Learning from Kohut: progress in self psychology* (Vol. 4). Hillsdale, NJ: Analytic Press.

Grotstein, J.S. (2000). *Who is the dreamer who dreams the dream?* Hillsdale, NJ: Analytic Press.

Joseph, B. (1975). The patient who is difficult to reach. In P. L. Giovacchini (Ed.), *Tactics and techniques in psychoanalytic therapy: Vol. 2. Countertransference* (pp. 205–210). New York: Jason Aronson.

Klein, M. (1923). The development of a child. *International Journal of Psychoanalysis*, 4: 419–474.

Klein, M. (1946). Notes on some schizoid mechanisms. *International Journal of Psychoanalysis*, 27: 99–110.

Kohut, H. (1979). The two analyses of Mr. Z. *International Journal of Psychoanalysis*, 60: 3–27.

Lombardi, R. (2009). Body, affect, thought: reflections of the work of Matte Blanco and Ferrari. *Psychoanalytic Quarterly*, 78: 126–160.

Matte Blanco, I. (1975). *The unconscious as infinite sets*. London: Karnac Books.

Matte Blanco, I. (1988). *Thinking, feeling and being.* London: Routledge.

Pine, F. (2006). The psychoanalytic dictionary: a position paper on diversity and its unifiers. *Journal of the American Psychoanalytic Association,* 54: 463–492.

Rayner, E. (1995). *Unconscious logic: an introduction to Matte Blanco's bi-logic and its uses.* London: Routledge.

Rayner, E., & Tuckett, D. (1988). An introduction to Matte Blanco's reformulation of the Freudian unconscious and his conceptualization of the internal world. In I. Matte Blanco, *Thinking, feeling and being* (pp. 3–42). London: Routledge.

Roth, P. (2001). Mapping the landscape: levels of transference interpretation. *International Journal of Psychoanalysis,* 82: 533–543.

Searles, H. F. (1951). Data concerning certain manifestations of incorporation. In *Collected papers on schizophrenia and related subjects* (pp. 38–66). Turin: Boringhieri. (Reprinted 1965, London: Hogarth Press)

Skelton, R. (1990). Generalization from Freud to Matte Blanco. *International Journal of Psychoanalysis,* 17: 471–474.

Tustin, F. (1981). *Autistic states in children.* London: Routledge, 1992.

von Domarus, E. (1944). The specific laws of logic in schizophrenia. In J. S. Kasanin (Ed.), *Language and thought in schizophrenia: collected papers* (pp. 101–114). Berkeley: University of California Press.

EMOTIONAL EXPERIENCE
AND INFINITY[1]

> *. . . like the mythological two faced-Janus. Look at it from one side. You will*
> *see the patients, their emotions, their thoughts, their actions, their bi-logical*
> *structures. Look at it from the other side and you will find that all these*
> *examples are also illustrations of fundamental philosophical questions which*
> *psychoanalysis is bringing to the fore.*
>
> —Matte Blanco (1988, p. 71)

The story of the infinite is rooted in the very origins of philosophical and scientific thought. As is well known, Aristotle's position, in response to Zeno's paradox, was that the infinite could never be realized in fact (actual infinity) but had to remain potential (potential infinity). This is because the reality of infinity exceeds the finite capacity of thought which can only proceed bit by finite bit towards infinity without ever being able to attain it as an entity.

Only with the 'new science' would thinkers of the stature of Galileo and Leibniz in the modern age pose the problem of actual infinity again. They proposed infinity as a totality, as a number, as a 'determinate quantity'. But in doing so, they came up again against those terrible paradoxes with which its structure is riven. Borges (1932/1984, p. 399) poetically called them 'the interstices of the absurd', testimony, he went on to say to the 'undivided divinity which works within us': the indivisible reality without parts, and yet infinitely divided.

In the masterpiece of his old age, *Discourse on Two New Sciences*, Galileo confronted the paradox that takes his name whereby the 'squares', a proper part of the infinite set of natural numbers, are as many as the natural numbers. Meditating on this paradox which is implicit in 'counting' infinity, Galileo concluded that: 'these are among the difficulties that we encounter in talking about the infinites using our finite intellects, giving them those attributes that we give to things that are finite and determinate; this is, I believe, an error in that such attributes of being greater or less or equal are not applicable to the infinites of which it cannot be said that one is larger or smaller or the same as another.'

In an interview shortly before his death, called 'An Infinity Within Us', Matte Blanco said, 'what mathematical logic hadn't managed to work out, Freud intuited with the discovery that the unconscious does not respect the laws of classical logic, and in particular that it fails to respect its basic principle, that of non-contradiction. We are convinced that this will give rise to the possibility of a new epistemology which will in some respects reflect the laws of classical logic, and in some, those of the infinite and the unconscious. This seems to me to have been Freud's fundamental contribution to human culture.'

It was in fact Freud (1900, 1915b) who recognized a particular function in the violation of the principle of non-contradiction. For Aristotle, this principle was his attempt to safeguard the divisibility of the world, and its violations signalled the presence of a confusional element at the heart of our logic. This is the expression of a specific modality of consciousness and meaning in part of the mind, alien to the distinguishing functions of consciousness. Freud recognized it in the apparent contradictions he encountered in his exploration of unconscious and emotional levels of mental functioning, and saw that it was not a defect which removed us from the realm of reason, which is what the concept of the irrational might suggest. The modality that it suggested was, on the contrary, no less essential to our survival than the differentiating function that we attribute to thought.

But it was Matte Blanco (1959, 1975) who, in an entirely original departure, took Freud's intuition of a structural unconscious absolutely seriously, and applied it to the inherent significance of the logical calamities of schizophrenic patients. He attempted to delineate a logic of confusion whose basis was in the identity between part and whole, element and class, rather than in pure and simple equivalence. This is the origin – in his contact with the logical disintegration of schizophrenic patients' experiences – of Matte Blanco's insight about an isomorphic connection between the structure of the unconscious – which involves a violation of the principle of non-contradiction posited by Aristotle as a guarantee of the differentiating function of thought – and the structure of mathematical infinity – which Dedekind (1888/1969) defines as a set in which it is possible to establish a bi-univocal correspondence between a proper fraction and the whole. In other words, infinity and the unconscious are revealed, according to this view, as the two most remarkable human attempts to capture in the net of space and time a reality, by its very nature indivisible and unthinkable, which is at the heart of our emotional being, and which *treats as a unity that which thought inevitably divides.*

Matte Blanco's bi-logic throws a powerful light on the nature of the unconscious and on that of the infinite. These two great symbolic constructions are woven together and testify to the human struggle to capture an indivisible aspect of being. This aspect is beyond any determination or predication. But it is at the same time, the source of any possible determination or predication. And the struggle is to capture it in a net whose mesh is made of time and space.

This bi-logical interweaving on which 'indivisible being' is founded, is also at the heart of our emotions, and here we are at the second step in Matte Blanco's theoretical framework. It constitutes the cognitive valence of our emotions which orientates them 'intentionally towards the world', and it prompts Sartre, whom Matte Blanco cites, to assert that 'what is constitutive of emotion is the fact that *it takes from the object something which infinitely overflows emotion*' from the instant that, he continues, 'every quality is conferred on an object only through *a step towards the infinite*' (Matte Blanco 1988, p. 457).

Emotions, bodily experience and the infinite

Thus, the logic of the unconscious, and the logics of the infinite and of emotion reveal a surprising structural isomorphism; and the processes of symmetrization with which the emotional unconscious operates are *processes of the infinitization of experience.*

It was the encounter with Cantor in the 19th century that put the actual infinite back on the map and defined an 'arithmetic of the infinite' which ventured towards the infinite levels of the 'trans–finite' (aleph). Then there was the definition of infinite sets by Dedekind as those sets in which a proper part could be put into a bi-univocal correspondence with the whole. This it was that permitted Matte Blanco to respond to the apparently irresolvable internal contradiction that Galileo had noticed, and to give back to the infinite a new

20

empirical foundation in the internal experience of the affects. *It is here that the unconscious encounters the infinite* because emotions structurally imply idealization, and idealization of objects or people, or of any other aspect of the environment, signifies, according to this logic, *the infinitization of its characteristics* or properties. This is what Sartre (1936) intuited.

We can say, with Matte Blanco, that the infinite – rooted, with its 'paradoxes', in our most primitive emotions which arise through corporeal experience – is in fact empirically grounded in the emotional unconscious. It is at this juncture that philosophical and epistemological thought are closely connected with clinical research, and the infinite becomes a 'mental operator', that colours the so-called 'emotional mind' and works with the 'separate' and 'differentiating' forces of our conscious, paving the way for a new definition of the relations between the unconscious and the conscious. These epistemological implications of Matte Blanco's thinking and its relations with mathematical theory were recognized by Partenope Bion Talamo (1999), who made it the subject of his degree thesis, in which Matte Blanco's logico–mathematical approach to the unconscious is considered in relation to W. R. Bion's theories about 'thinking', starting with the seminal contributions *Learning from Experience* (1962) and *Transformations* (1965).

Our aim, in this chapter, is to explore some clinical implications of Matte Blanco's discoveries, demonstrating a more explicit causative connection between his insights about the unconscious and the modes of mental functioning in the face of the impact of sensory data of a bodily nature, as well as in the presence of the turbulence of primitive emotions. We wish thereby to emphasize once more how it is that the unconscious and the infinite find their roots in the primitive experience of the body.

From his earliest contributions to his last work Freud (1893–95, 1911, 1915b, 1940) stressed, in a variety of ways, that the unconscious is grounded in bodily experiences and the mind has, most importantly, a 'need for work' (Freud 1915a) because of its connection to the body. Subsequently various authors have emphasized the relation between the body and the unconscious, including Tausk (1933), Scott (1948), Winnicott (1953), Marty (1976) and, more recently, Salomon Resnik (1979, 2001) and Armando Ferrari (2004). 'The intimate link between biology and bi-logic', Bria has written (1981, p. 47), indicating the connection between Resnik's concept of the unconscious

(1979) and Matte Blanco's, 'calls attention to a fundamental aspect of human nature, as a result of which every bi-logical structure, like every structure in our thinking, is supported by our biological equipment. Because of this inescapable link – the body-mind link – we can say that we are "body", hence biology, even in the most abstract and spiritual of our manifestations, in that our psychological being is rooted in our instinctual needs' (Bria 1981, p. 47). I suggested elsewhere (Lombardi 2000, 2002a) a rapprochement of Matte Blanco's formulations on mental functioning with Armando Ferrari's hypothesis of the eclipse of the body: both these authors underline the structural difficulty of achieving discrimination and thinkability in the face of the disturbing bio-psychological thrust of the emotions. The pressure the body exerts on mental functioning thus constitutes the one of the first structural element of infinitization, in that the mental trace in contact with the bodily matrix functions in a distinctly symmetrical way, in which the logical classes display the characteristics of infinite sets. The passage from turmoil to forms less dominated by symmetry and more varied by asymmetrical differentiation is mediated by a complex system of internal theories comparable to the vicissitudes of misconceptions in Money-Kyrle (1968) and to Bion's transformative processes (1962). These internal private theories can function as an obstacle to the progressive asymmetrization of the emotional matrices of thought.

It should be noted that, from a technical point of view, at this depth of mental functioning a psychoanalytic approach based on systematic transference interpretation is counterproductive to the extent that, in the deep unconscious, characterized by the emergence of somatic sensations (Freud 1940), the distinction between external and internal vanishes and the analyst finds himself functioning essentially as the analysand's counterpart, i.e. as a sort of imaginary twin (Bion 1950) who contributes significantly to the functions of containment and asymmetrization of the sensory-emotional experience that the analysand is going through (Lombardi 2002a, 2002b). In other words, when the logic of turmoil has the upper hand, the analyst performs his function by means of *reverie* (Bion 1962), giving precedence to the unfolding of the non-repressed unconscious and postponing to a subsequent period of the analytic working through the confrontation with the relational other, with all its attendant dynamics (Klein 1952/1975). This technical choice thus corresponds to highlighting the need to introduce the patient to himself (cf. Bion 1974, p. 40), or what Ferrari (2004) indicated as the urgent need to favour the vertical body–mind relationship, leaving the horizontal analysand–analyst relationship in the background for the moment. This emphasis on the patient's internal functioning is intended to avoid a displacement of cathexis onto the external object, which would make it easier to dodge confronting the confusion, disorganization and internal conflict typical of the primary areas and would also increase the risk of the analysand's resorting to compliance and imitation in his relation to the analyst (Gaddini 1969/1992). In the clinical material at the end of this article there is a clear focus on internal dynamics and a corresponding marginalization of transference interpretation. This choice should, of course, not be taken to indicate a disregard for the transference, which is still the mainstay of the analytic exchange: instead, transference interpretation is put off to phases in which the analysand has mental room for an opening to relational dynamics (Lombardi 2003). Indeed when internal turmoil and structural conflict seem to be resolved, work on the transference makes it possible to put back into perspective the symmetrization that characterized the analytic relationship, by working through the massive projective identification that can colour certain phases of analysis (Bon de Matte 1988).

Dialectic between the infinite and the finite

The step towards the infinite or infinitization comes to be constituted as a true and proper *mental operator* which makes possible the passage from the individual element (e) to the class to which it belongs (E), from the realm of individuals to that of classes: this is an astounding 'logical leap' whereby the individual, limited by time and space, is as if reabsorbed into or annulled in the infinity of the class. This is an *intensive infinity*, that is, one that is within finite limits which are none other than the 'borders' that define the class. Applied to the chain of inference that presides over human reasoning, its action is manifest as the introduction of 'symmetrical links' within the process of reasoning. These are areas of 'indivision' and so of infinitization, in which part is identical to whole, and which have the capacity to give rise to development, as is the case with delusional developments. Such developments appear completely incoherent and strange to the purely Aristotelian eye, but become perfectly legitimate and coherent to a bi-logical eye which finds reason and therefore meaning in what might otherwise seem irrational and nonsensical. Following Matte Blanco's intuition, Bria

23

(1999) have called such processes, marked by 'bi-logical rationality', *affective syllogisms* which are in clear competition or interaction with the better known processes of 'Aristotelian reasoning', bound by their respect for the principle of non-contradiction.

If we consider the world of *delusional perception* described so masterfully by Karl Jaspers (1959) and subsequently by Kurt Schneider (1950), we might say that 'delusional meaning', to use Jaspers's suggestive term, which knocks down the whole of the sensory and perceptive system, is entirely the result of a process of infinitization which renders part equal to whole. In this way, it becomes entirely legitimate, in terms of this new meaning which invades the field of consciousness and which, in Jaspers's words, is a radical modification in the awareness of meaning, that someone who is ill, to use his example, 'sees uniformed people in the road and says "those are Spanish soldiers". If he sees another uniform, he might say, "those are Turkish soldiers", and from this might deduce "all the soldiers are concentrating here, so there must be a world war". The same patient confronted with *a few* houses with *scaffolding* might say that *the entire city* must have been demolished.' In the same way, delusional inference led a schizophrenic patient of Storch's, much cited by Matte Blanco, to assert that opening a door, 'he was being eaten by animals.' The idea of being eaten by animals becomes 'valid' if the opening of the door is treated 'symmetrically' with the class of openings. In fact there is a shifting here from a particular to a general class, followed by a second shifting from a general to a particular class (the animals), but here the logical relation among elements is symmetrized to the point that opening the door becomes indistinguishable from opening a voracious mouth: the category of the fathomless chasm which includes the gaping jaws of a predator in search of prey, so that, in what Binswanger (1965) calls *delusional consequence*, the danger is infinitized.

Thus we have found (see, e.g. Bria 1985), that infinitization is the source of all conflict in the emotional unconscious since, when applied to the antithetical desires described by Freud, it translates these Aristotelian 'contraries' into 'contradictories', which are mutually exclusive (*a, not-a*). Such antithetical desires include love and hate, but also the paired opposites good and bad in Kleinian theory. The very existence of such contradictories — whereby, still in Kleinian terms, the same breast is the fount of (infinite) good as well as of (infinite) bad, and the object of (infinite) love as well as of (infinite) hate — violates the principle of non-contradiction. This is, for Aristotle, the principle of the *incompatibility of opposites*, important not only logically but also ontologically, placed as it is in the defence of the dialectic between opposites which is a constitutive property of the substantiality of the world. And it is precisely this emotional climate that gives birth to Aristotle's principle as the psychobiological necessity for making distinctions within that which infinite emotion tends to experience as 'one' and 'confused', whereby there is an *identity between opposites* and therefore a threat to survival: whence the spur to splitting and projection as Klein conceived them.

A brief clinical vignette will help to illustrate this: F had developed an omnipotent delusional system in relation to a severe depressive break down, organized around the pathological belief that he could nourish himself adequately on his own saliva. This allowed him to feel that he was a sort of divinity, and that he was completely self-sufficient and immune to any need or bodily desire for food. He would have allowed himself to die as a result of this gesture of self-affirmation. When we were obliged to feed him forcibly, his reaction was one of rage and desperation: he accused us of having killed him, of having made him impotent, and of having emptied him of all his own strength, despite the evidence that his body was meanwhile clearly recovering its strength. This apparent dissociation which was established in the delusion between the assertion of an infinite mind and the denial of the finite biology of the body is very reminiscent of the drama of countless anorexic patients who live out this persecuting and omnipotent delusion. It was the necessary consequence of the fact that the self-affirmation and the infinite autonomy that characterized the delusion, was *absolutely incompatible* with any sort of limitation or dependence, such as might be betrayed by his body and experience as infinite as well: there could be no midpoint between (infinite) autonomy and (infinite) dependency.

Staying in the Kleinian model, it is with the dawning of the *depressive position* (Klein 1940) that the breast is allowed to be both good and bad (partially and not at the same time or in the same respect), in virtue of the more mature processes of 'finitization', and this in turn permits the development of a capacity for mourning, which is no longer an obstacle, but a stimulus toward integration and thinking.

In this perspective, the interactive competition between the logics, and the dialectic between finite and infinite that characterizes the strata or levels of the mind, become more fundamental than the conflict between the drives which, in the Freudian description, always operates according to the principle of non-contradiction.

What emerges clearly from all this is that emotional experience furnishes the *prima materia* for the infinite and for the development of the function of thinking. And, as Figà Talamanca (1989) has asserted, far from being 'imperfections, the apparent contradictions of the infinite (as in Galileo's paradox) are an indication that it is possible to study the dimensions of symmetrical being which are manifest in our emotions, but which are not accessible via the ordinary logic of the finite'.

We are going to apply these concepts now to a clinical aspect of psychoanalysis.

Panic as a 'catastrophic experience': the infinite and the function of unfolding

The pathology of panic

Over recent years, psychiatry has increasingly subjected the phenomenology of panic attack to multifactorial aetiological explanations 'in which elements that contribute to a "biological vulnerability" on a genetic, neurophysiological and neurochemical basis combine with psychogenic factors to produce the "catastrophic" character of the bodily experience' (Gorman et al. 2000).

Both psychosomatic and cognitivist studies of panic have underlined the centrality of bodily experience and the mechanisms of 'somatosensory amplification' whereby unpleasant sensations are perceived and interpreted as 'catastrophic' (Clark 1986): this is a theory of *bodily turmoil*.

The premorbid personalities of these patients are characteristically based on the rigid control of their affects. Their principal traits are cutoff-ness and a contempt for the world of affects, together with an exclusive focus on their physical symptoms, so that any links with meaning, or with the affective context that might have generated them are severed; and the affects that are controlled or negated are those linked to loss, abandonment and to separation that might evoke the idea of their original attachments.

Furthermore, the dramatic immediacy of the crisis characterized by 'loss of control' and 'break down in security' ushers in a sense of grief and reproach in such patients towards an idealized body which had guaranteed them a perfection of well-being and security: an example of what Resnik (1986) has referred to as *narcissistic depression*.

Freud was the first to describe such a condition when, in *Inhibitions, Symptoms and Anxiety* (1926), he distinguished *signal anxiety* from *automatic anxiety*, whose prototype was the sensory catastrophe of birth and the sensation of impotence which was so overwhelming as to paralyze the mind. It is as if somatic sensation for some reason fails to reach the world of representation and remains confined to the body without being able to unfold into the propositional network which thought might offer it.

This brings us to an examination of the logic of chaotic experience which is the feeling of catastrophe that mind attributes to body, and which paralyses its functions of affect regulation.

The logic of turmoil

In *The Unconscious as Infinite Sets* (1975), Matte Blanco systematically confronts that aspect of emotion which is rooted in the body and which is expressed in terms of what he calls *sensation-emotion*. This in turn is nothing other than the way in which the emotional mind gets hold of the body, and which William James had equated to the whole of emotional experience. In other words, if we are frightened, we are first and foremost, frightened bodies, and the ensemble of sensations of fear that the body evinces is picked up somehow by the very mind which is representing the world in a threatening way. And Matte Blanco maintains in contrast to James, but in agreement with Sartre, that the cognitive or transformative element of this, the thought of fear, is essential to the phenomenon of emotion.

Matte Blanco developed a painstaking analysis of sensation, concentrating in particular on the idea of it as the interface which accesses the first inkling of 'feeling' into the area of the mental. Only as such can sensation be isolated, he suggests, as for instance in the case of the sensation of pain or in one of synaesthesia, or as part of a more complex emotion such as fear. But for mind to get hold of it, for it not to remain as a pure 'noumenon', it has to be 'clothed in thought', and so, with relations, as is the case when it makes up part of a given perceptual experience.

In his last work, *Thinking, Feeling and Being* (1988), he returns to this theme and suggests the notion that sensation can become the point of departure for 'symmetrical developments'. These developments are precisely those that make up the original experience of turmoil which is linked to the body and the bombardment of disorganized sensation that it generates. The ethological expectation is that such sensation be organized in the mind of a care-giver. In his concept of the *concrete original object*, Ferrari (2004) makes this the very foundation of the function and activity of thinking which unfolds in the world of representation.

It will be clear from what we have said that the symmetrical experience of turmoil recalls the infinite, and has the characteristics of 'infinite experience' (Rayner 1981). The symmetrical developments mentioned by Matte Blanco are processes of infinitization of experience which arise in the body and its sensations. So panic and the accompanying sense of helplessness result in the limitless re-emergence of feelings of infinity. These can no longer be held in a mind which was not originally constituted as an elaborative space in relation to them, but as a protective dyke. Following Matte Blanco, we might describe the collapse of this containing function on the part of the mind as the *unfolding function* becoming less critical. The task of this function of unfolding, which is never complete, is the translation – whence Matte Blanco talks about the *translating function* as well – of unconscious emotional experience into conscious experience. Personally, we find the term *unfolding* more satisfactory, because it implies not only discrimination or differentiation of what is lived as one and is precisely about emotional feeling, but also the unwinding into finite space-time of something that, in itself, shuns the limitations of space and time: it is an unfolding that is necessarily 'without end', potentially and only potentially, infinite.

Invoking these functions which endlessly extract asymmetrical relations from the emotional unconscious, Matte Blanco recasts Freud's famous dictum, 'where id was, there shall ego be' (1932) entrusting the task of enriching asymmetry and therefore the ego with a continuously flowing source to the 'unfolding' without end: the enrichment is one he adds 'does not reduce the size of the source, not simply because the source is infinite, but on account of the fact that the translation of symmetrical being into asymmetrical terms does not take anything *away* from symmetrical being : it only increases the total amount of asymmetry'. So he concludes: 'Emotion offers the intellect unlimited possibilities of development . . . Emotion is the mother of thinking' (Matte Blanco 1975, pp. 301–303).

A note on catastrophic change

In *Attention and Interpretation* (1970), one of his most inspired works, Bion takes up a work that he had read to the British Psychoanalytic Society, and formulates the concept of 'catastrophic change' as an abstract structure, and, therefore, as a class of equivalence made up of various configurations whose unchanging aspect is characteristic of a particular *transformation in the relationship of container contained*. This concerns the mental functioning of the individual and his function as thinker of the thought. It also concerns that of the group in contact with the new idea, with the 'mystic' who gives birth to or develops it in its 'body'. Pondering the catastrophic nature of such a transformation, Bion gives the configuration, container-contained, a connotation of explosiveness in the sense of the presence within it of *oppositional tension* between centrifugal and centripetal forces. These push towards destruction, the collapse or disintegration of the container through the action of the contained, or towards the annihilation or evacuation of the contained by the container. The *model of stammering* which he cites in chapter ten of the same book, and in which the oppositional tension concerns the emotions, is important in this regard. In it, the oppositional tension is between the emotions: its meaning and the way in which he expresses it are very close to our model of panic. He says:

> The man was trying to contain his experience in the form of words; he was trying to contain himself, as one sometimes says of someone about to lose control of himself; he was trying to 'contain' his emotions in the form of words, as one might speak of a general attempting to 'contain' enemy forces within a given zone.
> The words that should have represented the meaning the man wanted to express were fragmented by the emotional forces to which he wished to give only verbal expression; the verbal formulation could not 'contain' his emotions, which broke through and dispersed it as enemy forces might break through the forces that strove to contain them.
>
> (Bion 1970, p. 94)

> . . . The expression is lost in an 'explosion' in which the verbal formulation is lost.
>
> (Ibid., 95)

Bria (1989) reads Bion's catastrophic change as an abstract bi-logical structure whose basis was the *symmetrization of the relation container-contained*: a Simassi structure that Matte Blanco (1988) suggested could also be used for projective identification in which the model – to use Bion's word – was realized of a container into which an object might be projected, or a content that could be projected into a container. Here, there is a real subversion of topology in which at the same time, symmetrical aspects are present that require the distinction between part and whole, and between internal and external. Symmetry is also in evidence in aspects of in-division whereby there is an identity between internal and external as well as between container and contained. This is the result of part or aspects of the self being projected more or less wholesale into the object, and being felt to be indistinguishable from the object. In effect, catastrophic change is associated by Bion with phenomena of 'explosive projection' which characterize fear or psychotic panic, and which occur – as he asserts in line with Matte Blanchian thought – in a mental space that has no visual images to fulfil the functions of a co-ordinate system, either 'the "faceted solid" or the multi-dimensional, multi-linear figure of lines intersecting at a point' because the space is felt 'as an immensity so great that it cannot be represented even by astronomical space because it cannot be represented at all' (Bion 1970, p. 12).

If we apply all of this to panic and to the relation which it creates between mind and emotional experience, we will find there the same catastrophic transformation ('symmetrization') of the configuration container-contained, which, as we know, is an asymmetrical relationship, which thought requires. We can consider this catastrophic transformation, which gives rise to a sudden qualitative experiential change, to be the result of an actual 'mental operator' which, by operating on basic asymmetrical relations, such as that between the container and the thing contained, has – in Matte Blanchian terms – symmetrizing and hence infinitizing effects. Applied to the relation between mind and emotional experience, it might be termed the collapser of the container which fails to contain and transform that persecuting infinity that arises in the body. This is a useful spatial metaphor which makes use of explosive projection, as we have already seen, to describe the emergence of feeling from a deep level, feeling that as Bion suggests, does not achieve representation and is condemned in the failure.

We will illustrate these concepts with two clinical vignettes.

First clinical case: Mario

Mario is a young patient who presented for the first time in a state of panic, some time after his father's death. This had happened after a long illness that had slowly but inexorably 'rotted' his body away. At the time of his father's death, he was apparently devoid of emotions to the point where 'it was he who was helping everyone else' and comforting them. Two years later, his first crisis erupted in relation to an unexpected physical illness. This was characterized with physical wasting, uncontrollable fear, the terror of going mad, of no longer being himself, and of his own body literally rotting away. It was as if his father's body had returned like a ghost to announce his imminent death. Psychotherapeutic exploration revealed an omnipotent personality who exercised rigid control over his emotions. This was manifest in a perfectionist and self-aggrandizing attention to his body, with which 'he collected sporting trophies and extraordinary sexual exploits.' He lavished care on it on a daily basis, with exhaustive exercise so as to be invulnerable to any illness: an omnipotent carapace-container with which to confront the unpredictable and infinite threats that his body offered him. It was clear that the unexpected and painful experience of mortality with which his father had confronted him had not been adequately processed and had now reappeared like the bursting of a bank, or a dyke that had been precociously erected against any 'flood' of emotion linked with loss. And while the crisis put him in contact with *a tide of infinite emotion* linked to *the infinite vulnerability of his body*, it was also the case that the crisis found its force in his inability to think (*collapse of the container*), to 'contain' the infinite emotion which needed to be processed and so 'thought'.

Over the course of the therapy, M. kept a diary of his 'impressions' and 'sensations' which he punctually entrusted to me before each session. Here are some entries that are particularly significant and pertinent to our theme:

> I'm sure that my breakdowns start with a feeling of fear. If I can explain, I have been terrified for my father's life ever since I was a child. I sometimes managed obsessively and controllingly to hear whether he was breathing when he was asleep. His illnesses made him seem vulnerable to me to the point that as a child I insisted on taking care of him. After he died, I went to the cemetery for

31

12 days, not only to be close to him – too close, really – but as if I were still keeping up that instinct of protection like a mission impossible. It's probably obvious that I've never accepted his death, so much as death-as-the-end-of-a-life-of-suffering. I'm not frightened of death – that's a normal process – I'm terrified of bodily suffering. . . .

I'm getting used to emotions. Having them doesn't have to mean having to put the lid on them as I did for years . . . I had a really significant dream last night, I can tell you. . . . the day before I had a really nice day with my dad who was alive; next day, he died. I think that this is a real step in the direction of my accepting his death as the end of his life, not just as the end of his suffering.

My problem was emotions that I wasn't used to. Just a little makes me drunk as if I were a tee-totaller and you weren't – a little doesn't make you drunk. I'm like an emotional tee-totaller . . . I'm sure that given my obsessionality, there are often times that I misinterpret signs of tiredness even in my body and within the labyrinth of my fear . . . I so wish I could have fun and get some laughter back.

Panic, therefore, could be described in Matte Blanchian terms as a failure of the function of unfolding, this being essential for operating the processes of differentiation and integration that characterize conscious functioning (cf. Tononi 2002). This function is necessary for us to be aware of our emotions, so that we can know what they mean and modulate their intensity adaptively. The function of unfolding seems connected with an *activation of a dialogue between the body and the mind* ('I'm like an emotional tee-totaller') and with a *perception of time* ('the day before I had a really nice day with my dad who was alive'). Its failure, furthermore, together with the pressure of emotional reality exposes us to sensory and emotional 'catastrophe' which is saturated with infinity, so that we are in a vicious circle in which we are overcome or inactivated, increasing our sense of insecurity.

Second clinical case: Susan

Susan, a 40-year-old woman, was in four-session-a-week analysis because of severe panic attacks which she described as being like plunging into overwhelming physical sensations of feeling pulverized and then sucked up into a terrifying void. Over the years she had tried various kinds of psychotherapy (behaviour therapy, autogenic training, group analysis, etc.) without being helped at all thereby, before she came to psychoanalysis.

For the first few years of her analysis the approach of holiday separations provoked violent reactions including personal insults and screaming, as well as the repeatedly stated intention to break off her analysis for good. The situation had evolved thereafter to the point where S. could recognize the continuity of our relationship over the summer vacation. In correspondence with this evolution she showed a distinctly increased awareness of her own body and emotions.

We shall be dealing here with a clinical fragment from her sixth year of analysis. She asked if she could make up a session which she had had to cancel, but unfortunately her analyst was unable to grant her request. S. reacted by promising that she would never again make the mistake of asking her analyst for anything.

At her next session S. brought in a dream in which she saw her analyst in the midst of a group of people; he was engaged in writing a speech for a girl whom the others would be listening to. S., on the other hand, saw herself, wearing a little mini-skirt, in the uninhibited performance of somersaults which revealed her almost naked bottom, covered only by a G–string. At this point in the dream the analyst approached her and said that she was an 'apeiron'. In the dream she recognized this as an Ancient Greek word, but she didn't know what it meant. She had the impression that this scene had taken place in Piazza Indipendenza (Independence Square).

The morning after the dream she was at pains to dig up her old Ancient Greek dictionary from her schooldays to check whether the word in fact meant something like undisciplined, without limits; at the same time she found another similar word that meant 'someone who is far-sighted'.

Her analyst told her that, thanks to her dream, she could be far-sighted and become aware of her reaction to her frustration at her analyst not having been able to give her an alternative session: in fact she had felt betrayed by him since he was taking care of another patient and neglecting her, and she took her revenge by asserting herself through her acrobatic motion, while also asserting her independence of any sort of connection with him or with frustration or disappointment. S. answered in her customary excited tone that she needed to assert herself and that even in the first dream she had recounted to him in analysis she had seen herself turning somersaults in a room.

During the following session S. reported that she had just had an X-ray which revealed a sacro-coccygeal infraction, as a result of which she could no longer even sit. Thus she introduced a report of what had happened during a party in the country. For fun she had executed a long-jump. She had been very good at this sport when she was young. On this occasion, however, she took a running start and off she went, leaping and then landing right on her bottom with a shooting pain that left her breathless for several minutes. When she thought it over she realized that she had in no way considered the fact that it was thirty years since last she had jumped, and that where she was jumping now there was just earth covered with grass, a very different sort of thing from the sand on which one normally does the long-jump and to which she had been accustomed. She added to this report the detail that when she undressed for her X-ray she realized that underneath her trousers she was wearing only a G-string, leaving her bottom completely uncovered so that she felt very ill at ease in front of the radiologist. She said that she found that a G-string was extremely comfortable, contrary to what is generally believed, but on this occasion, when she had to show herself with so little covering, she had felt awful. Since she was no longer a young woman, if she had thought of it she would have put on a pair of ordinary knickers. She connected the G-string at the X-ray with the scene in her dream in which she turned somersaults, revealing her bare bottom.

At this point the analyst proposed a hypothesis with which he intended to knit together the phenomena that had emerged. He said that she had told him about two examples of how she did herself damage by adopting a position towards herself of an *apeiron* who takes no account of any sort of limit. In fact she took no account, when putting on her clothes, of the context in which she would find herself: consequently she was embarrassed when faced by external reality. The long-jump was a much more serious matter: here it was quite plain that she hurt herself by taking no account of real limits, such as, for example, the limits implied by the thirty years that had passed since her last jump, by her no longer being able to jump as if she were a young girl and by the fact that jumping on grass is quite different from jumping on sand. This behaviour was indicative of a general criterion which she used *in relation to her body*, involving doing away

34

with all perception of limits connected to it, just as she attempted to do away with all frustration connected *to the limitations of the analytic relationship.* Then she took no account of any sort of limit in relation to her analyst: consequently if he had no space to change her session, it happened only because he treated her impersonally, and not – more realistically – because he was subjected to time limitations. The result was that she left her body in the *apeiron*, i.e. in limitlessness, removed from the possibility of recognizing any sort of limit. Hence when her body was subject to intense emotions it charged right ahead without limits, creating just that infinite panic which so terrified her.

This material might perhaps have lent itself to a different type of intervention, which would have stressed that the patient may actually have wanted to bare her bottom to the analyst and that having injured her bottom was a sort of acting out of her guilt for having exposed it to the analyst in her dream. We, however, think that this kind of intervention would have involved the risk of eroticizing the relationship and deflecting the analysand from the conflictual area of her relationship with herself, her body and her emotions which was emerging in analysis, and the working through of what we consider the more urgent conflictual element needed to be fostered first. This is in line with our considerations about the need to favour *reverie* and the unfolding of symmetrical structures (Matte Blanco 1988), leaving a more particular focus on transference interpretation for a later stage. Reference to the transference is nonetheless present in the analysand's tendency to ignore the objective spatio-temporal limitations to which the analyst is subject in relation to his availability.

S. replied that she found what the analyst had said important because when she was seized by panic it was actually a catastrophe for her and indeed she wanted to be more careful so as not to hurt herself. This constructive answer astonished, given her tendency to reject her analyst's ideas, or at best to reply that whatever he was saying to her was something she had said already. In this sense S.'s acceptance of her own body and emotions seemed connected with her new acceptance of her analytic relationship. She went on to say that she now understood why she was so greatly drawn to the sea: it cannot, in fact, be confined, and one's body seems free of all limits in the water. One feels weightless, and the boundaries of one's body seem to disappear.

We have chosen this material because, through the reference to *apeiron*, it reveals *a tendency towards infinitization* which is implicit in *a* relationship with the body symmetrical feelings that are kept apart from the asymmetrical elements deriving from a connection with reality and thought. Progress in internal integration between symmetry and asymmetry is realized in analysis through the mediation of the analyst's *reverie* (Bion 1962), but only in the final stages of the analytic process can the analyst's contribution be clearly accepted and recognized (Lombardi 2003). The fracture between symmetry and asymmetry (Matte Blanco 1988), as well as the fracture between the body and the mind (Ferrari 2004), at the beginning of the analysis had as one consequence the inability to contain senso-emotional data, a feature of such syndromes as serious panic attacks, which show in their violence and the depth of this dissociation some distinctly psychotic aspects.

To paraphrase a biblical metaphor used by Freud (1893–95) ('it is easier for a camel to pass through the eye of a needle than for a rich man to enter the kingdom of heaven'), we might say that, in cases of this sort, the camel of the body and body-related symmetrized feelings has a hard time passing through the eye of the needle of thought and meeting asymmetry, because of the internal system of the patient's misconceptions (Money-Kyrle 1968), which is forcibly pulling corporeality in the direction of concreteness and infinitization.

At this point, Matte Blanco would say that to be at ease with ourselves, we need to be in good contact with both modes of being: to be capable of asymmetrical consciousness, but also and above all, of living the infinity of symmetrical experience. In conclusion, we find ourselves with our emotions in the midst of the infinite, and discover that, as a symbolic structure, it responds to the need to *transcend* the finite limits of our consciousness, but that it is at the same time, *immanent* in our psychic being, as Blaise Pascal (1670/1962) intuited. What is certain is that with Matte Blanco, infinity broke into the science of psychoanalysis, and it's here to stay; it should become a fundamental tool in the growth of our own consciousness and in the interpretation of clinical fact.

Note

1 Chapter written with Pietro Bria. A different version was published as Bria, P., & Lombardi, R. (2008). The logic of turmoil: some epistemological and clinical considerations on emotional experience and the infinite. *International Journal of Psychoanalysis*, 89: 709–726.

References

Binswanger, L. (1965). *Wahn*. Pfullingen: Verlag Gunther Neske.

Bion, W. R. (1950). The imaginary twin. In *Second thoughts* (pp. 3–22). London: Karnac Books, 1967.

Bion, W. R. (1962). *Learning from experience*. London: Karnac Books, 1984.

Bion, W. R. (1965). *Transformations*. London: Karnac Books.

Bion, W. R. (1970). *Attention and interpretation*. London: Karnac Books.

Bion, W. R. (1974). *Brazilian lectures part 2*. Rio de Janeiro: Imago Editoria.

Bion Talamo, P. (1999). *Metapsicologia y metamatematica en algunas teorias psicoanaliticas recientes*. Buenos Aires: Editorial Polemos.

Bon de Matte, L. (1988). An account of Melanie Klein's conception of projective identification. In I. Matte Blanco (Ed.), *Thinking, feeling and being* (pp. 319–330). London: Routledge.

Borges, J. L. (1932). Metempsicosi della tartaruga. In *'Discussione'. Tutte le opere I*. Milan: Mondadori, 1984.

Bria, P. (1981). Pensiero, mondo e problemi di fondazione [Thought, world, and problems of 'foundation']. Introduction to I. Matte Blanco, *L'inconscio come insiemi infiniti [The unconscious as infinite sets]* (pp. 19–111). Turin: Einaudi.

Bria, P. (1985). Freud e la contraddizione: un punto di vista bi-logico. In M. Pissacroia (Ed.), *Delle psicoanalisi possibili: Bion, Lacan, Matte Blanco*. Rome: Borla.

Bria, P. (1989). Il cambiamento catastrofico come struttura astratta bi-logica [Catastrophic change as an abstract bi-logical structure]. In P. Bria (Ed.), *Il pensiero e l'infinito [Thought and the infinite]*. Castrovillari: Teda.

Bria, P. (1999, July). *Los silogismos afectivos y la logica del delirio. Un enfoque bi-logico a la psico-patologia [Emotional syllogisms and the logic of delusion. A bi-logical approach to psychopathology]*. Paper presented at the IPA Congress, Santiago, Chile.

Clark, D. M. (1986). A cognitive approach to panic. *Behaviour Research and Therapy*, 24(4): 461–470.

Dedekind, R. (1888). *Was sind und was sollen die Zahlen?* In O. Taussky (Ed.), *Gesammelte mathematische Werke*. Berlin: Springer Verlag. (Reprinted 1969, New York: Chelsea)

Ferrari, A. B. (2004). *From the eclipse of the body to the dawn of thought*. London: Free Association Books.

Figà Talamanca, A. (1989). L'esperienza 'interna': base empirica per l'infinito. In *Il pensiero e l'infinito*. Castrovillari: Teda.

Freud, S. (1893–95). Studies on hysteria. *Standard Edition*, 2: 1–306.

Freud, S. (1900). The interpretation of dreams. *Standard Edition*, 4–5.

Freud, S. (1911). Formulations on the two principles of mental functioning. *Standard Edition*, 12: 213–226.

Freud, S. (1915a). Instincts and their vicissitudes. *Standard Edition*, 14: 109–140.

Freud, S. (1915b). The unconscious. *Standard Edition*, 14: 159–215.

Freud, S. (1926). Inhibitions, symptoms and anxiety. *Standard Edition*, 20: 75–176.

Freud, S. (1932). New introductory lectures on psycho-analysis. *Standard Edition*, 22: 1–182.

Freud, S. (1940). An outline of psychoanalysis. *Standard Edition*, 23: 139–208.

Gaddini, E. (1969). On imitation. In E. Gaddini & A. Limentani (Ed.), *A psychoanalytic theory of infantile experience: conceptual and clinical reflections* (pp. 18–34). London: Karnac Books, 1992.

Galilei, G. (1638). Discorsi e dimostrazioni matematiche intorno a due nuove scienze. In L. Geymonat & A. Carugo (Eds.), *Opere.* Turin: UTET, 1958.

Gorman, J.M., Kent, J.M., Sullivan, G.M. & Coplan, J.D. (2000). Neuroanatomical hypothesis of panic disorder, revised. *American Journal of Psychiatry*, 157(4): 493–505.

Jaspers, K. (1959). *Allgemein psychopathologie*. Berlin: Springer-Verlag.

Klein, M. (1940). Mourning and its relation to manic depressive states. In *Love, guilt and reparation, and other works 1921–1945*. New York: Delta, 1977.

Klein, M. (1952). Some theoretical conclusion regarding the emotional life of the infant. In *Envy and gratitude, and other works 1946–1963*. New York: Delta, 1975.

Lombardi, R. (2000). Corpo, affetti, pensieri. Riflessioni su alcune ipotesi di I. Matte Blanco e A. B. Ferrari [Body, feelings, thoughts. Reflections on some of the theories of I. Matte Blanco and A.B. Ferrari]. *Rivista di Psicoanalisi*, 46(4): 683–706.

Lombardi, R. (2002a). Primitive mental states and the body. A personal view of Armando B. Ferrari's concrete original object. *International Journal of Psychoanalysis*, 83: 363–381.

Lombardi, R. (2002b). *Through the eye of the needle: unfolding of the unconscious and the body*. Paper presented at the International Bi-logic Conference, Adelphi University, New York.

Lombardi, R. (2003). Mental models and language registers in the psychoanalysis of psychosis. An overview of a thirteen-year analysis. *International Journal of Psychoanalysis*, 84: 843–863.

Marty, P. (1976). *Les mouvements inividuelles de vie et de mort*. Paris: Payot.

Matte Blanco, I. (1959). Expression in symbolic logic of the characteristics of the system Ucs. or the logic of the system Ucs. *International Journal of Psychoanalysis*, 40: 1–5.

Matte Blanco, I. (1975). *The unconscious as infinite sets*. London: Karnac Books.

Matte Blanco, I. (1988). *Thinking, feeling and being*. London: Routledge.

Money-Kyrle, R. (1968). On cognitive development. *International Journal of Psychoanalysis*, 49: 691–698.

Pascal, B. (1670). *Pensées [Thoughts]*. Paris: Librairie Générale Française, 1962.

Rayner, E. (1981). *Unconscious logic*. London: Routledge.

Resnik, S. (1979). L'inconscio. In *Enciclopedia Einaudi* (Vol. 7). Turin: Einaudi.

Resnik, S. (1986). *L'esperienza psicotica*. Milan: Boringhieri.

Resnik, S. (2001). *The delusional person: bodily feeling in psychosis*. London: Karnac Books.

Sartre, J. P. (1936). *Idee per una teoria delle emozioni*. Milan: Bompiani.

Schneider, K. (1950). *Klinische psychopathologie*. Stuttgart: Gerg Thieme Verlag.

Scott, W. C. (1948). Some embriological, neurological, psychiatric and psychoanalytic implications of the body scheme. *International Journal of Psychoanalysis*, 29: 141–155.

Tausk, V. (1933). On the origin of the 'influencing machine' in schizophrenia. *Psychoanalytic Quarterly*, 2: 519–556.

Tononi, G. (2002). *Galileo e il fotodiodo*. Laterza: Bari.

Winnicott, D. W. (1953). Mind and its relation to the psyche-soma. In *Collected papers: through paediatrics to psycho-analysis*. London: Tavistock, 1958.

2

SYMMETRIC FRENZY AND CATASTROPHIC CHANGE

An exploration of primitive mental states in the wake of Bion and Matte Blanco[1]

The attempt to translate the non-spatial and timeless aspects of human nature into space-time is essential to thinking but it is always a form of 'thinkating'.
—Matte Blanco (1988, p. 316)

In this chapter I will be exploring several characteristics of primitive mental states in relation to some of the theories of Bion and Matte Blanco. It seems justified to weave together the perspectives of these two authors, given that each held the other in high esteem. Furthermore, Matte Blanco himself reflected on Bion's theories in relation to his own theory of the unconscious as infinite sets (1981) in an essay that was published in a *festschrift* to celebrate Bion's eightieth birthday. Clearly I will not be able to look at the whole of their work, as this would be an undertaking for a book, not a paper. Rather I will be focussing on some aspects of Bion's *catastrophic change* which have captured my attention, linking these to Matte Blanco's concept of *symmetric frenzy*. Introducing this idea (1988, p. 228), he writes: 'Here I think, it is essential to remember that as we go "deeper" we begin to enter the strata where time and space relations are dissolving, where asymmetrical relations begin to decrease, and we find ourselves confronted with increasing proportions of symmetrical relations.'[2]

Working within the length constraints, I will aim to set clinical material and theoretical ideas alongside one another. It should be noted that both of these authors write in very abstract terms, referring frequently to philosophical issues and leaving it to the reader to consider and weigh up the clinical significance and implications of their ideas. This has led to what Parthenope Bion called the impossibility of saying that we are 'Bionian', as this signifies, first and foremost, being ourselves: 'I have come to bury Caesar, not to praise him' as she used to say, quoting Shakespeare's Mark Anthony, during the preparations for the conference for Bion's centenary (see Merciai 2000). In the same way, Matte Blanco lays out a psychoanalytic epistemology based on bi-logic, without setting out the implications of his thought on technique, leaving ample room for personalized versions of his approach.

The approaches of Bion and Matte Blanco find a common focus of interest in the formal structures that organize thought. They also reconsider the functioning of the unconscious (Freud 1900, 1915, 1940) in current terms. Central to the analyst's interest is the conflict between the a-spatial and a-temporal nature of the unconscious (not to mention the a-dimensional abyss from which it is derived) and the organizing concepts of space and time. In particular, in the treatment of severe cases, this conflict can become the central core of the clinical work with the patient, as I hope to show later on.

I will start by presenting clinical material and will then consider the theoretical perspective, returning to the clinical context again at the end of the chapter. Since my reflections mainly come from experience, I hope that by starting with clinical material I can help the reader to obtain a practical understanding of the ideas explored. Indeed, the terminology used by Bion and Matte Blanco can end up seeming obscure and hard to understand, due to the limitations imposed by the nature of their subject: thought. Thought, by its nature, refers back to absence (Bion 1962a); and is in its own essence inevitably obscure and ineffable (Bion 1965).

The first part of the clinical material here examines the problems that the psychotic patient has with the capacity to think. As we will see more specifically in the theoretical part of the chapter, the first section deals with the emergence of *the patient's relationship with himself, as well as the activation of mental phenomena which can begin to contain the emotional chaos* (Freud 1911; Bion 1962b). By contrast, the clinical section towards the end of the article shows a more advanced stage of the working-through with the same analysand, in which he begins to *recognize the analyst as a separate object that he cannot control.*

The separation of the clinical material into two sections has been done purposefully to highlight the two distinct levels of analytic work, and to emphasize the importance of switching to interpreting the transference during the more advanced phases of the analysis. These phases are marked by the reduction of emotional turmoil and the expansion of a mental space with a well-developed capacity to symbolize.

Confronting the breakdown of normal perception of space and time in the psychoanalysis of psychosis

Gerardo, a twenty-five-year-old patient who is tall and athletic, is in his fourth year of analysis of four sessions a week. His childhood was characterized by schizoid and autistic periods. He suffered a first period of acute psychosis at the age of sixteen, but this subsided in the course of a few weeks following medical intervention. The seriousness of this episode was completely denied by his family: his parents even welcomed the rather strange suggestion of taking the boy swimming with dolphins in a tropical country, as an alleged therapy for his problem. The second phase of acute psychosis happened five years later, when G. was twenty-one. This time the danger signs were more pronounced; indeed the patient's state of insanity, his mental disturbance and suicidal tendencies lasted for over a year. The patient started in intensive psychoanalysis of four sessions per week immediately after the first appearance of the symptoms, when the confusion, madness and violence were still in their acute phase; the sessions continued without interruption even during very dramatic periods when it became necessary for the patient to be hospitalized. The analysis was accompanied by medication for the symptoms, administered by an analyst–psychiatrist, and a third colleague worked with the parents. During the years that followed, the patient gradually developed mental functioning and his behaviour and ability to relate improved, which enabled the more demanding analytic work to begin (see Lombardi 2007, which deals with the progress of the analysis in its early stages).

I am going to look at a particular phase of instability that occurred during the fourth year of the analysis, which triggered a fear of regression into madness. Up until this point, the sessions had been taking place with regularity; therefore I was quite worried when one day G. did not arrive for his Monday session. After about ten minutes I received a telephone call from his mother, saying that G. had suffered a rather strange breakdown a short distance from my consulting room, and was therefore being taken to hospital in an ambulance. I later discovered that G. had been overcome by a panic attack; his breathing was laboured and he had needed an oxygen mask. However, he was discharged from hospital the same day, thanks to the psychiatric medication administered by our team.

The fact that G. was unable to get to the consulting room, although he was only a few metres away, is a circumstance which can be considered in the light of one of the theories being discussed in this chapter, that is, *the dismemberment of spatio-temporal coordinates and the patient's collapse into the black hole of formless infinity*. Indeed, from the material which emerged during the following sessions, I discovered that on this occasion, G.'s perception of space dissolved into infinity so that he experienced complete mental disorientation and a sense of total paralysis and collapse. The patient was unable to cover the short distance, rather like how, in the paradox of Zeno of Elea, Achilles is unable to defeat the tortoise. Indeed, when the phenomenon which Matte Blanco called 'symmetrization' gains the upper hand over asymmetrization, the *encounter with 'the indivisible'* can make it impossible to cover a distance which, in purely objective terms would seem trivial. For his part, Bion (1967, p. 136) emphasizes that for certain patients 'measurements of time and space are based on psychic reality and not physical space or time.' In the psychic reality of the patient, a realistic conception of space and time relies, for Bion, on having mental apparatus that is capable of discriminating. Such a capacity can by no means be taken for granted with more damaged patients. In the same way, for Matte Blanco, it is unlikely that such patients will be able to articulate asymmetries when faced with the symmetrizations of the unconscious.

In the context of the psychotic panic experienced by G. during this episode, it was the relationship with me that was a stake, together with the *points* and the *lines* (as Bion would have said) that this relationship allowed him to construct in his mental space, in order to *work through the return after a separation*. This explicit emergence of otherness in the relationship will be treated in more depth in the second section of clinical material at the end of this article. Before examining this relational level, it was first necessary to deal with the re-surfacing of G.'s emotional turmoil and the fragility of his capacity for representation and thought. His emotions made themselves

43

known through acting–out, as had been the case in the early stages of the analysis.

In the course of the subsequent sessions it therefore became necessary to work through this experience, 'unfolding' the infinity of the real emotion in terms of the main finite elements which constituted it (Matte Blanco 1975). I will try to illustrate several aspects of this work.

I will start by describing an extremely difficult session, the first part of which was taken up with shouting and insults, threats to destroy the furniture in the room and animal-like cries of despair. Every attempt I made to try to find meaning in his actions seemed at first to fail. Towards the middle of the session, my work of containment seemed to show some effect and his rage started to subside. Still acting as if he were a wild beast in a cage, G. said to me: 'Inside me there is someone who is screaming in despair and I'm not able to handle him.' As he was saying this, he made a shape with his hands to indicate on his T-shirt an area on his thorax, which went from below his uvula to a little above his belly button, giving the idea of a kind of *homunculus (little man)* which was screaming at him inside. And after a pause he added uncomfortably, 'I am mad.'

I was very impressed by his spatial reference to the 'little man' inside his thorax: this was the first example of representation emerging from the chaos. It was a kind of picture which described a psychic space. In this development, the experience of despair which could not be thought seemed to place itself within an internal space, appearing as something like a part of himself. That is, it seemed that the state of despair and disintegration were now positioned in the context of a 'capacity to recognize a boundary or an asymmetry' (Matte Blanco 1975), or of a 'container/contained relationship'. And this appeared to be an entirely new acquisition for the patient, in spite of the analysand's own confused interpretation of this as a sign of getting worse. His own view assimilated his current despair into his earlier madness, not recognizing the very different quality of his present experience in comparison with the earlier ones.

Therefore I said to him: 'You are now able to recognize inside yourself the violence of your emotions, whereas before you did not see any difference between inside and outside. In fact, you are recognizing your own hatred, your own despair, your own fear of going mad, as things that are yours. But this is happening because you are now *not* mad. Now you are able to recognize your feelings and your

44

anguish, whereas before you could not recognize anything, you only went to pieces.' The patient's response appeared to confirm my interpretation, because G. immediately became calmer. I wanted, through my comments, to underline a difference – an asymmetry – between G.'s current state and his previous condition, which was characterized by paranoia, in which it was others who saw him as 'bad' and hated him: a distinction, which, in its simplicity, had escaped G., threatening to make his suffering worse and to weaken his already fragile ego.

In the next session, G. brought me one of his paintings which represented a face. It evoked Edward Munch's famous painting 'The Scream' – with a mouth that was wide open and screaming and concentric circles of dark and violent colours moving outwards from it. At the same time, G. started to yell at me, insulting me, as he had done during the time of his serious illness. I said to him that now when he cried out in a violent and desperate way, he was overlooking the fact that he had the capacity to represent and to think about what he was feeling, as the picture he had given me demonstrated. Almost amazed, G. stopped yelling at me, he looked in my direction and said that when he had drawn that picture he didn't have any idea what was happening to him and only after drawing it did he realize. I had the impression that in so saying, G. felt himself to be 'dreaming' (Bion 1992) everything that was happening in the session between us, so that his capacity to represent through the drawing had started to exist in his mind only when this fact was highlighted by my saying so. Then I said to him that now he could see himself and think about himself, see his hatred and his despair, just as in his own time he had discovered himself to be capable of representing himself in the drawing, in order to manage his explosive feelings. G. seemed to be able to take in my comments as, after this, the session no longer had the threatening and explosive quality that had been there at the beginning.

By referring to his earlier experience of having no idea of what was happening to him, G. highlighted to me the tendency to hold oneself outside of consciousness and perception of self. This state had characterized the early part of his acute psychotic crisis, during which a sort of black cloud had engulfed him, *annihilating almost the whole of his capacity for self-recognition*. The picture, however, introduced to the session a capacity to represent feelings of despair and hatred: in the absence of this ability to represent there was nothing else for G. to do but act out his emotions concretely, evacuating them from himself. It was therefore a turning point that I as the analyst verbalized to him the existence of these resources, transforming his act of giving me the picture *from the concrete to the realm of the abstract* (Freud 1915; Bion 1962b) so that it became possible for him to think about himself. The activation of self-perception and abstraction saved him from relapsing into madness, which he felt as a very real threat.

Again, in this second clinical context, increasing the patient's capacity for asymmetric representation (Matte Blanco 1975), or his ability to make significant mental links (Bion 1957, 1970), is an important technique to create the conditions for containment and to establish the conditions for learning from experience which will act as a catalyst for mental growth.

At this point, I am going to refer to a brief episode earlier on in the analysis to enable us to observe the first explicit signs of the activation of mental functioning. On this occasion, G. unexpectedly interrupted his confused discourse and, seated on the couch, he fixed his gaze on my eyes, saying: 'We have never been to the cinema together!' Recovering from my surprise with some difficulty, I replied, 'There is something that we can see together, like a mental cinema which represents what is going on for you inside.' And G. said 'I can see red cascading from the ceiling down the walls . . . it is blood which is running down the walls . . . it is all red.' As the analysand was saying these words, I felt my blood freezing in my veins from blind terror. At the same time, almost paradoxically, I felt a sense of relief as though G.'s emotional haemorrhage was starting to find a boundary, containment within the walls of the consulting room, as if he was starting to find the capacity to represent. A scene from Bergman's *Cries and Whispers* came to mind, in which the black and white of the film is momentarily tinged with red.

To return to more recent events, other factors contributing to G.'s panic attack included the break in the analysis coming up with the approach of the summer holidays, his parents' recent decision to sell the house where G. grew up – which posed an imminent problem of working through the *mourning* – as well as a recent professional failure, as he had failed at the end of an important qualification. There were other factors too. This 'amorphous mass of unconnected and undifferentiated elements' as Bion would have described it (1992, p. 46) needed to be processed by an *alpha-function* (Bion) or by a translation function (Matte Blanco). The lack of this caused G.'s perception of the space between my room and the place where he was, just a few steps away, to become exploded and fragmented. If the analysis had not been able to take care of working through these elements during the following sessions, the pressure they exerted would have mounted until it caused a new psychotic explosion, with dramatic consequences that can be imagined – on both the organizing structures of the mind and the course of the analysis.

A change of direction in psychoanalysis: from the contents of the unconscious to the abyss of the infinite unknown

The clinical episode I have described may help to illuminate a passage in the latter pages of *Second Thoughts* in which Bion affirms that: 'The idea of infinitude is prior to any idea of the finite. The finite is "won from the dark and formless infinite". Restating this more concretely the human personality is aware of infinity, the "oceanic feeling". It becomes aware of limitation, presumably through physical and mental experience of itself and the sense of frustration' (1967, p. 165). Citing 'the dark and formless infinite' of which Milton speaks in *Paradise Lost*, Bion sees the birth of thought as the defining of 'finite' mental boundaries which emerge out of infinity. In another context, Bion wrote that mental links are elements that are won from the dark and amorphous infinite. In this way, in the asystematic manner that struck him as being right, Bion redefined *the relationship between conscious and unconscious in terms of a relationship between infinite and finite*. Emerging from infinity coincides, for Bion, with the activation of a function for generating experience (the alpha-function). From this position, an inexhaustible production of unconscious happens, which in its turn plays a role in the process of mentalization and in the transformation of the mind from infinite to finite.

Bion's view of the unconscious should not be viewed in terms of Freud's repressed unconscious, but instead should be thought of as the unknown – Oedipus and the Sphinx, which we come up against when we try to achieve some form of experience. A decade after *Second Thoughts*, Bion wrote in the *Brazilian Lectures*: 'Most of us think that psycho-analysis is important, not because it is good (we know that even the whole of existing psycho-analytic theory does not get much further than scratching the surface of our problem), but because if we are right in thinking that we have minds we shall have to do something about them' (1974, p. 96). This affirmation seems to echo the key role of negative infinity for the development of knowledge, highlighted by renaissance philosophers such as Nicholas of Cusa.

Bion's interest in centring his thinking on the idea of an oscillation between the infinite and the finite puts him very close, theoretically, to the thinker who, more than any other psychoanalyst, has dedicated his research to the infinite: Ignatio Matte Blanco. Focussing his work on the infinite, Matte Blanco places Freud's revolution in the context of work by other revolutionary thinkers, such as Parmenides and Galileo (Matte Blanco 2006). Thus he locates psychoanalysis within a wider epistemology, which reveals the intimately existential, emotive and cognitive background to his subject matter.

For Matte Blanco, as for Bion, the Freudian conceptualization of the unconscious, typically categorized in terms of the repressed unconscious, was found to be insufficient. In particular this was felt to be the case with regard the widening of the psychoanalytic undertaking to encompass patients with defects in their capacity to think. Thus, the unconscious is viewed more in terms of its structural aspects than its content. In fact the structuring of the mind involves the unconscious dimension, and not a particular part of its contents. This finding led Matte Blanco to say: 'In truth we are on a raft. Our thought does not have foundations from which everything emerges' (quoted by Bria, 1981a). This is an affirmation which echoes Bion's above-mentioned comment that 'The finite "comes out of the dark and formless infinite".'

This journey from the infinite to the finite raises the issue of the understanding of 'symmetric frenzy', where the mind is in greater contact with the sensory and formless world of the id (Freud 1923).

A poem by the German poet Heinrich Heine – '*Die alten boesen Lieder*', from the cycle entitled *Dichterliebe* ('*The poet's love*'), lends itself well to demonstrating this deep conflict, which is by nature intrinsically psychotic. The great scale of the objects in the poem demonstrates the tendency of emotions to become infinite. Out of this circumstance arises a conflict between emotions and the rejection of emotional life, which is aggravated by the intensity of the emotions. The poet is seeking a coffin that is the size of a bridge over the Rhine and is so heavy that it can only be lifted by twelve giants. In the coffin he will bury his emotional life at the bottom of the sea, as it is intolerable.

> The old songs filled with anger
> The bad dreams filled with woe

Let's bury them now – get hold of
A mighty coffin, – ho!

(...)

(And bring a bier as sturdy)
Of planks hewn thick and strong;
It must be even longer
Than the bridge at Mainz is long.

And bring twelve giants also –
They must be brawnier
Than in his Rhine cathedral
Cologne's St Christopher.

Bear it out and sink it
Beneath the deepest wave;
For such a mighty coffin
Befits a mighty grave.

Do you know why it's so heavy,
So great and long and wide?
I put my love and sorrow
And all my pain inside.[3]

Conflict and catastrophe at the origin of thought

The transformation of the instinctual drives into a format that can be represented is, for Bion, a function of the capacity to tolerate frustration. Such a transformation, however, is invested with conflicted content. 'Since thought liberates the intuition there is conflict between the impulse to leave the intuition unexpressed and the impulse to express it. The restrictive element of representation therefore obtrudes in transformation T alpha → T beta of pre-verbal material' (Bion 1970, p. 11).

The restrictive element of representation therefore constitutes for Bion a kind of claustro-agoraphobic conflict, whereby the subject feels almost suffocated as he or she approaches a thinking-transformation. In order for the subject to think it is necessary to enable the apparatus for making meaning and communicating from a virtually undifferentiated world of sensations and feelings. This type of conflict is particularly evident in the psychoanalysis of psychosis. 'Thinking makes me feel trapped' affirmed one of my female analysands, while still very much in the grip of an acute phase of psychosis. In these contexts, the role of the analyst is firstly, on an emotional level, to share the patient's 'claustrophobic' suffering (emotional reverie), but also, at the same time, to operate a cognitive reverie, showing the patient, for example, that it is exactly the 'not-thinking' which leads him to fall into the trap of insanity. In this way the analytic reverie takes care of the patient's needs on a number of levels, and this acts as a catalyst for change. In work which uses the cognitive element of the reverie to address the needs of a patient with a defect of thought, interpretative work must be made a secondary priority. It is necessary to put the interpretation of the transference to one side in order to prioritize therapy that facilitates the development of the patient's 'mental structure'. In the absence of this mental structure, there is much less opportunity for the mind to grow and to have experiences.

As a counterpart to the conflict introduced by the restrictive element of representation, Bion underscores the potentially catastrophic role of very strong emotions in the context of the development of the mind. To do this, he uses the model of the stammer and of boredom, as alternative configurations which derive from an impairment of the container-contained relationship. The mental model of the stammer is characterized by an excess of feeling, while for boredom it is the reverse – there is an emptying of emotion from the analytic exchange. In both cases, the ability to learn from experience is paralysed. The task of the mind faced with very strong emotions is compared by Bion to the work of the general who attempts to 'contain' the enemy forces in a certain zone: a metaphor for the way in which the role of thought and words is to organize and contain the emotional chaos. Bion writes, following on from his military metaphor: 'The words that should have represented the meaning the man wanted to express were fragmented by the emotional forces to which he wished to give only verbal expression; . . . the meaning is too powerful for the verbal formulation; the expression is lost in an 'explosion' in which the verbal formulation is destroyed' (Bion 1970, pp. 94–95).

Later on, Bion explores further the problems posed by the transformation of sensory events into thought experiences when he looks at the relationship between the subjective experience of mental space and the objective spatial-temporal order which is necessary for the organization of thought. When the organizing capacity of the mind is diminished or emotional forces overwhelm the resources of containment, the experience of space becomes fragmented and tends towards the infinite. Not even the immensity of astronomic space can help us to represent these experiences, because they cannot be represented at all.

'Mental space is so vast,' writes Bion (1970, p. 12), 'compared with any realization of three dimensional space that the patient's capacity for emotions is felt to be lost because emotion itself is felt to drain away and be lost in the immensity.'

If it is true that an excess of emotion can lead to the paradoxical configuration of an apparent absence of emotional life, this fact could lead us to reflect on conceptualizations such as Alexithymia, which attribute, in a self-evident manner, an absence of emotions to certain groups of analysands (Sifneos 1967). In these conditions of psychotic panic, Bion writes (1970, p. 12) that 'the patient may bleed to death in his own tissues': however, this type of implosion is not equated with a lack, but rather an excess of emotion.

From the symmetrical to the asymmetrical

For Matte Blanco, the importance of drives as the origin of the unconscious is placed alongside the significance of the mechanisms of symmetrization in the impairment of the capacity for thinking. Also important is the affirmation of an emotional logic dominated by 'infinitized' experiences and by infinite anguish and loss of boundaries, which are linked (Rayner 1981; Grotstein 2000).

In the *Outline of Psychoanalysis* (1940), Freud affirmed that 'the unconscious is the real and true psyche ... In spite of this, it is, however, not said that the quality of consciousness has lost its importance for us. It remains the only light in the shadow of psychic life which illuminates the way and guides us.' If Freud compares the unconscious to the shadow, Matte Blanco translates the evocative nature of this image into the specificity of the functioning of the 'Principle of Symmetry', which leads to the cancelling out of distinctions, producing confusion and disorganization. Meanwhile, the asymmetrizing activity of the conscious mind brings perception and the ability to discriminate. The role of the conscious mind is accentuated by Matte Blanco. It is instrumental in terms of its relationship with the world of the emotions. This mode of thought anticipates the increased attention given to the conscious mind in contemporary psychoanalysis (Busch 2004).

The symmetric–asymmetric oscillation is, for Matte Blanco, constantly involved in mental functioning. Phenomena of sensory saturation, linked to emotional intensity, lead the mind to a continuous slide towards infinitization of emotions, to the point of jeopardizing the work of the unfolding function. This function is adept at transforming phenomena which are largely 'symmetric' into phenomena that are largely 'asymmetric'. The work of leaving behind the symmetric and creating asymmetric functioning which is compatible with the spatial–temporal organization of the conscious mind involves for Matte Blanco the same kind of conflict highlighted by Bion in relation to restricted representation and explosive emotional chaos.

In Gerardo's case, we have seen some first attempts at visual representation that express a first moment of freedom from the experience of fragmentation in an 'empty and formless infinity'. This happened when the analysand coloured the walls of the consulting room with his emotions, and later when he managed to paint the watercolour that was reminiscent of Munch's painting, producing a self-portrait in which emotions were very much in evidence. In the first episode, the real walls of the consulting room remind one of the frame of containment offered by the analytic reverie, onto which the analysand can paint his own proto-experience of an emotional world which is still formless. This is an essential process of mediation to make the experience 'thinkable'. The next achievement, a separate representation of himself in the painting, shows how the various potential activities of the mind – from imaginative creation to intellectual and abstract thought – are forged out of the formless magma of emotional turbulence. As Matte Blanco would have said, 'feeling is the matrix for thought' (1975, Italian version p. 335).

Regarding catastrophic change in terms of the organization of the mind, Bion considers the role of the analysis when an upset of spatial and temporal perception happens: 'the total analysis can be seen as a transformation in which an intense catastrophic emotional explosion O has occurred' (Bion 1970, p. 14).

This conception of catastrophic change and the connected emphasis on the upsetting of the spatial–temporal order comes very close in meaning to Matte Blanco's description of the deep layers of the mind, where symmetric frenzy dominates. In this region of the psyche, 'the amount of symmetrization is so great that thinking, which requires asymmetrical relations, is greatly impaired. The conceptual end is the pure indivisible mode, where everything is everything else, and where the relations between things are all theoretically contained in any single thing which the intellect can grasp. The endless number of things tends to become, mysteriously, only one thing' (Matte Blanco 1988, p. 54).

The experience of indissoluble unity within variety which Bion calls 'O' – 'ultimate reality, absolute truth, the godhead, the infinite, the-thing-in-itself' is for Matte Blanco the one thing which the indivisible mode of being tends towards in its pure state. Both authors underscore the conflicted nature of the most primitive parts of the mind, those parts which involve, for Bion, 'a losing of the self in immensity' and for Matte Blanco, a tendency towards indivisibility and difficulty in maintaining the vital dialectic of symmetric-asymmetric in the face of powerful emotional forces (Ginzburg 2007).

Primitive mental states and symmetric transference

As previously indicated, Matte Blanco's concept of infinite sets and Bion's catastrophic change refer to the early experience of feeling – a chaos of indistinct physical sensations – and also to the experience of thinking in its nascent state. This is a dialectic which seems particularly important when considering the boundary between mind and body.

This relationship between catastrophic experience/symmetric frenzy and the origins of thinking from the body's sensory matrix is important because it shows that the phenomena considered here are not only relevant to experiences of acute psychosis but are actually common dynamics in analytic practice. Such phenomena are relevant in all situations where emotion comes to the fore, or where emotion has overwhelmed the patient to the point of impairing the faculties of thought and experience – a widespread occurrence even in less damaged patients.

Various writers have developed Matte Blanco's contribution with different emphases: Bria (1981a, 1981b, 1999), Di Benedetto (2000), Ginzburg (2004, 2007) and myself (2000, 2006). All of these have highlighted the conflict and at the same time the creative possibilities that arise from combining the world of sensation and the world of thought. They have pointed out the existence of a correspondence between body and mind, whereby the bodily foundations of emotion become the empirical origin of the infinite, or indeed of the infinite sets which constitute the unconscious from Matte Blanco's perspective.

In this interpretation of Matte Blanco's ideas, the body's feeling of infinitude is put in parallel with the incongruence between thinking and feeling, which marks the human animal as a kind of ontological conflict. This same fact has been emphasized on the philosophical front by Emilio Garroni (1992), who reformulated the epistemological problems posed by Thomas Nagel (1981) in 'What Is It Like to Be a Bat?' Garroni considers the conflict between feeling and thinking as a constant in the development of Western philosophy and ethics. This is the same conflict that in *Thinking, Feeling and Being* Matte Blanco (1988) placed at the root of his own conception of the fundamental antinomy between the two modes of being, divisible and indivisible, which recall thinking and feeling. It is a contradiction which summarizes Matte Blanco's point of view on the philosophical and epistemological implications of Freud's discoveries about the unconscious. It is also, in part, found in Bion's reading of the phenomena which constitute catastrophic change.

Whilst focussing on the importance of the conflict between thought and feeling, infinite and finite, non-thinking and thinking, it is important not to neglect certain aspects of analytic technique. The bi-personal nature of the meeting requires a joint commitment of analyst and analysand in order to maintain a profitable link with the emotions; it is necessary to maintain care of the patient alongside the verbal transformation of the experiences that are taking place. The urgent need to organize the mind for the purpose of thinking and the continuing risk of a collapse of the container require the analyst's work to be something other than a systematic interpretation of the transference. Rather, it should be thought of in terms of the ability to maintain some kind of unity when confronted with the deep emotional dynamics of the patient. In Matte Blanco's terms, we can say that at these deep levels we are essentially faced with phenomena of symmetric transference – to handle this, the analyst functions mainly as the patient's 'imaginary twin' (Bion 1950), contributing a constant support as the thinking function for these transference elements. Little by little, the flood of symmetries begins to subside, as the analysand's mental growth progresses with the strengthening of mental resources for asymmetric differentiation. As this happens, the analytic work can address more consistently relational dynamics and a separation of identity takes place in the context of the analytic couple. An example of this journey will be presented in the last part of this chapter.

By accepting the symmetric transference and avoiding a precocious introduction of the recognition of the other, the analyst can facilitate the analysand's encounter with himself as the first interlocutor of his mental functioning. Bion (1988, p. 239) seems to affirm this need to prioritize the relationship of the subject with himself when he states: 'The oracle of Delphi was supposed to have carved into the stone, "Know thyself". So the idea that it is useful and helpful to "know thyself" is not new. In that sense we are trying to say, "I will help you to know yourself. If you tell me something. I will tell it back again to you in a way in which you may be able to see yourself. I am trying to be a mirror which doesn't tell you who I am – that is of no importance whatsoever – but who you are".'

This view is consistent with the emphasis introduced by Bion on the function of the analyst's reverie as a catalyst towards new experiences and understanding for the analysand. The analyst problematizes the patient's utterings and stimulates a continuous enlargement of mental space, valuing in particular the routes into new and un–thought depictions. As Bion affirms, 'Any one of many facets of the patient's statements may be noticed rather than any other. It can be considered as a statement or as a transformation; as multi–dimensional or multi–faceted; it could be represented by a visual image of a figure in which many planes meet or lines pass through a common point. I can represent it to myself by a visual image of a geometric solid with an infinite number of surfaces' (1970, p. 8).

Thus the analyst becomes in Bion's view as well as in Matte Blanco's, a sort of surveyor of the infinite, or as Paul Valéry said, with an expression that emphasizes poetically the meeting of opposites, *'un algébriste, au service d'un reveur affiné'* / 'an algebraist, in the service of a subtle dreamer'.

Otherness as a source of asymmetry and containment

I am now going to return to Gerardo's story, to consider some developments that followed concerning the recognition of otherness as a source of containment for catastrophic symmetrizations encountered in primitive states.

With just over two weeks to go until the summer break, G. presented himself at the penultimate session of the week with a serious and professional air, dressed in dark colours, giving me the impression that he had unexpectedly made progress. He told me that he had that day had a job interview and was now awaiting a response. After a few minutes he received a phone call during the session, to let him know that he had been accepted for a trial period. Processing this news, G. commented straight away, 'It's responsibility that I can't handle. I don't know if I'd manage to stay in a building without running away.'

I felt that recognition of his competence – as he had just been considered capable of working – caused an edgy and claustrophobic reaction from the omnipotent psychotic parts of himself, which were anxious to keep him far away from reality. Therefore I said to him: 'When you are approved of, a reality is introduced, which has limits. At this point, you feel hatred and attack your responsibility and its links with reality – you run away. But in so doing you are brought close to madness.' I saw that G. reacted with an expression of worry on his face and said, 'I no longer want to be attached to my mother, but then I feel that there's a void. . . .' And he went on, making a sign with his hand as though his brain was falling out of his head. I noted that G. had passed from feeling claustrophobia of an enclosed space to agoraphobia of the void, introducing the theme of anxiety about separation from his mother and in parallel, from me, in the maternal transference. This theme seemed to be perceived in very concrete terms, given that G. felt that the separation meant an abyss of noth-ingness, not for a moment considering the possibility of using his mental resources, or of representing his experience of separation in space and time. I responded, 'There is no void, nor a loss of your brain, if you use your mind to recognize that you are separate from your mother, as you are also from me, here in analysis.' At this point, G. stopped roaming about the room and seated himself on the couch. I saw that he was suffering a great deal as he said to me, 'I am afraid of sitting down. If I sit I fear I am sinking, I feel like I'm falling, it's a ter-rible feeling.' I noticed that G. had shed his protective armour and was in contact with his feelings of falling and loss. In this way he seemed to be experiencing what we had just said about separation, but he was falling into a kind of primary agony (Winnicott 1974) linked to his difficulty articulating feeling and thinking.

I said to him, 'If you are able to recognize your feelings of loss, you can also bear them, as you are doing now. "Feeling as though you are falling" is the expression of the capacity of your mind to have feelings, such as the feeling of sadness about a separation – it is not an actual fall.' Saying this, I was trying to stimulate an asymmetrization between concrete and abstract, whereas for him the 'feeling of falling' was symmetrically confused (Matte Blanco 1975) with a concrete falling. After I had spoken, G. appeared more settled, he turned towards me, looked at me and said straight at me, 'there are only ten sessions left.' I did a quick calculation and realized that there were indeed ten sessions until the break. I was struck by his return to reality and at the precision of his statement. It seemed to me that this discrete number was the constructive response that G. was giving at the risk of sliding back into the abyss of undifferentiated immensity. This response was therefore the outcome of a capacity to recognize separation and otherness. I said to him, 'there are indeed ten left. And this is an example of how you can be capable of accepting separation from me and the feelings that go with it.' And G. immediately replied, 'I don't want to think about it because I feel as though then too much hatred overcomes me and I can't bear that.' Saying this, G. spoke to me of his terror of not managing his feelings of hate, but also of his defect of thought (Bion 1962b) linked to an idea that 'non-thinking' seemed to offer a better solution than 'thinking'. I replied, 'we have seen at other times that you are capable of bearing your hatred: furthermore, thinking allows you to put boundaries on our separation, both in terms of how many sessions are left, and in terms of when we will see each other again in September. In this way you will be able to recognize me mentally even when I am not there.' Thus I was describing to him how thinking gave him boundaries to help guard against sinking into the abyss, leading him to consider the real space and time in which he could position his experience of an absent object (Bion 1962a). G. appeared satisfied and he finished the session in a particularly calm mood, stopping to rearrange the couch carefully after he got up to go; this too was another sign of his capacity to accept separation.

In the last session of the week, too, the atmosphere in the consulting room seemed collaborative. But let us look at the start of the following week, where we can see the provision G. had made for the experience of separation. 'Do you know Martignano Lake?' G. asked me, whilst walking around the room, without yet settling on a place to sit down. 'It's a small lake, near Bracciano Lake, which is a volcanic lake. It seems that Martignano is a secondary crater. I went there at the weekend; there were lots of people.'

My attention was caught by the reference to a geographical phenomenon in which there was a link between elements that were similar and different at the same time. In G.'s image, what had once been explosive volcanoes were now fresh and welcoming lakes. This appeared to me to be a constructive communication, an indication that, in spite of the limits imposed by narcissism, he was recognizing the relationship with me in an explicit way. Therefore I said to him: 'You seem to be able to recognize a continuity of the link with me even when we are apart, accepting yourself and me as separate people, as we are separate, but also as associated, like the lakes of Martignano and Bracciano. Having recognized your volcanic, explosive hatred for the separation from me, now your tears have cooled, giving way to a calmer mood.'

G. stopped walking, sat down on the couch and said to me, in a simple and wise tone, 'I feel that I have explored the abyss of my emotions. I feel that I have been to the very bottom of this void. I am no longer afraid of falling into the abyss: it is as if I had touched the bottom.' I appreciated his response, so coherent and transparent, but I also had the impression that he was still leaving out the containing role played by recognition of our relationship; therefore I replied, 'Now you recognize that there is an edge to the abyss, because you are able to recognize that a limit exists, rather than making it disappear by not thinking. But this boundary is also the fact of recognizing me as your travelling companion through the volcano of your emotions. Even if I am a companion that you feel you cannot control, and from whom you must accept separation.' This comment, too, was received well by G., showing that the analytic work was moving towards addressing separation with a knowledge of the duality between us, which had not stood out as clearly, or been as acceptable as it was now, before this moment in the analysis.

I hope that these two later fragments provide insight into the gradual mental growth of G. from a very undifferentiated and inchoate condition which echoes the formless abyss to which Bion and Matte Blanco refer, to a condition marked by a development of asymmetric logic and links between thought, feelings and human relationships. G.'s mind passes from an uncertain and confused conceptualization of space and time, exposing him to claustrophobic and agoraphobic suffering and the re-emergence of the panic of the abyss, to a recognition of separation and otherness in a relationship. This is accompanied by a gradual detoxification of the emotions, which move from volcanic explosiveness verging on madness to a more peaceful form. An intersubjective relationship impregnated with realism has formed.

The analyst's interventions accompany the internal movements of the analysand, pointing out the attacks on linking and the destructive fascination of non-thinking (Bion 1959/1967), correcting the cognitive distortions (Bion 1962b) and the non-viable symmetrizations (Matte Blanco 1988), to facilitate the processing of feelings and a more explicit role for the relationship.

The set of clinical fragments seem to me to show the many levels on which the analytic process operates (Gabbard 2007). Work on the conditions of 'containment' and on the defect of thought (Bion 1962b) – which aims to enable to patient to think about the infinite and unconscious space of the internal world – happens, at a certain point in the process, through the appearance of a relational other. In this way, the transference-countertransference aspect of the analytic relationship interweaves itself with the multidimensionality of the deep layers of the mind. This allows us to put the work of processing the transference into a context of greater complexity, which is called for with a clinical condition in which the thinking function and the patient's relationship with himself can never be taken entirely for granted.

In this piece I have attempted to demonstrate my own personal way of relating to the work of Bion and Matte Blanco: authors who invite one to conceive of psychoanalysis as an experience which, through the tolerance of doubt and the unknown, can put boundaries of space and time around the dark and amorphous immensity that the analysand encounters in the most primitive areas of his mental functioning.

Notes

1   This chapter was previously published as Lombardi, R. (2009). Symmetric frenzy and catastrophic change: a consideration of primitive mental states in the wake of Bion and Matte Blanco. *International Journal of Psychoanalysis*, 90: 529–549.

2   As his theories evolve, Matte Blanco begins to distinguish between a bi-logical frenzy and a bi-modal frenzy (1988, pp. 266–284). In the context of this piece I will not deal with this late distinction, seeking instead to develop the implications of this first, general definition which broadly captures the changes in the organization of the mind as one goes "deeper". However, the term which is most relevant in my paper is *bi-logical frenzy*.

3   English translation of 'Die alten boesen Lieder' from Hal Draper, *The Complete Poems of Heinrich Heine: A Modern English Version by Hal Draper* (p. 75). Oxford: Oxford University Press, 1982.

References

Bion, W. R. (1950). The imaginary twin. In *Second thoughts* (pp. 3–22). London: Karnac Books, 1967.

Bion, W. R. (1957). Differentiation of psychotic from the non-psychotic personalities. In *Second thoughts* (pp. 43–64). London: Karnac Books, 1967.

Bion, W. R. (1959). Attacks on linking. In *Second thoughts* (pp. 93–109). London: Karnac Books, 1967.

Bion, W. R. (1962a). A theory of thinking. In *Second thoughts*. London: Karnac Books, 1967.

Bion, W. R. (1962b). *Learning from experience*. London: Karnac Books, 1984.

Bion, W. R. (1965). *Transformations*. London: Karnac Books, 1984.

Bion, W.R. (1967). *Second thoughts*. London: Karnac Books, 1984.

Bion, W. R. (1970). *Attention and interpretation*. London: Karnac Books.

Bion, W. R. (1974). *Brazilian lectures parts 1 & 2*. Rio de Janeiro: Imago Editoria.

Bion, W. R. (1988). *Clinical seminar and other works*. London: Karnac Books.

Bion, W. R. (1992). *Cogitations* (F. Bion, Ed.). London: Karnac Books.

Bria, P. (1981a). Pensiero, mondo e problemi di fondazione [Thought, world, and problems of 'foundation']. Introduction in I. Matte Blanco, *L'inconscio come insiemi infiniti* [*The unconscious as infinite sets*] (pp. 19–111). Turin: Einaudi.

Bria, P. (1981b). Catastrophe and transformations. Geometries of the mind in the Bion's transformational perspective: consideration in terms of bi-logical epistemology. *Rivista di Psicoanalisi*, 26: 503–522.

Bria, P. (1999, July). *Los silogismos afectivos y la logica del delirio. Un enfoque bi-logico a la psico-patologia* [*Emotional syllogisms and the logic of delusion. A bi-logical approach to psychopathology*]. Paper presented at the IPA Congress, Santiago, Chile.

Busch, F. (2004). A missing link in psychoanalytic technique: psychoanalytic consciousness. *International Journal of Psychoanalysis*, 85: 567–572.

Di Benedetto, A. (2000). *Prima della parola: l'ascolto psicoanalitico del non detto attraverso le forme dell'arte* [*Before words: Psychoanalytic listening to the 'unsaid' through artwork*]. Milan: Angeli.

Freud, S. (1900). The interpretation of dreams. *Standard Edition*, 4–5.

Freud, S. (1911). Formulations on the two principles of mental functioning. *Standard Edition*, 12: 213–226.

Freud, S. (1915). The unconscious. *Standard Edition*, 14: 159–215.

Freud, S. (1923). The ego and the id. *Standard Edition*, 19: 1–66.

Freud, S. (1940). An outline of psycho-analysis. *Standard Edition*, 23: 139–208.

Gabbard, G. O. (2007). 'Bound in a nutshell': thoughts on complexity, reductionism, and 'infinite space'. *International Journal of Psychoanalysis*, 88: 559–574.

Garroni, E. (1992). Che cosa si prova ad essere un uomo sapiens? [What does it mean to be a human being?]. Introduction in A. Ferrari, *L'eclissi del corpo* [*Eclipse of the body*]. Rome: Borla.

Ginzburg, A. (2004). Jekill e Hyde gemelli identici [Jekyll and Hyde – identical twins]. In P. Bria & F. Oneroso (Eds.), *La bi-logica fra mito e letteratura. Saggi sul pensiero di Matte Blanco* [*Bi-logic between myth and literature. Essays on Matte's Blanco's Thought*] (pp. 154, 161). Milan: Angeli.

Ginzburg, A. (2007). Da Bion a Matte Blanco: lo scandalo dell'indivisibilità [From Bion to Matte Blanco: the scandal of indivisibility]. *Psiche*, 1: 69–80.

Grotstein, J. S. (2000). *Who is the dreamer who dreams the dreams?* Hillsdale, NJ: Analytic Press.

Lombardi, R. (2000). Corpo, affetti, pensieri. Riflessioni su alcune ipotesi di I. Matte Blanco e A.B. Ferrari [Body, feelings, thoughts. Reflections on some of the theories of I. Matte Blanco and A.B. Ferrari]. *Rivista di Psicoanalisi*, 46(4): 683–706.

Lombardi, R. (2006). Catalizzando il dialogo tra il corpo e la mente in un analizzando psicotico. Una prospettiva bilogica [Facilitating the dialogue between body and mind in a psychotic analysand. A bi-logical view]. *Rivista di Psicoanalisi*, 52: 743–765.

Lombardi, R. (2007). Shame in relation to the body, sex, and death: a clinical exploration of the psychotic levels of shame. *Psychoanalytic Dialogues*, 17(3): 385–399.

Matte Blanco, I. (1975). *The unconscious as infinite sets.* London: Karnac Books.

Matte Blanco, I. (1981). Reflecting with Bion. In J. S. Grotstein (Ed.), *Do I dare disturb the universe? A memorial to Wilfred R. Bion* (pp. 489–528). Beverly Hills, CA: Caesura Press.

Matte Blanco, I. (1988). *Thinking, feeling and being.* London: Routledge.

Matte Blanco, I. (2006). Aristotele, Parmenide, Galileo e Freud: via regia verso una nuova epistemologia [Aristotle, Parmenides, Galileo and Freud: the way towards a new epistemology]. *Rivista di Psicoanalisi*, 52: 711–723.

Merciai, S. (2000). Ripensando il percorso analitico con Parthenope Bion Talamo [Rethinking the analytic journey with Parthenope Bion Talamo]. *Psychomedia.* Retrieved from www.psychomedia.it

Nagel, T. (1981). What is it like to be a bat? In D. R. Hofstadter & D. C. Dennett (Eds.), *The mind's I. Fantasies and reflections on self and soul.* New York: Basic Books.

Rayner, E. (1981). *Unconscious logic. An Introduction to Matte Blanco's bi-logic and its uses.* London: Routledge.

Sifneos, P. (1967). Clinical observations on some patients suffering from a variety of psychosomatic diseases. *Psychosomatic Research: Proceedings of the Seventh European Conference on Psychosomatic Research*, 13: 339–345.

Winnicott, D. W. (1974). Fear of breakdown. *International Review of Psycho-Analysis*, 1: 103–107.

THROUGH THE EYE OF THE NEEDLE

The unfolding of the unconscious body[1]

In his *Studies on Hysteria* (1893–95, p. 291) Freud stated, making use of a New Testament image, that it is as difficult to pass from the unconscious to the 'defile' of consciousness as for a camel to pass through the eye of a needle: this metaphor, which highlights the dissimilarity of the two substances – the physical body and linear, symbolic thought –, seems newly relevant today because it evokes the difficulty in passing from the concrete physical body to symbolic thought which we now encounter with increasing frequency in our patients. Freud (1893–95), in his work with hysterical patients, noticed a connection between the body and the unconscious, such that the entry into the conscious of the relevant repressed material made possible the resolution of the physical hysterical symptom. Today we are faced with a widening scope of analytic practice, being more common today to work with more disturbed patients. Consequently we meet clinical situations in which we cannot assume the presence of a clear link between body and mind, as in Freud's day: a link that seems, in these cases, fraught with obstacles and conflicts which require specific working through (Liebermann 2000; Lombardi 2002; Aisenstein 2006). This peculiarity of contemporary clinical practice prompts us to devote particular attention to the body and its place in our idea of the unconscious. In this chapter I shall be drawing inspiration from some of Matte Blanco's epistemological theories and bi-logic, in order to deal with certain aspects of the mind–body relationship.

In addition to the well-known repressed unconscious, Freud intuited the existence of a 'non-repressed unconscious', since, for example, he specifies that 'the *Ucs.* does not coincide with the repressed;

it is still true that all that is repressed is *Ucs.*, but not all that is *Ucs.* is repressed' (1923, p. 18), and he further states that we can look upon 'an individual as a psychical id, unknown and unconscious' and that 'the repressed merges into the id as well, and is merely a part of it' (1923, pp. 23–24). Freud developed this broader understanding of the unconscious particularly when attempting to describe the more disorganized levels of the mind which are involved in *profound emotions*. More recently Matte Blanco (1975, 1988) developed and systematized Freud's insight, devising the model of a 'non-repressed unconscious' or 'structural unconscious' as a normal human mental system which is continuously active and completely impervious to the common coordinates of space and time that organize thought. As I see it, this rearticulation of the idea of the unconscious gives new relevance to Freud's contribution by relating it more clearly to what we see in today's patients, who increasingly present strong signs of non-differentiation. In other words, our more serious patients, instead of presenting limited areas of repression and specific defence mechanisms (A. Freud 1937), seem, particularly at the beginning of analysis, almost 'swamped' by their unconscious, so that a significant part of the analysis consists in activating mental differentiation and organizing resources of consciousness. It is no accident that Bion (1962) noticed that the mind needs an orientation (an alpha function) for the unconscious to be able to organize itself and then be subjected to conscious unfolding; such an orientation can by no means be taken for granted.

In this chapter I shall contend that the existence of a non-repressed unconscious, unrelated to the mental categories of space and time, implies that the body itself is originally unknown to the conscious and therefore unrepresentable for the mind. The unfolding of the non-repressed unconscious that takes place in the course of analysis leads to the development of an awareness of the body, and this level, in many serious cases, becomes something requiring psychoanalytic working through more urgently than defences and conflicts of a more developed nature.

Mental processing of the body

The importance for psychoanalysis of the body and the body–mind relationship was obvious to Freud starting as far back as his first study of hysteria (Breuer & Freud 1895), in which the body and somatic sensations seemed like a compass that could serve for orientation in the working through. From then on, throughout the course of Freud's studies the body constantly emerges as an essential reference point that organizes his principal psychoanalytic concepts, from his notion of psychosexuality (1905) and the theory of thinking conceived as a function of the containment of somatic discharge (1911), to the concept of instinct as a measure of the 'demand for work' that connection with the body makes on the mind (1915a), and to the re-emergence of the 'enigmatic Ucs.' in narcissistic psychoneuroses, where 'the whole train of thought is dominated by the element which has for its content a bodily innervation (or, rather, the sensation of it)' (1915b, p. 198). At a turning point in the 1920s, Freud (1923) declares that 'the ego is first and foremost a bodily ego' (p. 26), an idea elaborated in a footnote added to the 1927 English edition and authorized by Freud: 'the ego is ultimately derived from bodily sensations, chiefly from those springing from the surface of the body. It may thus be regarded as a mental projection of the surface of the body' (p. 26 n.1). Finally, in his last writings in 'An Outline of Psycho-Analysis' (1940), Freud states that 'the physical or somatic processes . . . concomitant with the psychical ones' are 'the true essence of what is psychical,' thus confirming the fundamental role of bodily sensations for psychoanalysis (p. 158). Many authors other than Freud have investigated the role of the body in psychoanalysis, from Tausk (1933) to Schilder (1950), Scott (1948), Deutsch (1954), and Greenacre (1971), with more recent contributions from Lichtenberg (1978), Anzieu (1985), Ogden (1989), Meissner (1997, 1998a, 1998b, 1998c), Bion (1979/1988) and Ferrari (2004), who variously underline the importance of the body in mental functioning and the development of object relations.

The characteristics of Matte Blanco's structural unconscious, which include the unconscious processes being extraneous to space and time, lead to the consequence that unconscious manifestations, in their extreme form, result in the disappearance of that basic human spatio-temporal structure, the body. This absence of bodily space–time that characterizes the unconscious world appears in various known psychoanalytic manifestations, such as the fantasy of not having been born and of still inhabiting the maternal belly, which M. Klein describes (1923/1977, 1928) in small children, or in the omnipotent fantasy of being God, as it appears, for instance, in the case of Schreber (Freud 1910), where God, by definition, is extraneous to the limits of space-time and is for this reason, in certain traditions, unrepresentable. From the point of view of the unconscious, which takes no account of the parameters of logic or reality as they are normally understood, an integrated and 'embodied' mental life is by no means to be taken for granted, but is the result of a specific mental development.

a) The invisible man can make his own body visible

'The child has only her/his body to express mental processes. . . . An inner world begins. The child feels inside his/her body that there are objects, persons and parts of persons, and that they are alive and active and can influence or be influenced by him/her.' This statement by Paula Heimann (1952, quoted by Matte Blanco 1975, pp. 155–160) receives the following comment from Matte Blanco: 'It is from this experience of the body and the external world that our psycho-analytic study begins' (Matte Blanco 1988, p. 143). Interest in the mind–body relationship does not permeate Matte Blanco's research, but this statement makes explicit his assumption of the importance of the role of the body in clinical and psychoanalytic research.

The body, although it always exists in external reality, comes onto the individual's horizon *only when* it becomes in some way an *object of mental processing*. With regard to indivisibility, which can only be known when clothed in bivalent logic, Matte Blanco, in his work on dreams (1984), refers to Wells's invisible man, who could only be perceived when dressed. Invisibility obviously refers to the body. If we use the model of the invisible man with reference to the body/mind relationship, we can say that *the body can be mentally seen only when clothed in asymmetrical elements*: an unfolding which can be brought about by bivalent logic, or through that mixed product of the two logics, bi-logic. In the clinical part of this chapter I shall give some examples of the mind's discovery of the body. The way mental operations hook onto the physicality of the body is extremely important and can, if neglected, be transformed into a contributing element to impasse in the psychoanalytic process.

b) Sensation, sensation-feeling and thought

It is often through the emotions that the body indirectly makes its presence felt. Matte Blanco finds emotion to be 'the expression of a corporeal state' (1975, p. 242), which shows itself either as such or as a drive to action, and he calls the psychological apprehension of corporeal events *sensation-feeling*. To the sensation arising from the bodily matrix he adds *a propositional activity* which introduces relationships more proper to thought activity. Emotion is thus conceived by Matte Blanco as *a composite of sensation-feeling and thought*.

Although Matte Blanco sees the setting up of relationships as an essential part of sensation, he is punctilious in defining an extreme case of *pure sensation*, where sensation presents itself to consciousness in a state of absolute nudity: it is felt to be simple and indivisible, outside time and all the other distinctions which characterize the phenomena of thought; if such distinctions appear, it is only because we have covered the sensory event with our thought (Matte Blanco 1975, p. 259).

The distinction between *pure sensation, sensation-feeling* and *thoughts connected with sensory activity* I hold to be a significant one, above all in the light of the different paths which lead from each of these single components, creating the conditions for the dominance of symmetrical or asymmetrical components in every single experience of life.

Using these distinctions, we can for instance hypothesize that pure sensation might close itself off and stagnate to the point of becoming infinite and indivisible, or rather an exclusive area radically dissociated from the possibility of being registered by thought, as happens, for example, in drug addictions. When these sensory states are actually experienced, even in certain normally integrated patients, *the presence of sensation in the mind tends to saturate it and block any participation of thinking activity*, as is the case in clinical situations of erotic transference, particularly in patients in whom even simple experiences of emotional contact activate confusion and uncontainable excitation tending towards acting out. In these states, which are distinguished by the dominance of the symmetrical component, the analyst's most urgent task is to help the analysand to differentiate asymmetrically among the sensations he/she is experiencing. Thus *bodily experience can pass through the eye of the needle of thought*, allowing the analysand, for example, to distinguish within his/her emotional turmoil what can be defined verbally: excitation, fear, curiosity, relaxation, trust, aggressivity, desire for possession, etc. Freud, in his essay on the two principles of mental functioning (1911), had already distinguished between a *primordial sensory level proper to the pleasure principle* and a second level consisting of *consciousness linked to the sense organs*, the activation of which can lead to obtaining pleasure through the mediation of the recognition of reality. Freud thus seems to emphasize that the pure sensory level, when the primordial level is not integrated with the conscious, tends to assert itself *outside* of the differentiation proper to thought. The best-known development of this hypothesis of Freud's is Bion's distinction (1957) between psychotic and non-psychotic areas, in which the psychotic area needs to be integrated with the non-psychotic area to bring about emotional containment. In this context the action of the non-psychotic area provides differentiation of a realistic kind: a form of differentiation which is altogether foreign to the psychotic area. In all these authors – Freud, Bion, Matte Blanco – a polarity is set up: (1) pleasure principle, psychotic area, pure sensation; (2) reality principle, non-psychotic area, thoughts connected with sensory activity. The interaction of these conflictual areas leads to the possibility of integrated mental activity allowing for the containment of primitive sensory data which, by dint of their original intensity (Klein 1932), know no boundaries and structurally tend towards the infinite (Matte Blanco 1975).

c) Infantile catastrophe and body-mind dissociation

The systole and diastole proposed by the oscillation between sensations and feelings on the one hand and the asymmetric activity of thought on the other, can thus become the support of the mental circulatory system proposed by psychoanalytic experience: a system which is often set in motion by analysis, but which is not terminated at its close, becoming instead part of that interminable analysis spoken of by Freud (1937). Right from birth, the body provides us with feelings and emotions which are difficult to contain and originally extraneous alike to space-time boundaries and to asymmetrical differentiation.

The body-mind relation is formed at a very early stage of life, when the ego is not yet structured and is subject to the impact of external traumas (first of all separation from the mother) and to traumas caused by shortcomings of the maternal *reverie* (Winnicott 1953/1958; James 1960; Gaddini 1980/1992; Mahler & McDevitt 1982). It is not always possible during analysis to reconstruct these subjects' trauma histories; at the same time this aspect of reconstruction does not have the same importance it has in other more evolved types of mental disturbance. Various authors have noted how trauma affects mental integration, causing differing degrees of dissociation (Krystal 1988; Laub & Auerhahn 1993; Bromberg 1998); they have also pointed out how the body takes it upon itself to be the repository of whatever the mind has not succeeded in working through and integrating (Balint 1987; van der Kolk 1996; Kaplan 2006). Matte Blanco (1988) stresses the importance of Melanie Klein's insight about 'memories in feelings': in fact, he maintains that in analysis, in certain conditions, we find ourselves working through the sensory-emotional implications of traumatic memories, which are presented as densely symmetric zones that are not integrated with the normal asymmetric functioning typical of verbal thinking. What is most important in more serious disturbances of body-mind relation activated by trauma is the *experience* one has in analysis; this allows the subject, with the help of the analyst's *reverie*, to draw closer to his/her physical and emotional being: a meaningful and concrete change which also influences the patient's way of being in the world.

Of all the periods of life, adolescence is perhaps that in which the relationship with one's body becomes most important, due to the changes brought about by puberty and to the transformation of a child's body into the body of an adult (Laufer & Laufer 1991). In this stage of life the subject finds, with peculiar intensity, that he/she must get to know and come to terms with his/her own actual body as an expression of the changes that have taken place through the passage of time. This requires a particular working through that often leads the adolescent to analysis.

First clinical vignette: adolescence and the discovery of the body

I shall first be discussing an 18-year-old adolescent, Giorgio, who presented anxiety attacks, hashish dependence and psychogenic sexual impotence. This clinical material seems interesting because it renews our sense of adolescence as the birth of a new body and also suggests the importance of the activation of a connection with the body in this phase of life. During the entire initial phase of his analysis, communication with G. was rather stiff, thanks to his tendency to remain as superficial as possible and to avoid facing situations that evoked anxiety. The countertransference seemed problematic, since it was often virtually impossible to follow his confused remarks and find logical elements in what he communicated.

The development, in the transference with me, of a trusting relationship led G. to tell me after a while about his intense agoraphobia and suicidal fantasies. He was haunted by the fantasy of throwing himself off his balcony, because he experienced the limits represented by the railing as a prison that was suffocating him and that he wanted to escape from. At the same time G. spoke of his almost delusional conviction that his legs would be elastic enough to withstand the impact of his fall from the fifth floor. G. in fact tended to be unaware of his body, thus placing his very life at risk.

In subsequent sessions other material confirmed his unconscious suicidal tendencies. He reported that he had, at the last moment, avoided a serious crash on his motorcycle when he turned the wrong way into a one-way street. He was apparently in a sort of trance brought about by the excitation of driving at high speed, so he hadn't noticed the No Entry sign at the corner. Thus he suddenly found himself about to run into a car, which he just managed to avoid, convinced that it was the other driver who was going the wrong way. Only later was he able to reconstruct what had actually happened. I confronted G. directly with the fact that he was running the risk of fatal accidents, since I wished to stimulate his perception of his resorting to acting out.

'Clearly,' I said, 'you have such hatred for yourself and for your actual body that you want to destroy it, in part as a means of doing away with the limits of reality that your body imposes.' G. answered, 'It is not my intention to go that far.' And I replied, 'But if it were to happen, you obviously have an omnipotent fantasy that you could keep on living even after a fatal accident: as if you could live independently of your body.' G.'s response to this approach was 'I often have the fantasy of going backwards in time to when I was a baby.' G.'s association revealed his confusion about the existence of realistic temporal limits and also his being trapped in a structural unconscious on which time and space tended to have no bearing. So I said, 'You arrange your mind as if time and corporeal space didn't exist: thus it not only is unable to protect itself but, however unwillingly, it even attacks itself.'

Among other things, the fantasy of being able to continue to be a baby seemed very closely connected with his sexual impotence. The working through of the existence of both time and a real adult body – as 'asymmetrical' elements of mental *functioning* – therefore played an important role in the resolution of his symptoms.

After about two years' work, when we were on the brink of the summer separation, G. brought in a dream which signalled an

69

important evolution. *He dreamt that he was in a sort of tube in which he could hardly move. At a certain point he overcame his feeling of paralysis and suffocation, and in his dream he picked up a pair of glasses he had dropped, put them back on, and again shouldered a rucksack that had slipped off. Thus he was able to move his arms and make room for himself as he moved forward. To his great surprise G. found that he was emerging from the suffocating tube.*

His first association was that he would never have thought he could get out of an enclosed space so easily, and he connected his dream to a sort of 'birth'. I was struck by his ability to interpret his dream in relation to his claustrophobia. I sought to stress the value of the evolution (Bion 1970) that was taking place, and said that whereas he had previously tried to do away with any sort of closing off – the railing of the balcony and the No Entry sign – now he was able to accept the fact that he was in the 'tube' of his sensations and could discover that he had his own resources of thought (the glasses resting on his nose) and action (moving his arms in a coordinated manner): resources that he had generally tended not to recognize in himself. In this way he was trying to revalue his tolerance for his anxiety about the helplessness he experienced in the dream and his openness towards forms of mental representation, instead of acting out.

At this point G. replied, 'The rucksack is my body: a body I feel I'm constantly on the point of losing when I feel swallowed up by my fantasies. The glasses are my mind, which I need in order to be aware of myself and of what's happening to me. I continually run the risk of losing my body and my mind. But, unlike before, now I realize it.'

I was struck by the precision with which G. stressed the danger of losing contact with his body and his mind: a perception that coincided with his tendency towards dangerous acting out. I added that in dreaming of his birth, he was also representing his separation from me in analysis, as an occasion for separating himself from me, taking with him the body and the mind that he used to cause to disappear, in part so as not to realize that he was a separate person. I attempted with this statement to maintain a link between his reacquired connection to his body and his acceptance of separation in the context of the transference relationship, and it was only in a later comment, after the patient had given me an indication of his active mental participation, that I introduced a reference to the transference.

After the session featuring the dream, G. showed sexual interest in a foreign girl, particularly an intense physical attraction to her body, and he had a brief relationship with her that ended with her departure. Thus G. activated a connection with his body and his sexuality which had vanished after his episodes of impotence.

The case of G. brings us up against denial of the body during adolescence, aimed at avoiding the anxiety of bodily changes and new experiences. Faced with a state of nondifferentiation in which the patient is unaware of his body, the analyst can fulfil, tolerating difficult feelings in his countertransference, the important function of stimulating the development of a sense of reality (Freud 1911), indicating the real mortal dangers to which the patient subjects himself by ignoring his corporeal existence. The analyst thus fosters a responsible relationship between the analysand and his mental apparatus (Bion 1970) as well as the activation of an asymmetrical relationship (Matte Blanco 1988) with his body and his mind. The working through of actual experiences the adolescent has had – such as sexual and emotional experiences – provides, later on, a further source of growth and of consolidation of the body–mind relationship, in a stage which is particularly exposed to the risk of dissociation of the mind from bodily experience.

Second clinical vignette: a method for finding oneself

In all cases of failure to make a vital connection between indivisibility and the dividing modes within the body-mind organization, the *body-mind conflict* plays an important role. Body and mind position themselves as two infinites which remain mutually extraneous, two totally separate classes with nothing linking them. The conflict fuels drastic forms of separation and denial, to the extent that in certain clinical situations the body remains absolutely impervious to asymmetrical elements, as I noted apropos of Wells's invisible man. With this separation it clearly becomes impossible to operate the motor discharge deferral function (Freud 1911; Bion 1962). At this point we can look at some aspects of a case in which the body acted out destructively in a mental state which was extremely unbalanced, listing heavily towards intellectualization and abstraction.

Rita was a 19-year-old woman when she began her four-session-a-week analysis because of severe alcoholism: she would find herself in front of the fridge compulsively downing bottles of wine. Although very intelligent, R. was unable to come close to any form of

71

emotional experience and her speech was always on such an abstract level that it was hardly ever possible to understand what she was talking about or trying to get at. She often did not seem to know where she was and moved in a kind of automatic trance, which was alarming as it exposed her to risks such as losing control of her moped or being hit by a bus. She also conducted her sex life in a promiscuous and almost ethological way; indeed she got pregnant and had to have an abortion simply through omission to take contraceptive precautions. In addition she was frigid and anorgasmic. With her compulsive verbalization, R. made me feel as if I were sharing my office with a plastic effigy, while her symptoms, not the least of which were unconscious suicide attempts, put one in mind of a seething cauldron of emotions from which she herself remained aloof. My countertransference reaction involved my feeling that something was blocking my thinking in R.'s presence; I felt as if I were in a thick fog, and I could hardly focus on the patient's communications or my own sensory responses. Goldberg (1995), in particular, has described the analyst's singular difficulty when faced with cases characterized by the absence of spontaneity and affectivity and by the patient's evident dissociation from his or her body and sensations; in such situations the analyst is in danger of duplicating the patient's withdrawal from the sensory environment.

The first change came after a session in which, as if moved by exasperation, I interrupted her empty discourse to ask, 'Excuse me, but have you ever asked yourself what your feet are telling you?' My interruption was a provocation aimed at eliciting some kind of emotional response we could consider together in analysis, rather than risking its being discharged in further acting out. R. at first responded with a long silence, after which she said she was amazed that I should ask her about her feet since she had noticed that when she was able to feel them she felt better, adding that she was unable to account for this strange fact. I told her I was thinking of the expression 'to have your feet on the ground', meaning to be in touch with reality, which was precisely what she lacked when she forgot she had two feet and a body and instead operated in abstract mode, as if she were all head. After this episode R. began to use the sessions differently, with a very concrete sense of her physical presence through continual attention to the feelings stirring inside her, even if she did not understand what they might mean. One day she told me she had been feeling particularly bad, as if she were falling into the void without being able to stop herself, and she felt the urge to go back to swigging alcohol grabbed out of the fridge. It was at this point that she decided to lie down on the bed, just as she generally lay on the analytic couch, and try to feel her feet, then her stomach and finally her breathing. She told me she had found 'a method for finding herself', which she called a 'register', the term used for the roll call in school, when the teacher would call out the pupils' names at the beginning of the school day, and each pupil there would reply 'present'. She used this method on her various body parts, until she could perceive their tangible presence and the boundary where her body ended. This discovery was in the nature of a Copernican revolution for R., to the extent that eight years later, nearing the end of analysis, she still considered her 'register' one of her fundamental discoveries, the most precious tool she brought away from her experience of analysis. 'The body is like a subway train,' she told me during one of our last sessions, 'if you don't follow the directions to get there, you can't take it. And you have to get to know all the different lines and connections. Analysis has been useful in bringing me closer to all this.'

This case history shows us how necessary a *specific working through* is in order to place *the body on the perceptual horizon of the mind*. The register enabled R. to make her body representable. Without this active investigation, her body remained indivisible and hence extraneous to any asymmetric element that could represent it. The analytic *reverie* catalyzed this perceptual drawing-closer, detoxifying its link with feelings of primitive terror, which otherwise could have led to an interruption of the body-mind connection. To a mind not used to bearing the weight of sensations, experiencing contact with sensory areas can be likened to crossing a minefield, where feelings and emotions are like explosions one has no control over, nor any means of filtering out and which, once they have occurred, will keep occurring. The case of R. lends itself to considerations of the *limits* to the realistic possibilities of healing areas traumatized early in life, limits that exist even when the psychoanalytic experience reaches the deeper levels and the analysis is on balance decidedly positive. In these cases the aim of analysis is to make the subject aware of the characteristics and limitations inherent in one's internal organization, in order to actively defend the continuity of the body-mind relationship and to maintain the unity of the personality, which would otherwise be exposed to the risk of fragmentation.

Third clinical vignette: symmetrization and clinical evolution

Now we can consider the clinical case of an adult patient who presented serious problems both mental, with symptoms of paranoia, and physical, with a diagnosis of a severe neurological illness made a year before analysis began.

Jodie was tormented by noise coming from the apartment above her. She likened her situation to that depicted in Roman Polanski's film *The Tenant*. Her apartment was in an exclusive building in an upmarket neighbourhood and was to have been the fulfilment of the dream of a lifetime. Instead, it had given rise to a state of persecution and claustrophobic anxieties. J. was not without insight, describing herself as an efficient puppet intent on carrying out her weekly tasks, which could not be put off for any reason. She felt that a transparent wall separated her from what was happening around her and that people and places were far off and unreachable. She likened all the feelings and emotions of her inner world to a stain which ruined her ideal of having inside herself the equivalent of a white napkin, perfectly pure and immaculate: all strongly reminiscent of the *psychose blanche* described by André Green (1983). Any form of unfolding which could have translated physical and sensory experiences into mental events was absent. Consequently, the atmosphere this patient evoked was one of remoteness and complete emotional impassivity, as if everything had just come sliding monotonously onto her, without her being in the least involved. It was as if J. had wandered by chance into an analyst's office: she showed no trace of emotional involvement in the analytic relationship, even when she spoke about the seriously menacing persecutions of which she felt herself the victim.

J. had already gotten well into her working through when she recounted the dream she had had on her first night in the new apartment. 'I'm out in the garden and I close the French windows from outside, then I close the shutters. I find that I'm outside the house: locked out.' The moment she takes possession of her own house, which may coincide with an internal house, Jodie performs the inverse operation (what Bion would call 'minus K') of locking herself out of the house, i.e. locking herself out of herself. The dream became even more disturbing when the patient associated it with the sporadic onset of her neurological illness: she stood up in a perfectly

74

normal-seeming situation and found that her arm did not respond, as if it were no longer hers. She reacted with extreme *sangfroid*, as if it had nothing to do with her.

The advent of this dream was also consistent with certain aspects of the transference relationship at the time. A short while previously I had had to deal with her urgent request to cancel one of her four sessions so that she could take part in some 'unmissable' event. I was very determined in interpreting her attack on analysis and not changing the setting. As she recounted the dream, she seemed to allude to her attempt to keep herself out of analysis and out of herself, exactly as she had dreamt of actively keeping herself out of her own house.

Afterwards there started to appear certain forms of evolution, which I am inclined to consider J.'s first coherent unfolding of sensation-feelings emerging from the corporeal matrix. On the next Monday, the first session of the week, J. appeared looking disturbed and upset. She had been feeling terrible since the last session and her persecution by the neighbour on the floor above had again become acute. She added that during the last session she had been very much shaken and annoyed by a comment I made on her attitude. She claimed I had said 'You must stop thinking of yourself as a small defenceless child, totally at the mercy of a big bad daddy.' I felt the patient was attributing a peremptory manner to me that wasn't at all like me. She had experienced this phrase as an order which she had to carry out without question or comment. She had then thought that my expression was exactly the one her father used when she was little: 'you must stop it.'

I decided not to correct J.'s apprehension of my attitude but to accept the role that she, albeit in a quasi-hallucinatory way, was attributing to me in the transference, since I thought this role coincided with something inside her that was struggling to get out and be dealt with in analysis. In this way we could work through the reappearance of her discomfort in relation to her hatred towards me, whom she was seeing as the severe and implacable father of her early childhood who scolded and bullied her. Thus it was possible to proceed with the working through of the paternal transference onto me, in conjunction with the conscious representative integration of her feelings of hatred. J. pointed out that when she managed to *correlate* the panic and terror of those days with my phrase, she began to feel better. Before, her feelings had been closer to *pure terror*, with *no link to any representation whatsoever*.

What J. was experiencing here in relation to me was the possibility of making room for an inner life which was exploding with concrete, chaotic and boundless emotions; later she was *able to introduce a layer of thought* which allowed that affect to find a place within her inner world, inside her inner house, and then be linked to a representation, so that what she experienced could be communicated in analysis and enter into the realm of the phenomena of consciousness, thinkability and experience. This type of unfolding was revolutionary in the light of her tendency to place herself outside her body-house, making herself impervious to her emotions, just when her body was proposing new emotions for her to receive and work through. In such a context of artificial separation of body and mind, it was hardly surprising that bodily feelings tended to stagnate, making their weight felt wholly at the somatic level, without any mental reception or registration.

The role of the transference in this context thus consisted primarily in offering, in the person of the analyst, an object that allowed her to connect bodily affect and representation; the kind of transference to which I refer here is closer to Freud's early conception of it (1900), in which he emphasized the establishment of a representative connection with an unconscious trace that, precisely because it is unconscious, was originally not represented at all. Emphasizing the evolution of the body-mind connection leads to making the most of the transference component as an intrasubjective mechanism whereby an unconscious trace becomes expressible through transference onto an external object or preconscious idea (for the correlation between the intrapsychic and relational levels of the transference, see Loewald 1960; Green 1984; Lombardi 2002). It is by no means my intention, in stating the above, to deny the value of the analytic relationship and regress to a one-person perspective. Instead I would emphasize the variety of levels on which intersubjective action takes place.

In a subsequent session J. related an episode which turned out to be very significant. She said she had been feeling very unwell after a run-in with a colleague – I won't go into the details – which she considered a grave, unpardonable offence that she took personally. She portrayed herself as a sort of queen whose pride had been deeply wounded as a result of being replaced when she considered herself irreplaceable. In the context of the clinical evolution of the case, what seems important to me in this episode is not so much J.'s anger and narcissistic wound as her *completely new way of locating and relating to an inner feeling*, in the sense that she was able to experience it within her, recognize it and talk about it in analysis with complete coherence and precision.[2] This was something totally revolutionary for her: previously she had felt absolutely nothing and let every episode slip by as if it had nothing to do with her, or else, at the other extreme, she could be suddenly devastated by an explosion of emotions, as had been the case in a particular period in her life, so that an episode of this kind would have led to insults and an irreparable breaking off of the relationship. In this episode we can see how J. *used inner space* to make room for the infinite experience of emotions, using representation as a crucial go-between so that asymmetrical organization and containment of the symmetrical explosion could take place at the level of pure emotion. One significant aspect here was J.'s ability, at the end of the session, to correlate the noises from the apartment above her with the crushing emotional weight of her feelings, to which she usually refused to give space, with the result – which she was only now coming to understand – that she constantly felt persecuted. I told her that in analysis she was starting to build *an inner room for her emotions*: emotions she had previously 'locked herself out' of, as in her dream of locking herself out of the house, or had assigned to the floor above, as in her attack of desperate rage towards her neighbour.

In a subsequent session there was an important dream, which further depicted the characteristics of the patient's inner world. In this dream she saw the inside of her chest in a series of successive images, as in a CAT scan, and was able to make out distinct spheroid shapes. Someone told her it was cancer. J. immediately associated this with the recent increase in her tobacco addiction: she was up to two packs a day and had been warned by an acquaintance of the attendant dangers for her health. I cannot here go into most of the interesting implications of this dream, but while the anxiety charge it provoked was very strong, it nevertheless elicited important perceptions, most significantly regarding her general state of internal death, dominated by obsessive organizing, which left no space for recognizing or dealing with any vital manifestation, whether an unexpected external event or an emotion. This marked the start of an important working through of her father's death, about which she had up to then been in denial. Her state of inner death seemed correlated to the objective link with her father, whom she treated like an unburied corpse she had to hold on to, as had actually happened – she told me – during the ethnic conflict between Slavs and Italians at Istria. Historically, the Italians who had refused to leave the region after it became part of Yugoslavia were tortured, tied to a corpse and left to die and rot with it in a common grave. The handful of survivors, including a relative of J.'s, went mad. This description chillingly captured the symmetrical state of non-differentiation between death and life (see Chapter 8) deriving from her denial of her father's death. There was a correspondence between, on the one hand, this mental state bordering on madness and psychic death and, on the other, the physical and concrete reality of the neurological illness the patient had been suffering from recently and which, though only hypothetically, might be linked to the putrefaction of J.'s inner world. However, the concrete nature of her disease by now belonged to the physical order of reality and was presumably, in the absence of proof to the contrary, no longer influenceable by recovery at the level of psychic organization.

I have chosen to dedicate considerable space to this case because of its particular interest. It offers us a graphic illustration of the pathogenic role played by the separation of mind and body, which seriously jeopardized both physical and mental health. Feeling unconnected to her own body co-existed with J.'s feeling psychologically separated from the world by an impassable transparent screen.

As occurred with Giorgio and Rita, J. was dissociated from her body, keeping it at a distance and meanwhile feeling persecuted by her neighbour's heavy footsteps, which represented exactly the foot-body-emotion she was unable to locate inside herself.

It is interesting to note that the dissociation that took place as a psychological mechanism, through paranoia, is repeated in another level in the body-mind relationship. Obviously body-mind dissociation must not be confused with either hysterical dissociation (Freud 1893–95) or the schizoid mechanism (Klein 1946), both of which are, in any case, concerned with modes of treating, at the fantasy level, an emotional sphere that is already in some way mentally organized. J.'s tendency to dissociate was also acted out in analysis in her various requests to reduce the number of sessions and later, as the case evolved, in attempts to break off analysis altogether. In a context where integration of somatic and psychic manifestations is still a long way off, the phenomena of delusion and acting out may offer – when worked through in analysis – an initial connection with the area of representability (Lombardi 2003, 2004, 2008), allowing internal positions adopted by the analysand (in this case, primarily the shutting oneself out of one's own body) to become regularly recognizable. Awareness of these positions may prompt the patient to acquire responsibility and consequently trigger a stimulus for change and integration.[3]

Concluding remarks

In the course of this work I have hypothesized that the unfolding of the body acts as a three-dimensional organizer of thought operations: in this sense, corporeal space-time becomes the starting-point for the translation of unconscious processes into representation data. Two clinical cases show the devastating effects, at both the psycho-phenomenological (alcoholism, suicide risk) and the physical (impotence, frigidity and destructive acting out) levels, of serious damage to the body-mind link in adolescence.

From another point of view the body appears also as the source of strongly disorganized emotions which press to be contained and unfolded at the conscious level. The third case, an adult patient suffering from a serious physical illness, shows a severance of the body-mind connection leading to the subject's becoming quite unaware of her own body. Thanks to analysis the patient managed to dream of this disconnected state, photographing it in the action of locking herself out of her house. The clinical evolution that followed not only led to a restoration of the mind-body link, but also brought to light very primitive emotions with an exacerbation of narcissistic feelings. Far from being an indication of regression, these manifestations marked the beginning of an ability to listen to inner feelings and a diminution of imitative attitudes which had formerly alternated with impulsive acting out. This point should be carefully considered when one is dealing with the so-called negative therapeutic reaction (Grabel 2008; Horney 1936); it is important to determine whether certain clinical manifestations are in fact regressive or rather have an evolutionary significance. This case history also shows the emergence of a strongly symmetrized nucleus of emotions regarding the patient's relationship with her father, which had hitherto existed beyond the realistic limits of space and time, with consequences so destructive as to border on madness. Restoring the link with her body made possible the unfolding of inner feelings.

In this presentation I have particularly stressed the idea of time. In the case of Giorgio, the discovery of his body and the activation, in his mind, of a capacity for spatio-temporal organization proceeded in tandem, making possible the resolution of complex clinical symptoms and freeing him from his recurrent unconscious suicide attempts. In the case of Rita, time allowed her to explore sensory experience and to record changes in her inner condition. Finally, in the case of Jodie, time linked the patient to reality, just as it linked her to her body: time marks life's changes as well as ultimately bringing death, aspects which the patient had tended to deny.

I hope that the clinical perspective I have attempted to illustrate can lead to greater interest in the manifestations of more serious cases, with emphasis on the *structural difficulty* involved in making primitive feelings and emotions thinkable. Several authors have demonstrated the importance in this regard of the lack of a symbolizing capacity, especially in so-called psychosomatic patients (Marty & De M'Uzan 1963; Sifneos 1967; Taylor 1987; etc.). In this context Rizzuto pointed out the significance of bodily metaphors and of their development in analysis conducted so as to further 'a prolonged fantasized *enactment*': 'the metaphors unfold as several scenes of a particular scenario/story, revealing a self experienced as a body self, *a body for psychic habitation*, in which the patient has not managed fully to dwell' (2001, p. 565, my italics). I would, however, emphasize the importance of the *link with the concreteness of the body* for the development of ineffable experiences (Bion 1965) that are the source of a representational activity on the part of the mind, rather than emphasizing the role of the *mental mechanism of metaphor as such*. Hence in the third clinical case I have opted to present material from the beginning of the analysis, a phase in which the patient's tendency to keep herself aloof from her own body was very evident, to the detriment of the capacity to promote the body–mind relationship through the integrative use of metaphor. In addition it is my intention to underline, by means of this distinction, the essential importance of *reality* – the reality of the body – in the development of the analytic process, which is hence understood as *not* primarily oriented towards investigating fantasies.

Thus, it seems essential to inquire into the possible dangers of regarding clinical material exclusively in terms of unconscious fantasy and symbolism, while ignoring the fact that our difficult patients have only a limited capacity for working through. It was not by chance that Freud wished never to lose sight of the connection of his psychology with reality and the somatic processes, and that he assigned a specific but circumscribed importance to fantasy (see Symington 2007). It seems to me that the process of releasing psychoanalysis from the trap of a dangerous one-sided emphasis on the psyche, to the exclusion of all else, can be furthered by greater attention to the actual body as the starting point for sensations and emotions – the connecting link with the id – as well as of perceptions – the connecting link with the ego – all of which are determinant in autonomous mental functioning.

The body seems to have earned the right to be considered the Cinderella of contemporary psychoanalysis, since it makes no appearance whatever among the important topics explored over the past half century (see, e.g. Cooper 2008). The reasons for this exclusion and the resistance that supports it could do with some examination. We cannot rule out the possibility that a revaluation of the body in psychoanalysis – as a dimension that is not thought, and yet precedes and consistently generates it (Bion 1979/1988) – might be awkward, in that it would get in the way of a tendency toward omniscience and intellectual control, both of which are rather well established in our discipline and in its basically authoritarian tradition (Reeder 2004). On the other hand, the drive to liberate ourselves from the body to the point of repudiating it altogether is a constant in Western intellectual history, in which a disembodied brain is a popular philosophical fantasy. It is nicely summed up in Descartes's *Meditations* (1642), in which he considers the possibility that the existence of the body and the external world are to be attributed to the action of an evil and very powerful demon (Hofstadter & Dennett 1981).

In psychoanalysis today it is notable that – even for those who are concerned with the body – either Freud might just as well never have had his momentous insights (see, e.g. Aron 1998), or else the body can be recognized only within the limited spheres of the relationship to the mother, sexual identity and oedipal working through (Laufer 2002; Fogel 2006). Meanwhile there is virtually no reference to the body in studies of shame, in which much is generally made of the more developed levels bound up with oedipal fantasies (Kilborne 2002; Lansky 2005), while neglect is the fate of the more primitive determinants on the paranoid level, which stand in the way of recognition both of one's own real body and of appearance as an expression of one's physical self (Lombardi 2007). In none of these contexts is any notice taken of the irreplaceable and continuous contribution the body makes to our existence as actual persons, to the dawning of affects, to discovering the borders of the self, to establishing a link with reality by means of the sense organs. Even those who study dissociation are capable of entirely ignoring the specific ways in which the patient uses the body and bodily processes, as Sands (2007) has noted apropos of Bromberg (1998, 2006). This partial blindness that excludes recognition of the body in relation to dissociation involves overlooking the fact that body–mind dissociation has a specific natural basis, the essential separation inherent in the 'substance dualism' that characterizes *Homo sapiens* ethologically, and according to which we *are* physical matter, thanks to our bodies, but at the same time our minds are not (Nagel 1974; Damasio 2003, pp. 183–191).

In a cultural atmosphere of this sort, where the body–mind relationship is marginalized in favour of stressing more evolved and symbolic levels of mental functioning, it can happen that the patient's need to organize his or her mental growth chiefly around the body is not recognized (see, e.g. Kantrowitz 2008, who takes as hostile her patient's need to spend money on clothes rather than on a higher fee for the analyst; in the light of what I have just been saying, the patient's choice seems instead to give real substance to her discovery of having a body of her own, clothed, at last, in asymmetrical elements). Alternatively, that need is read as a form of perversion (see, e.g. Good 2006) or can be faced only after having at length worked through the realm of the analytic relationship (as in Wrye 1998), thereby slowing down the course of the analytic process by several years.

With my clinical examples I have tried to show the dynamic contribution the body makes to the formation and dissolution of organized thought. This focus should not, however, be taken to indicate a reluctance to recognize the centrality of the relational matrix, in which the analyst's reverie and the relational dynamics of the analytic couple fulfil the important function of catalyzing the analysand's internal transformations. Building on Matte Blanco's hypotheses, I have tried to present my way of regarding body–mind dissociation. I believe this perspective may have interesting implications and could improve the evaluation of material in which corporeality contributes to the psychoanalytic process.

Notes

1 A former version was published as Lombardi, R. (2009). Through the eye of the needle: the unfolding of the unconscious body. *Journal of the American Psychoanalytic Association*, 57: 61–94.

2 This is an example of how I understand an integrative change fostering the body–mind relationship. This type of change seems to me in line

with a psychoanalytic technique guided by changes in thought processes, that is not in what patients think about, but in *how* they think about and how they organize internal links (Bion 1962).

3   Obviously, when I refer to evolution in this type of patient I am not talking of being cured of a somatic illness, which is regulated by a biological system quite independent of mental stimuli; to think that such an illness could be resolved mentally would indeed be an omnipotent fantasy! What I *am* talking about is a change in the body-mind relationship, which can in certain cases play an important role in the evolution of some physical illnesses, favouring a constructive relationship with the body through the development of tolerance for the limits imposed by reality. A greater attunement to body/ physical symptoms can for example allow an individual with a neurological disease to better identify his/ her internal condition, allowing for earlier intervention that can reduce severity of symptoms and course.

References

Aisenstein, M. (2006). The indissociable unity of psyche and soma: a view from the Paris Psychosomatic School. *International Journal of Psychoanalysis*, 87(3): 667–680.

Anzieu, D. (1985). *The skin ego*. New Haven, CT: Yale University Press.

Aron, L. (1998). The clinical body and the reflexive mind. In L. Aron & F.S. Anderson (Eds.), *Relational perspectives on the body* (pp. 3–37). Hillsdale, NJ: Analytic Press.

Balint, E. (1987). Memory and consciousness. *International Journal of Psychoanalysis*, 68: 475–483.

Bion, W. R. (1957). Differentiation of the psychotic from the non-psychotic personalities. *In Second thoughts*. London: Karnac Books, 1967, pp. 43–64.

Bion, W. R. (1962). *Learning from experience*. London: Karnac Books, 1984.

Bion, W. R. (1965). *Transformations*. London: Karnac Books, 1984.

Bion, W. R. (1970). *Attention and interpretation*. London: Karnac Books.

Bion, W. R. (1979). Making the best of a bad job. In *Clinical seminar and other works*. London: Karnac Books, 1988.

Bion, W. R. (1988). *Clinical seminar and other works*. London: Karnac Books.

Breuer, J., & Freud, S. (1893–95). Studies on hysteria. *Standard Edition*, 2: 1–306.

Bromberg, P. (1998). *Standing in the spaces: essays on clinical process, trauma and dissociation*. Hillsdale, NJ: Analytic Press.

Bromberg, P. (2006). *Awakening the dreamer: clinical journeys*. Hillsdale, NJ: Analytic Press.

Cooper, A. (2008). American psychoanalysis today: a plurality of orthodoxies. *Journal of the American Academy of Psychoanalysis and Dynamic Psychiatry*, 36(2): 235–253.

Damasio, A. (2003). *Looking for Spinosa. Joy, sorrow and the feeling brain.* London: Heinemann.

Deutsch, F. (1954). Analytic synesthesiology – analytic interpretation of intersensory perception. *International Journal of Psychoanalysis*, 35: 293–301.

Ferrari, A. B. (2004). *From the eclipse of the body to the dawn of thought.* London: Free Association Books.

Fogel, G. I. (2006). Riddles of masculinity: gender, bisexuality and thirdness. *Journal of the American Psychoanalytic Association*, 54: 1139–1163.

Freud, A. (1937). *The ego and the mechanisms of defence.* London: Hogarth Press.

Freud, S. (1893–95). Studies on hysteria. *Standard Edition*, 2: 1–306.

Freud, S. (1900). The interpretation of dreams. *Standard Edition*, 5.

Freud, S. (1905). Three essays on the theory of sexuality. *Standard Edition*, 7: 130–243.

Freud, S. (1910). Psychoanalytic notes on an autobiographical account of a case of paranoia (dementia paranoides). *Standard Edition*, 12.

Freud, S. (1911). Formulations on the two principles of mental functioning. *Standard Edition*, 12.

Freud, S. (1915a). Instincts and their vicissitudes. *Standard Edition*, 14: 109–140.

Freud, S. (1915b). The unconscious. *Standard Edition*, 14: 159–215.

Freud, S. (1923). The ego and the id. *Standard Edition*, 19: 1–66.

Freud, S. (1937). Analysis terminable and interminable. *Standard Edition*, 23.

Freud, S. (1940). An outline of psychoanalysis. *Standard Edition*, 23.

Gaddini, E. (1980). Notes on the mind–body question. In *A psychoanalytic theory of infantile experience* (pp. 119–141). London: Routledge, 1992.

Goldberg, P. (1995). 'Successful' dissociation, pseudovitality and inauthentic use of the senses. *Psychoanalytic Dialogues*, 5: 493–510.

Good, M.L. (2006). Perverse dreams and dreams of perversion. *Psychoanalytic Quarterly*, 75: 1005–1044.

Grabel, S. (2008). When analysis makes patients worse: the negative therapeutic reaction revisited. *Journal of the American Psychoanalytic Association*, 56: 583–594.

Green, A. (1983). *Narcissisme de vie, narcissisme de mort.* Paris: Editions de Minuit.

Green, A. (1984). Le langage dans la psychanalyse. In *Langages.* Paris: Les Belles Lettres.

Greenacre, P. (1971). *Emotional growth: psychoanalytic studies of the gifted and a great variety of other individuals.* New York: International Universities Press.

Hofstadter, D.R., & Dennett, D.C. (1981). *The mind's I: fantasies and reflections on self and soul.* New York: Basic Books.

Horney, K. (1936). The problem of the negative therapeutic reaction. *Psychoanalytic Quarterly*, 5: 29–44.

James, M. (1960). Premature ego development. Some observations on disturbances in the first three months of life. *International Journal of Psychoanalysis*, 41: 288–294.

Kantrowitz, J. I. (2008). Employing multiple theories and evoking new ideas: the use of clinical material. *International Journal of Psychoanalysis*, 89: 355–368.

Kaplan, S. (2006). Children in genocide. *International Journal of Psychoanalysis*, 87: 725–746.

Kilbourne, B. (2002). *Disappearing persons: shame and appearance*. New York: State University of New York Press.

Klein, M. (1923). Early analysis. In *Love, guilt and reparation, and other works 1921–1945*. New York: Delta, 1977.

Klein, M. (1928). Early stages of the Oedipus conflict. In *Love, guilt and reparation, and other works 1921–1945*. New York: Delta, 1977.

Klein, M. (1932). *Psychoanalysis of children*. London: Hogarth Press.

Klein, M. (1946). Notes on some schizoid mechanisms. In *Envy and gratitude, and other works 1946–1963*. London: Hogarth Press, 1975.

Krystal, H. (1988). *Integration and self-healing*. Hillsdale, NJ: Analytic Press.

Lansky, M. (2005). The impossibility of forgiveness: shame fantasies as instigators of vengefulness in Euripides' *Medea*. *Journal of the American Psychoanalytic Association* 53: 437–464.

Laub, D., & Auerhahn, N. C. (1993). Knowing and not-knowing massive psychic traumas: Forms of traumatic memories. *International Journal of Psychoanalysis*, 72: 63–71.

Laufer, E. (2002, April). *The body as internal object*. Paper presented at Centro di Psicoanalisi Romano, Rome.

Laufer, M., & Laufer, E. (1991). Body image, sexuality and the psychotic core. *International Journal of Psychoanalysis*, 74: 287–302.

Lichtenberg, J. (1978). The testing of reality from the standpoint of the body self. *Journal of the American Psychoanalytic Association*, 26: 357–385.

Liebermann, J. (2000). *Body talks. Looking and being looked at in psychoanalysis and psychotherapy*. New York: Aronson.

Loewald, H. (1960). On the therapeutic action of psychoanalysis. *International Journal of Psychoanalysis*, 41: 16–33.

Lombardi, R. (2002). Primitive mental states and the body. A personal view of Armando B. Ferrari's concrete original object. *International Journal of Psychoanalysis* 83: 363–381.

Lombardi, R. (2003). Mental models and language registers in the psychoanalysis of psychosis. An overview of a thirteen–year analysis. *International Journal of Psychoanalysis*, 84: 843–863.

Lombardi, R. (2004). Three psychoanalytic sessions. With commentaries by J. Grotstein, V. Bonaminio, J. Greenberg and a response. *Psychoanalytic Quarterly*, 73(3): 773–814.

Lombardi, R. (2007). Shame in relation to the body, sex and death: a clinical exploration of the psychotic levels of shame. *Psychoanalytic Dialogues*, 17(3): 385–399.

Lombardi, R. (2008). The body in the analytic session: focusing on the body-mind link. *International Journal of Psychoanalysis*, 89(1): 89–110.

Mahler, M., & McDevitt, J. (1982). Thoughts on the emergence of self, with particular emphasis on the body self. *Journal of the American Psychoanalytic Association*, 33: 827–848.

Marty, P., & De M'Uzan, M. (1963). La 'pensée operatoire'. *Revue Française de Psychanalyse*, 27 (suppl): 345–356.

Matte Blanco, I. (1975). *The unconscious as infinite sets*. London: Karnac Books.

Matte Blanco, I. (1988). *Thinking, feeling and being*. London: Routledge.

Meissner, W.W. (1997). The self and the body: I. The body self and the body image. *Psychoanalysis and Contemporary Thought*, 20: 419–448.

Meissner, W.W. (1998a). The self and the body: II. The embodied self – self vs. nonself. *Psychoanalysis and Contemporary Thought*, 21: 85–111.

Meissner, W.W. (1998b). The self and the body: III. The body image in clinical perspective. *Psychoanalysis and Contemporary Thought*, 21: 113–146.

Meissner, W.W. (1998c). The self and the body: IV. The body on the couch. *Psychoanalysis and Contemporary Thought*, 21: 277–300.

Nagel, T. (1974). What is it like to be a bat? In *Mortal questions* (pp. 165–180). Cambridge: Cambridge University Press.

Ogden, T. H. (1989). On the concept of an autistic-contiguous position. *International Journal of Psychoanalysis*, 70: 127–140.

Reeder, J. (2004). *Hate and love in psychoanalytic institutions. The dilemma of a profession*. New York: Other Press.

Rizzuto, A. M. (2001). Metaphors of a bodily mind. *Journal of the American Psychoanalytic Association*, 49: 535–568.

Sands, S. H. (2007). Dissociation, the analyst's vulnerability, and the body. Review of *Awakening the dreamer: clinical journeys* by Philip M. Bromberg. *Psychoanalytic Dialogues*, 17(5): 741–751.

Schilder, P. (1950). *The image and appearance of the human body*. New York: Wiley.

Scott, W. C. (1948). Some embryological, neurological, psychiatric and psycho-analytic implications of the body scheme. *International Journal of Psychoanalysis*, 29: 141–155.

Sifneos, P. (1967). Clinical observations on some patients suffering from a variety of psychosomatic diseases. *Psychosomatic Research: Proceedings of the Seventh European Conference on Psychosomatic Research*, 13: 339–345.

Symington, N. (2007). *Becoming a person through psychoanalysis*. London: Karnac Books.

Tausk, V. (1933). On the origin of the 'influencing machine' in schizophrenia. *Psychoanalytic Quarterly*, 2: 519–556.

Taylor, G.J. (1987). *Psychosomatic medicine and contemporary psychoanalysis*. Madison, CT: International Universities Press.

Van der Kolk, B. A. (1996). The body keeps the score: approaches to the psychobiology of the post-traumatic stress disorder. In B. A. van der Kolk, A. C. McFarlane, & L. Weisaeth (Eds.), *Traumatic stress* (pp. 214–241). New York: Guilford Press.

Winnicott, D. W. (1953). Mind and its relation to the psyche-soma. In *Collected papers: through paediatrics to psycho-analysis*. London: Tavistock, 1958.

Wrye, H.K. (1998). The embodiment of desire. In L. Aron & F. S. Anderson (Eds.). *Relational perspectives on the body* (pp. 97–116). Hillsdale, NJ: Analytic Press.

THE BODY EMERGING FROM
FORMLESS INFINITY[1]

The psychoanalytic revolution introduced by Freud is in some ways related to Darwin's epistemological revolution that unequivocally placed man in the context of the animal kingdom. Unveiling the undeniable connection that the human being has to the biological force of animal instincts, Freud places the operations of the human mind in relation to an irrefutable link with the body. That fundamental assumption of psychoanalysis seems to have passed into the background as a consequence of the growing relevance that research has attributed to the object relationship and intersubjectivity. Although there is no doubt that the intersubjective emphasis has definitely enriched clinical and theoretical psychoanalysis, at the same time it must be recognized, as I stated also in Chapter 3, that psychoanalytic research still lacks a full integration with the importance that the body holds, especially in relation to the deepest areas of mental functioning.

The body as a compass for psychoanalytic
working through

I would like to reconsider two brief quotations from Freud, in order to locate them in the most current vein of psychoanalytic reflection and research (Anzieu 1985; McDougall 1989; Lieberman 2000; Aron & Anderson 2003; Ferrari 2004; Lombardi 2002, 2009a) that finds a pivotal element of elaboration in the relationship between body and mind. In doing this I will utilize clinical material stemming from the analysis of a psychotic patient, accompanying my presentation of the material with comments and reflections stimulated by the clinical evidence.

With the passing of years and the accumulation of clinical experience, I have become ever more surprised by the strength of Freud's intuitions in his first clinically important work, of which I will quote a brief but very significant passage, from which I derive inspiration for the title of this article. Freud writes:

> Her painful legs began to 'join in the conversation' during our analyses. . . . *I came in time to use such pains as a compass to guide me*; if she stopped talking but admitted that she still had a pain, I knew that she had not told me everything, and insisted on her continuing her story till the pain had been talked away.
>
> (1893, p. 148, my italics)

And twenty years later, tackling his maximal effort at systematization of his clinical discoveries, Freud (1915a) wrote:

> It is only the analysis of one of the affections which we call *narcissistic psychoneuroses* that promises to furnish us with conceptions through which *the enigmatic Ucs. will be* brought more within our reach and, as it were, *made tangible.*
>
> (Ibid., p. 196, my italics)

> *Some reference to bodily organs or innervations* is often given prominence in the content of these remarks.
>
> (Ibid., p. 197, my italics)

> I would call attention once more to the fact that *the whole train of thought is dominated by* the element which has for its content *a bodily innervation* (or, rather, the sensation of it).
>
> (Ibid., p. 198, my italics)

In these passages, it seems to me that, in a single, clear conceptual network, Freud holds together the *body*, the *unconscious*, and *the psychotic levels of mental functioning*, and that he considers *bodily sensations to be a privileged 'compass' with which to establish a pragmatic relationship with the unconscious in the context of clinical working through*. To me the choice of this compass seems consistent with his assumption that psychic life finds its origin in the world of drives (*Triebe*). The models for elaboration of affects and thought are located in the body due to the 'demand for work' (*Arbeitsanforderung*): 'as the psychical representative of the stimuli originating from within the organism and reaching the mind, as a measure of the demand made upon the mind for work in consequence of its connection with the body' (1915b, p. 122).

From an analytic point of view, the deepest psychic levels coincide with a close proximity to the confused and boiling cauldron of the id. In the psychoanalytic lexicon, the adjective *psychotic*, then, in addition to a psychiatric diagnosis, has come to indicate an internal disposition in which the relationship between the ego and the id is privileged over that between the ego and external reality (Freud 1924; Bion 1957/1967). This fact seems to emphasize that the utility of clinical experience with psychosis pertains not only to the specificity of this dimension, but also has general interest for the treatment of all our patients, from the moment that we consider that *the psychotic levels are involved in every psychoanalytic treatment that may include among its objectives an improvement of the relationship between the subject and his or her emotional and instinctual world* – or, rather, more integrated communication between the ego and the id.

In my clinical experience, the importance of the body and the body–mind relationship is particularly clear in relation to the treatment of so-called difficult cases; this has been a 'found' element, rather than one that I specifically looked for on the basis of a theoretical expectation (Lombardi 2005). These experiences have triggered my more attentive consideration of the implications of body–mind dissociation and the specific modalities of clinical approach with which to catalyze a change in these conditions that are particularly vulnerable to situations of impasse (Lombardi 2003a, 2004, 2008a).

The clinical material drawn from the psychoanalysis of a psychotic patient that I will consider in this paper appears to me significant in demonstrating the *importance of bodily experiences* in the context of the psychoanalytic session *for the activation of a relationship with the unconscious and of 'learning from experience'* (Bion 1962b).

The body is the point of origin of the ego (Freud 1923a), as well as the subject's first vital 'object' of reference (Ferrari 2004), and so it seems indispensable to activate an elaboration of this area. In treating difficult patients, we must often confront explosive disorganization and uncontainable acting out, as well as a strongly 'de-emotionalized' orientation, resulting in the patient's having the 'texture' almost of a zombie deprived of life, of a mechanical automaton or a puppet made of ice, who often remains estranged from symbolic requests made to him by the analyst, with the consequent risk of an arrest of analytic elaboration. In his experience, Bion had to confront the same difficulties when he posed himself the problem of modifying the Freudian perspective centered around the working through of the repressed unconscious – in which symbolic interpretation, principally of the oedipal level and the analysis of defences, is central – in order to introduce his own model of the *alpha-function*, in which the principal task of analytic work becomes that of producing thinkable elements, on both conscious and unconscious levels. In this way, for Bion, the *most urgent* clinical necessity is not that of revealing the unconscious to the conscious, but of utilizing and producing the unconscious in order to permit the conscious mind to function. Alluding to the dramatic dehumanization and de-emotionalization that the analyst finds himself confronting in his clinical work, Bion noted that 'the attempt to evade the experience of contact with live objects by destroying alpha-function leaves the personality unable to have a relationship with any aspect of itself that does not resemble an automaton' (1962b, p. 13).

A contemporary perspective on the body

According to my hypothesis, the 'attempt to evade contact with life objects' to which Bion alludes is not to be understood only as a reference to the object relationship – or rather, to the sphere that, for example, has been explored in the post-Kleinian tradition by various authors, such as Joseph (1988), who described so-called difficult-to-reach patients in the context of the transference relationship – but also as a reference to the *subject's relationship with his or her own body*, that is, with the simultaneously biological and psychological object that has characterized him or her since birth, and with the diversified sensorial and emotional world that derives from it. In this perspective, the analyst must be considered not so much as an object to be interiorized as the first organizational core of the ego, but as an external facilitator who carries out his or her role through *reverie* (Bion 1962b).

With respect to Freud's discoveries, my conception of the body as a compass for working through is characterized, then, in a different way. In Freud's conception, the body is the repository of repressed content waiting to become conscious: the bodily symptom has a focal meaning, with *specific contents of anxiety, conflict and defences*. My conception of the body, by contrast, reflects clinical experience with patients of the nonneurotic sector, who – even when they seem to be well integrated with reality – suffer from defects of representation, profound splitting, and an incapacity to freely associate, as well as being continually confronted with annihilation anxieties. In such a context, the *sensori-perceptive experience of the body corresponds to the beginning of an early mental autonomous functioning and to the capacity to exist as a separate subject.*

Thus, *the body* does not express an unconscious repression to be interpreted in symbolic terms, but *is a central, driving factor of liberation from the whirlpool of an unrepressed unconscious* (Matte Blanco 1975), *from a 'dark and formless infinite'* (Milton cited by Bion 1970). These patients' primary anxiety does not correlate with the pressure of the drives, but with the annihilation anxiety that derives from the shattering or absence of spatiotemporal parameters (Bion 1970; Bria & Lombardi 2008; Lombardi 2009c; Matte Blanco 1975).

In my conception, the analyst has a prominent leading role, much greater than in the Freudian conception, from the moment that the birth of self-awareness is set in motion in the context of a deep intersubjective exchange. The analyst welcomes *transference as the total situation*, in the sense introduced by the clinical work of Klein and Bion – at the same time, however, paying attention not to rush transference interpretation – as *he or she utilizes the relationship to de-saturate the patient's internal experience through reverie* (Bion 1962b), *and facilitates the analysand's transference onto his or her own body* (Lombardi 2005).

A psychoanalytic focus on the internal experience helps the subject emerge from an undifferentiated internal turmoil, as he or she develops the capacity for representation of this sensorial turmoil and the ability to differentiate his or her own feelings internally. This working through is accomplished jointly with the exploration of the internal layout and unconscious theories that influence and regulate the patient's body–mind relationship (Bion 1962b; Lombardi 2003a, 2003b).

In this sense, we can understand *an approach toward the relationship with the body as the precondition for the activation of the analysand's alpha function*, and, as a consequence, for promoting the analysand's orientation to mental growth, to the world of object relationships and to change. It seems to me that a perspective that places the body and sensorial working through in the foreground highlights the most well-known and widely shared aspects of Bion's approach – that is, those centered on thinking and intersubjectivity – reaffirming in a new key the link between body and mind, which has characterized psychoanalysis since its origins.

I think that this emphasis on the body may permit us to avoid the stumbling block of transforming Bion's hypotheses on thinking into a system of self-referencing abstractions. Some contemporary Bionian authors, in fact, seem to conceive of the mind only on an abstract plane, a relational and narrative one, risking loss of contact with the primarily conflictual, wild and irreducible nature of an unconscious of a bodily origin, and with the mysterious psychosensorial experience of being ourselves.

My reference to the body thus does not aim to return to the past through obeisance to a reverent orthodoxy, but is rather an attempt to place value on the fundamental and generative role of the body with respect to a mental dimension constantly in evolution and potentially infinite: an area that can perhaps help us in orienting psychoanalysis toward the future.

The clinical material drawn from the psychoanalysis of a psychotic patient that I will consider in this paper appears to me significant in demonstrating the *importance of bodily experiences* in the context of the psychoanalytic session as first expressions of self-consciousness, and *for the activation of 'learning from experience'* (Bion 1962b).

The first psychoanalytic session

With these brief reflections in mind, I will present some highlights of the clinical case of Simone, a tall and athletic young man who began analysis at four times per week at the age of twenty-one, in the context of his second acutely psychotic episode. The first episode had appeared five years earlier and had been treated only at the pharmacological level. He now presented as delusional, with hallucinations and paranoid symptomatology, and with violent anxieties of annihilation related to feeling he was being watched. While he was in this acute, full-blown phase, the analysis was set in motion at its full rhythm, following a technical approach that I have explored in particular on other occasions (Lombardi 2003b). Treatment during this period was supported by my collaboration with another psychiatrist who, besides seeing to the medications and maintaining a connection with the patient's family, took care of the hospital management during the more dangerous phases;[2] moreover, the patient's mother

93

initiated a parallel personal analysis with a third colleague. A few months after the beginning of analytic treatment, the risk of suicide appeared very high, and a hospitalization was organized according to a modality that permitted the patient to continue to attend sessions with me. A very dangerous development occurred at the moment in which his murderous impulses – sometimes of self-murder, i.e. suicide – had infiltrated the transference, and the analysand had declared homicidal ideation toward me as well.

In this case, the relationship with the body appeared central in initiating an analytic process of change and the activation of a capacity for self-containment. I will not describe the initial period of analysis, which I have addressed elsewhere (Lombardi 2007a), and instead will present some vignettes from sessions that took place during the second and third years of analysis.

I will begin with a Thursday session, the last of the week, from the second year of analysis. At this point, it has not been long since the acute phase of psychosis has receded clinically. Simone enters with his head held high, displaying a challenging air. He sits rigidly on the couch. He begins to speak: 'I feel cold. I don't know what's happening to me. I'm becoming a piece of ice.' I notice with alarm his extreme coldness, which manifests itself in a mechanical aspect to his gestures and way of speaking, and I begin to fear an arrest in the process of working through, and a downward slide toward regression of an autistic type. I reply to him: 'You're making yourself into a piece of ice out of a fear that your hate may become a dangerous explosion that will again overwhelm both you and me.' At this point, Simone wheels his head around toward me, and says to me with a carefully pronounced and articulated voice, 'Why don't you look at me?'

I notice a wave of hate and a strong sense of challenge emanating from him and, at the same time, I am aware of the importance of not refusing this challenge, which appeared to represent an important occasion for an encounter between the two of us. I raise my head – which, until that moment, had been bent in concentration, as I tried to find an internal space in which to think – and face toward him in order to look directly into his eyes, and I say to him: 'Certainly, I look at you. And I am here with you even though I am not always looking at you.' Simone looks fixedly at me, as though to scrutinize me, and says: 'It's strange that I'm not afraid to look at you. . . . It isn't like other times when I've felt dangerous eyes.' At this point, I begin to understand the intersubjective meaning that Simone attributes to the gaze: *in looking into my eyes, he is in reality looking, first of all, into his own eyes*, which speak to him of himself, of his body, and of the hateful emotions that live within it. I realize with a shiver of emotion that I am witnessing an important development, and so I say to him: 'Now you are looking at me, and you see in my eyes your hatred, and you feel that it is not the uncontrollable hatred that you fear, because now you see it. And in seeing it, you can withstand it and think about it.' At this point, I see that the lines of Simone's face have softened, and in his left eye a tear is forming, which remains there, halted, like a tiny sac deposited in his eyelashes. Gazing fixedly in front of himself, he says: 'I feel heat, something hot that moves within me. . . . I feel pain inside. I don't understand what it is, but I feel pain that grabs me inside. . . . Maybe it's sadness.' And I say: 'When you accept your hate, the ice melts inside of you. You find the warmth of your acceptance and can refresh yourself with your tears.'

At this point, Simone appears to have adopted a more relaxed posture, almost as though he has become a different person with respect to the rigidity of a mechanical automaton that was displayed at the beginning of the session. He moves very slowly, and transitions from crouching on the far corner of the couch to lying down upon it, relaxed. It seems to me that time has become less dense, to the point that every instant seems an eternity to me. After a period of silence, he says to me: 'What are these dead things . . .? Dead things that I feel inside.' I notice a profound anguish, and I have the impression that Simone's discovery of feeling himself sensorially alive has opened him up to the devastating perception of his internal state of death, resulting from the paralysis of an internal being made up of emotions and thoughts. At the same time, I notice with anxiety that his thinking may be starting to lean in the direction of concreteness (dead things), and I fear that a downward slide toward concrete thinking could paralyze him. Thus I try to locate, inside myself, *a formulation that might give symbolic connotations to the emotional working through* that I feel is being activated inside him, and so I say: 'You recognize the pain of death, of experiences that come to an end, but this is a way of being alive and of allowing live emotions to run their course inside of you.' At the same time that I say this to him, I realize the end of the session is drawing near, and we are thus confronting 'death' together; in fact, the session has been an experience of life that we must now prepare to relinquish. After a long silence, Simone begins to move about on the couch in slow, sideways movements, though he remains lying down. Then he says to me softly, with an almost suffocated voice: 'Few people could understand what I am suffering.' I feel a rush of compassion in realizing that Simone is acknowledging an experience shared together with me – in 'at-one-ment,' Bion (1965) would have said – in which his relationship with himself accompanies a relationship with an otherness located on the same emotional wavelength. At the outer reaches of my mental space, Wolfgang Goethe's lines echo in my mind, those he gave to the delicate character of Mignon and to which Franz Schubert gave incomparable musical substance: '*Nur wer die Sehnsucht kennt, weiss was ich leide*' ('Only he who knows longing, can guess at my suffering'). Keeping my own tone of voice subdued as well, I said to Simone: 'To feel that you are understood in the relationship with me makes your pain tolerable, because you know that you are no longer the only one to feel it.' He remained silent, as though in assent; and after a moment, I stood up to signal the end of our meeting.

In this session, Simone transforms himself – through the mediation of analytic reverie (Bion 1962b) – from an icy automaton oriented toward 'evading the experience of contact with life objects,' into a human person characterized by sensations and feelings. 'I feel heat, something warm is moving inside me': through this sensorial experience, not unlike Elisabeth von R's painful legs as described by Freud, an elaborative carrier has been set in motion, capable of advancing the analytic working through and the growth of the nonpsychotic part of the personality (Bion 1957/1967). At the same time, through the sensorial register, the enigmatic unconscious is rendered 'tangible', so to speak, caught in its first-born dimension: 'dead things . . . dead things that I feel inside.' And the unconscious experience becomes our shared legacy in the intersubjective space.

After this session, I felt inside myself the almost inexplicable unblocking of an oppressive sense of paralysis, which for some time had been associated with my feeling exhausted, as though from an enormous physical effort. I felt that I regained my internal energies, which had been momentarily 'used up' inside me, as though from an unknown illness that deprived me of every strength. These experiences validate the *massive bodily and unconscious participation* that is required of us by the analytic processes that proceed along the most obscure levels of psychic depth, in which *the sharing of sensorial states deprived of a corresponding representation* sets the stage for developments that cannot be realized in the absence of this ample sensorial, internal territory, mutually shared by the analytic couple.

Commentary

Tustin (1981/1992) emphasized the minimal capacity to regulate sensorial experience that is connected to hypersensitive states in psychotic children, and the parallel tendency to activate rigid and impenetrable, protective armour in confronting waves of sensual experience that come to be feared as potentially catastrophic. The sensorial world – at these levels of functioning – is characterized by an 'all–or–nothing' modality, for which the subject is either deprived of sensations or is overwhelmed by them. Tustin writes: 'Thus, bodily sensations have been transformed into *psychological* experience through reciprocal and rhythmical activity between mother and infant. The stage is set for percept and concept formation. But this is a mysterious process' (1981/1992, p. 101). In analysis, such processing involves contact with levels that precede those of projection and introjection, which imply some sense of bodily separateness, in order to leave a place for states characterized by what Tustin defines as a 'flowing–over–at–oneness': 'mysterious' and unconscious states experienced in the analytic relationship. Through the 'hardness' of the transformation into a piece of ice at the beginning of the session, and the 'softness' of an internal warmth, Simone's experience comes close to internal levels that – from Tustin's perspective – can be likened to autistic levels of the personality, in which the integration and differentiation between opposing sensorial orbits (like hard and soft, cold and hot, etc.) play a central, driving role.

For Ferrari (2004), too, the experience of internal contact with sensations, and the collapse of an overarching and chaotic sensoriality caused by a decline in internal containment (Bion 1962b), implies – in the processing that characterizes the analytic relationship – an approach toward a '*vertical relationship*' between body and mind, which is understood to pre-date the phenomena of projection and introjection, which had been conceived by Klein (1952/1975), in contrast, as the earliest levels. With respect to the levels of functioning that Tustin related to autistic problems, we could say that Ferrari tends to consider them, instead, to be in some way structural, that is, as typical elements of the human being as a Darwinian, 'ethological' subject. In other words, for this author, *the conflict and the dialogue between body and mind* characterize the deepest levels of mental functioning and determine the constitutively 'catastrophic' nature of thinking acts, in the sense that had already been pointed out by Bion (1970). With respect to the undifferentiated sensorial flood that characterizes the primordial sense of self according to Tustin, Ferrari's emphasis on the *role of sensorial perception*, furthermore, appears particularly significant as the starting point of mental functioning. Sensorial perception, in fact, breaks the 'all-or-nothing' system and parcels out (we could say 'asymmetricizes,' in Matte Blanco's sense) the undifferentiated sensorial world into discrete and recognizable phenomena.

In the same way as Tustin and Ferrari, Matte Blanco (1988) highlights the inadequacy of a point of view that limits itself to projective-introjective dynamics and to the description of transference-countertransference dynamics, in order to emphasize the *'symmetrizing' impact that derives from an approach to the deep unconscious*. In fact, that level is characterized by an augmentation of the proportions of symmetry with respect to the asymmetrical and differentiating resources of thinking. Approaching *the experience of indivisibility* as an expression of deep aspects of human nature, for Matte Blanco, implies abandoning the external-internal antithesis – in which analyst and analysand are differentiated persons – and instead coming closer to non-tridimensional aspects of the being, where the confused logic of the dream is dominant and where an individual may trespass on the other in a disquieting way. The symmetrical experience of transference, or *symmetrical transference* (Lombardi 2009c), implies a conception of transference that is not a duplicate of past parental relationships, but is an essentially generative process in which new experiences are put into play, characterized by an openness to the future rather than a reorganization of the past. From this point of view, a different way of looking at the role of transference interpretations also emerges – which, when used at these levels, can imply a dangerous iatrogenic role of anti-developmental 'impingement,' to use an expression dear to Winnicott. Instead, what counts is the use of the experience of the analytic relationship as an instrument to give substance and visibility to the subject's internal experience – in the sense of that intrasubjective transference (*Übertragung*) emphasized by Freud (1900) in relation to dream formation – as happens, for example, in the session with Simone, when I correlate his *looking into my eyes* with *seeing his own hate*. The analytic relationship, more than a setting of 'transference' – in the classical sense of a new edition of past parental relationships, which has been attributed to it in the Freudian tradition – is thus a place where an *intersubjective relationship* unfolds, one of sharing new experiences, which, when it moves into the really 'deep levels' of the unconscious, assumes the connotations of indivisibility and lack of distinction that stem from the dominance of the 'principle of symmetry' (Matte Blanco 1975).

Likewise, I should like to observe that Freud's point of view regarding the body-mind relationship never moved away from a perspective that took continuity for granted, leaving undeveloped the problems connected to the clinical phenomenology of body-mind dissociation. Consistent with his personality that led him to 'have no use for other people's ideas when they are presented to [him] at an inopportune moment' (1923b, p. 287), the founding father of psychoanalysis remained deaf to the revolutionary implications of Tausk's (1933) writings on the 'influencing machine,' in which for the first time some clinical cases of dissociation of the body were described in a specific way. We can perhaps fully appreciate the relevance of these descriptions only today, thanks to the current epistemological models of authors like Bion, Tustin, Ferrari and Matte Blanco, who updated and reformulated the Freudian point of view in the light of urgent situations arising in contemporary psychoanalytic practice.

In this sense, a communication such as 'I feel heat, something hot that moves within me . . .' is an important indicator of an early internal dialogue between the analysand's body and mind, which contrasts with the body-mind dissociation and the paranoid split of his hatred. And as a whole, the entire session – which I have discussed in some detail up to this point, in order to consider its implications – was shown to be important in preparing the way for a more ample involvement of sensorial experiences in Simone's analysis – an experience that rooted the analysand in his body, no less than in his unconscious, confronting him with the need to tolerate the unknown that he was encountering inside himself, and permitting him to accept an early form of awareness of being a separate person.

I would also like to emphasize that, as we simultaneously move closer to anxieties tied to the sensorial and bodily experience of the self, *the analysand achieves an important relational experience*. In opening himself to eye contact with me, Simone asks me to confront his paranoid expectation of being destroyed by an external gaze. In fact, in the past, he had felt me to be 'the devil,' and so he absolutely could not look at me without fear of being destroyed. The new experience of

99

the mutual gaze that Simone achieves in this session transmits important inter-human contact, and this relational experience of acceptance and human communication is sensorially perceived inside him as an internal warmth.

In my verbal intervention, however, I decide not to emphasize the relational component in order to focus on the patient's new capacity to *use his eyes to look at and to see* his internal feelings, rather than to control and destroy. This clinical passage is an example of what I mean by working through that approaches and modifies the patient's unconscious theories influencing and regulating the body–mind relationship.

In fact, this analytic development permits the *modification of an important internal theory inherent in the visual function*, through which *the eye* is no longer considered in the light of *primitive sensorial functions* linked to the pleasure principle (possession, control, etc.), but begins to align with the *perceptive* functions linked to the reality principle and thought. This evolution – from concrete affects subjected to motor discharge, toward an abstract representational function – permits Simone to *begin to contain his paranoid violence of hate through his own mind* (Bion 1962b; Freud 1911).

To put it another way, in refusing to centre my intervention on myself as a transference object, I do not wish to negate the importance of this 'moment of meeting' – as Stern would say – but I am trying to protect the development of the delicate and complex arrangement of *internal experience* that the patient is beginning to actualize: in fact, he begins to utilize his bodily resources (his eyes) in a perceptive way, constructing new and decisive links between body and mind, between affect and representation (Freud 1915a).

From this point on, Simone can proceed to the point of perceiving his internal state of devitalization ('dead things that I feel inside'). The painful discovery of death leads him to discover, furthermore, how it may be possible to share these burning internal experiences with another human being. With these movements, the analytic couple reaches experiences of at-one-ment that gradually open up to a depressive organization and a recognition of otherness (Klein 1936/1975).

Further clinical developments

In light of the clinical material I have just described, a session appeared significant in which Simone began by saying: 'I feel something in my

stomach, like an emptiness, like when you ride a roller coaster.' In telling me this, the analysand was communicating to me that his incipient tolerance of sensations was furthering the ego's early resources of
containment, offering in parallel an early representability and con-
tainability of his feeling of falling into an annihilating void on the
occasion of breaks in the analysis. (This subject had already been
addressed in sessions and contexts that I will not describe more specifically here.) The void was no longer what it had been in earlier
phases of the analysis – a black hole into which the patient fell, feeling himself to be annihilated, in the sense described by Matte Blanco
(1975) as the infinite sets dominated by the principle of symmetry, or
in the sense discussed by Bion (1967) when he evoked the "dark and
formless infinite" described by Milton, or by Winnicott (1974), when
he referred to the so-called primary agonies. Instead, the void had a
new element, in that 'falling forever' immediately followed a phase
of internal support – as happens on a roller coaster, in fact – from
the part of his sense of self that derived from contact with his bodily
experience. The experience of falling into undifferentiated symmetry
is here immediately followed by the activation of asymmetry: a sort
of epistemological see-saw (Matte Blanco 1988) in which symmetry
and asymmetry are harmoniously interconnected.

In this way, the internal experience of registering the sensorial
data permitted a *comparison with absence on the relational level* (Klein
1936/1975), which was mediated by the *constant trustworthiness of
a sensorial internal presence: the contact with absence*, as a condition for
the structuring of a capacity to think abstractly (Bion 1962a/1967),
met an important antecedent in the intrasubjective relationship that the
subject came to establish with *the organizing layout of his own bodily
sensations*.

To return to the same session, after a little while, Simone added
that a friend of his had told him: 'There are those who succeeded
in surviving the concentration camps.' At this point he had thought:
'Maybe I, too, can succeed in overcoming my fears.' This is an affirmation that opens a perspective on the *resources of faith* that the registration of bodily sensations can activate in relation to the catastrophic
impact of the more primitive, unthinkable anxieties and terrors without a name. At the same time, the experience of the body can appear
in some way – to these archaic levels – indistinguishable from the
horror of a concentration camp, inasmuch as it forces him to confront the discovery of the *limits* of space and time, and, almost in

contradiction, the anxiety of the unknown and *infinite* unconscious that lives inside us.

Second psychoanalytic session

Let us turn to a session in a subsequent period, a Monday – that is, the first session of the week – in which Simone presented with a big smile. He took off his jacket and put it on the chair. He then immediately got up from the couch to pick up his jacket and put it on again. I asked myself whether he wasn't trying to modulate a relational distance between the two of us, utilizing the jacket almost as a way to define the border between our two identities that risked being mixed up. Simone then begins to tell me about being happy to have spoken with a friend about the problems of young people. 'We understood each other,' he added. It seemed evident to me that this was a reference to our analytic exchange and to the fact that facing his problems together might set in motion an experience of his feeling understood. My choice, however, was not to interpret these relational movements, waiting to see which directions he took in his elaboration.

At a certain point, Simone suddenly asked me, 'Have you seen *Neverland?*' In this way he introduced a reference to Marc Foster's film, '*Finding Neverland*' (2004), winner of seven Academy Awards, which at that time had just appeared in local theatres. The film tells about the famous Scottish playwright James M. Barrie and the story behind the creation of *Peter Pan*, his most famous work. Four children who have lost their father in Victorian England meet a writer, who, while visiting the family, begins to write the famous play mostly to speak to the emotional needs of the youngest child, the one suffering the most from grief for his father. Later on the children lose their mother as well.

I remained struck by his reference to the movie, which had impressed me very much for its depth, and I answered affirmatively, asking him what had interested him. Simone answered: 'The fantasy. It is something that can be used.' Having in mind the constructive value that fantasy has in the film in portraying dramatic situations, I said to him that fantasy could be helpful to him when he was dealing with self-expression in relation to painful situations. At this point, he answered, 'I can't stand taking showers. I don't know what to think. Maybe I should put some music on, then I would think of that.' From the subject of fantasy, the analysand was moving on to consider a very concrete element like showers, and I thought that his reference to showers might indicate an occasion of *meeting with the body*, as well as with sensations and emotions, according to a *non-'oceanic' modality*, as distinct from the overwhelming and infinite dimension that he found himself living in when sensations and emotions had felt inundating (for more on the relationship between the body and the infinite, see Lombardi 2009b, 2009c). At the same time, I caught in the background a reference to our relationship as well, now more defined in the spatio-temporal realm in which the analytic session, which put him in emotional contact, was 'a shower': a vital shower, but which at the same time was felt to be – concurrently with the blossoming of a binomial of life-death opposites (Lombardi 2007b) – potentially deadly. For my part—perhaps not by chance—I noted the tragically famous showers in concentration camps, recalling Simone's previous reference to 'those who succeeded in surviving the concentration camps'.

The emphasis that he introduced on 'not being able to stand it' seemed to hearken back to an 'attack on linking' with the body, with that link being a potential source of emotions. Considering this, and also having in mind his initial association to *Neverland*, I said to him: 'Evidently you hate your body, which is *the land that is* and where you really live. If you recognize this body of yours, then it can cease being *the land that is not*' – Neverland. And at this point, Simone referred to his experience over the weekend: 'I didn't do well on my trip to England. I couldn't look people in the eye. I left a pub where there was music, and I started to cry. Desperation came over me. Maybe it wasn't worth it.'

His contact with an area of depressive feelings (the music and the tears) seemed to me the sign of a very positive development, and I tried to show him its value, underlining his capacity to master this emotional experience, which was – I said – 'certainly worth it.' Conversely, Simone risked underrating the value of the experience of feeling bad, of crying and desperation that pulled him along toward the depressive position. Inside myself I thought that, in some way, Simone – in communicating this episode to me – was also living it: he was, in other words, using the session to have contact with his emotions (through the emotional experience that was shared between us as well), detoxifying his expectation of being left annihilated by emotional contact. In this way, Simone demonstrated a beginning capacity to *interweave ways of being with feeling and thinking* (ways of being that are indivisible and dividing, respectively, according to Matte Blanco 1988), tolerating the impact of an integrated mental functioning.

At this point, in an unexpected way, Simone asked me: 'Can you become a paedophile because you don't recognize your own sexuality? I saw a little girl of six, maybe eight, and I felt strange.' I thought that the analysand was fantasizing a paedophilic component in the relationship of the adult with the children described in the film *Neverland*, and this seemed to permit access to a representation of his personal paedophilic instincts. The reference to paedophilia brought up the risk of a destructive act of expulsion of his desire for contact with the emotional world onto the body of a child. It was an expression of his omnipotent denial of his real body and his adult sexuality, as well as of his deadly hate of the real passing of time. The risk of paedophilic acting out had been one of my concerns in the analytic management of this difficult case, especially when the analysand's discriminating capacities had appeared particularly weakened by psychotic devastation. I tried, then, to read his reference to paedophilia in relation to a disavowal of his relationship with his own body, characterized by real limits, and so I said to him: 'If you deny having an adult body and deny that time has passed, as though it could always be so in a *Neverland*, then you have a '*body that isn't*.' At this point, you can discharge sex and hate through paedophilia.' Simone, however, corrected me: 'It is *Neverland*. It isn't 'the land that isn't.' It is 'the land that never was.'' In saying this, Simone seemed to me to be alluding to his tragic lack of integration with the body as a fact that had been inexorably missing from *all* his personal development, and to the revolutionary and innovative meaning of the new experience that was being realized in the analysis (cf. Williams 2007). At that point, searching for a communicative bridge with what was circulating inside him at that moment, I answered: 'In this sense, you are right that you need to construct the relationship with your own body, a body that for you never was. Because, if you are there with your body and your emotions, it is also certain that you are there as a person.' And Simone said: 'I was thinking that when there's a good film playing, you see it.' Appreciating the recognition that the patient was indirectly offering me for my emotional participation in his personal experience, I said: 'Well, in a certain sense, here in the session, we are watching a movie together that permits feeling and thinking. And so you discover how useful it is to be able to look at experiences that you feel inside your body – just as at the cinema, where it is not enough only *to feel*, but it is also useful *to watch*, to be able *to talk* together here in analysis, and to be able *to think*.'

Commentary

In the context of this session, which appeared to me at intervals to be very moving, it emerges that the analysand, starting from his experience of being understood by me, is progressively giving space to his experience of his own body, endowed with a sensorial and emotional, live flow that provides him with a substantial base of identification, with which he can also face the experiences of separation from analysis. *The working through of his hate for the connection with his body* ('I can't stand taking showers') *permits a defence of the bodily framework of Simone's emotional working through* – in the sense of what I have reaffirmed of Freud's view in regard to the 'demand for work' that connects the mind to the body – facilitating the constitution of a *thinking connection* with one's own body. The body is for Simone a land 'that never was,' and one that it is for the analysis to approach and discover in its sensorial music and its emotional scenery.

In this phase of the analysis, the experience of a body inhabited by vital and tolerable sensations became ever more frequent in Simone's experience, as we have seen in the experience of internal warmth and in the tolerance of his stomach sensations. This achievement diminished the pressure to use an evacuative projective identification – for example, through the investment of his external body into the figure of a child, wanting to then destroy it and to re-animate it at the same time through paedophilic acting out. Simone's body was becoming a real 'land', a truly possible place, where he was discovering the ability to live without fear of being destroyed by his catastrophic annihilation anxieties.

In this session, encountering his own real body seems to Simone to be an indissoluble experience of the appropriation of his own real story and of the cumulative trauma of his childhood history. The unthinkable, buried childhood pain inside the patient at a sensorial level – memories *in feelings*, according to Klein's brilliant intuition – can be approached thanks to the mediation of my analytic reverie, just as the child's grief for the loss of his parents in the film could be tolerated thanks to Barrie's mediation. The fact that the playwright invents a character whom we could define as *psychotic* (Peter Pan) shows us the protective function that psychosis has with respect to childhood catastrophe, and, at the same time, how important it is that the analyst keeps clearly in mind that psychosis has an important creative function of survival, without repudiating the destructive components of this.

At the same time, an *awareness of the intersubjective relationship* has to be growing in Simone. In his separation from analysis during the trip to England, he regresses to the point of feeling himself incapable of looking other people in the eyes, and he must immediately leave a pub. In this way, the analysand experiences the difference between moments of mutuality constructed in analysis, and other moments – like the weekend – in which he is separated from the analyst, and in which his paranoid anxieties re-emerge. The analytic relationship contributes, with its alternation of presence and absence, to the creation of a *living experience of temporality*; and thanks, too, to these experiences, it becomes possible for Simone to liberate himself from the negation of real time that characterizes his 'land that never was.'

In this session, I find the working through around Marc Foster's *Finding Neverland* – a film of great emotional and aesthetic quality – very moving. Simone's association induces him to think of the role of fantasy as an expression that permits the translation of internal, ineffable sensorial states, which otherwise lack equivalent representations. Furthermore, when the expression of internal emotional states risks paralysis – as in the case of the young protagonist of the film, paralyzed in the grief he cannot elaborate – there is someone who succeeds in translating his internal emotional states for him, as the writer Barrie does.

The psychotic patient's receptivity to works of art can be very acute, and this gift may enrich the analytic experience in a profound way. The empathic capacity to appreciate a film dominated by the spirit of grief and loss, one that focuses on the creative implications that can be derived from grief, is striking in a patient dominated by paranoid symptoms. This fact strikes me less intensely when I remember that this patient, on his own, demonstrated significant creative tendencies in design, music and cinematographic short subjects. These creative tendencies encouraged the support of the hard psychoanalytic work required by these patients to reach their recovery and their return to normal life.

Equally moving is the sequence in which the patient speaks of his trip to England, when he finds the strength to cry, leaving a pub where external music was being played in order to find a personal way to express, through crying, his internal music, his 'unheard melodies' (Keats) (see Chapter 8).

After he has reappropriated his emotions, Simone can approach the topic of paedophilia, disquieting for its dangerous and destructive implications that derive from the denial of his actual, adult sexual body and from the missing elaboration of his grief for the end of his childhood. Keeping up an active verbal elaboration of this topic every time the occasion arises has permitted the avoidance of dangerous paedophilic acting out, which is again addressed on several occasions in the course of this analysis.

Third psychoanalytic session

At this point, let's move to a later session in which the violent conflictuality pertaining to recognition of the body reappears. I will describe this session by emphasizing the sequence of analytic dialogue. As soon as he lies down on the couch, Simone begins:

PATIENT: Returning home, I looked at myself in the mirror and I felt as though I were in prison.

ANALYST: [I feel very positively struck by the patient's capacity to look at himself in the mirror: it is a way of establishing a relationship with himself and a possible avenue toward symbolic self-reflection. But I am equally struck by the violence of his claustrophobic reaction, through which the body, in the same moment that it is assumed, immediately comes to be felt as a prison to be evaded. I also notice a claustrophobic feeling in the physical form of a limitation of my own breathing range. I set about exploring whether the analysand already has some hypothesis about his experience that he brings to the session.] What would this come from, in your opinion?

PATIENT: The hatred, the hatred that I recognize.

ANALYST: [I notice a sense of relief of my respiratory oppression, as though his verbal allusion to hatred permitted me to begin 'dreaming' (Bion 1992) the sensorial precursors of hatred that were already circulating in the session.] You keep your hatred imprisoned and so also yourself.

PATIENT: [He begins to move more freely on the couch.] When I work at the bar and I'm behind the counter, I don't want

107

to do anything. Maybe it's hatred that makes me fall into boredom. [His voice changes and he becomes more energetic.] You are a shit!

ANALYST: [My initial physical discomfort is at this point replaced by a clear perception of the hateful emotions that are circulating. I observe within myself that cohabiting with hatred may be less oppressive than feeling oneself oppressed by unrepresentable obscure elements.] You recognize the hatred toward me. If you are prepared to recognize your hatred, you can also think about it, instead of discharging it into boredom.

PATIENT: I have so much hatred that I make my body disappear. [pause] My cock is bugging me. It's peeling. A while back the urologist gave me a cream that cured me, but then I didn't put it on any more. Now it's peeling again; I always forgot to put on the cream.

ANALYST: [Simone returns to his hatred of his body, alluding to concrete and symbolic damages caused by his denial of it. I try to alert him to the destructive implications of his denial, which leads him not to take care of himself.] In not worrying about your body, you then damage it in acting out hatred against yourself.

PATIENT: [after a silence] I'm not paying attention. I should pay more attention. Today I had wet hands and I pulled out a plug. I noticed an electrical discharge. [pause] I feel like I'd like to die: when I'm bored, I feel that I want to be dead.

ANALYST: [I note that Simone's level of awareness and explication with respect to his internal violence is improving. The patient recognizes his attitude of not thinking, of being inattentive, with all the risk of leaving space to unwittingly act out against himself – with suicide – all the hatred that he doesn't think about.] In not paying attention to your body, you believe you can make homicidal hatred toward yourself disappear. But instead it is really cancelling out your body, so that you can continue to be a victim of your hatred, to the point of being capable of killing yourself in reality through an act of carelessness.

PATIENT: [with a more relaxed and reflective voice] Going back home, I stopped at Piazza Venezia with my Egyptian friend. There was a homeless man outside a bar, and a barista came out to give him a cappuccino and a croissant. The man thanked some people who were there.

ANALYST: [After a moment in which the hatred seemed to me to be hypersaturated and almost paralyzing, I notice that the tension is diminishing. Simone's communications seem more oriented in a reparative direction, and not exempt from a shade of gratitude for the 'analytic cappuccino' that I was serving up to him with my analytic propositions. I leave aside these relational implications in regard to me, however, and I decide to intervene by continuing to focus on the relationship that the patient entertains with himself, appreciating the development of feelings of self-acceptance that are taking the place of the initial claustrophobia at dwelling inside himself and in his own body.] When you are prepared to recognize your tendency not to live, as happens to a homeless person, you can accept yourself and take care of yourself.

PATIENT: I didn't feel superior to the homeless man outside the bar. Other times I have felt superior.

ANALYST: [I notice in him a certain sincerity, and a clear reduction in the destructive narcissism and the omnipotent push to dissociate from the self. The figure of the homeless man helps me put into focus the abandonment anxieties of precariousness and solitude that the patient gives evidence of when he sets about living inside his body and recognizing it, and so I make the following remarks.] You don't feel superior to your body, to the fragility of a needy body, as you do when you cancel it out or wish yourself dead. Now you can make use of the sense of coming close to it as your real self.

PATIENT: I remember when I was at university and I went crazy. I was walking along and I saw people who looked at me with very bright eyes. They hated me. It makes me angry to remember this.

ANALYST: [I feel that his hatred here does not have expulsive connotations, but rather that he is in constructive contact with himself. I find a very positive, elaborated element in his memory of his acute phase, toward which the patient finds a certain reconciliation, approaching his paranoid hatred that was not processed or digested at the time.

109

Simultaneously, I find that he is speaking to me of the horror that he feels when he recognizes madness in his previous experience: a body lacerated by explosive emotions devoid of containment. A condition that the patient seems to feel is worse than that of a homeless person, abandoned and without hope.] Now you are ready to recognize your madness and your precarious state when you do not succeed in thinking, but if you tolerate your hatred, you can take care of yourself, you can think in order not to go crazy. The situation today can be different from what happened to you in the past.

PATIENT: Yesterday my father left me 100 euros on the table. They were for me. I thought that I didn't want them. I want to know how to count on what I earn myself. I hate my parents.

ANALYST: [It seems to me that Simone's discovery of being capable of thinking about his self-hatred, and of containing it, activates in him a sense of pride that encourages him to take a certain distance from his parents, whom he feels are hyperprotective and infantilizing. At the same time, I notice that the subject of separation begins to assume currency in the transference, as we approach the end of the session.] When you agree to separate yourself, like today in separating from me, then you hate me. And this hatred of yours is a price you are prepared to pay in order to recognize yourself as differentiated from your parents, and also from me.

PATIENT: I feel proud that this summer I was alone in a foreign city.

ANALYST: [It seems to me that Simone is looking at his capacity to be alone with a realistic perspective. His attitude is barely tinged with a manic tendency, which I decide not to interpret in order not to disturb his positive orientation toward assuming differentiation.] Also here, in some way, you can be proud of yourself for placing yourself here, facing me, as though you are a foreign country that has its own identity and its own differentiation with respect to the different country that I am – a differentiation that you can take away with you as well, when we separate for interruptions in the analysis.

110

Commentary

The material in this session demonstrates an analysand capable of discovering his body in the mirror in an autonomous way, as a development of a previous stage in which the function of the mirror had been performed especially through analytic reverie and through self-reflection in the person of the analyst, as we saw in the material from the preceding session on the reflection of the self in the analyst's eyes, in order to see and perceive his own hatred. In the moment in which Simone recognizes *his own body*, this *comes to be seen as a prison from which to escape,* because it confronts him with the limits of reality, and, again, with his own hatred of reality. The activity of the personality's psychotic area (Bion 1957/1967) generates intense claustrophobic anxieties and pushes for denial of the body. Conversely, recognition of the body furthers the working through toward a sense of reality (Freud 1911) and the assumption of personal responsibility, creating the conditions for tolerance of deep anxieties of impotence.

When, for example, the analysand takes care of his body by using the ointment to protect his genitals, this genital protection seems to assume a *concrete value*, referring back to the protection of his body and of his real sexuality, and at the same time to a *symbolic value* of mental 'potency'. The penis seems correlated with the function of a *skin-thought* endowed with containment functions (Bick 1968): the penis is then felt to be 'peeling,' just as Simone feels his own mind is also 'peeling' in the absence of a protective membrane provided by the function of thought.

In these dynamics, it becomes important to emphasize the active relationship that exists between the working through of hatred and the capacity to integrate oneself on the level of the body-mind relationship: 'I have such hatred that I make my body disappear.' This demonstrates to us, in other words, that the body-mind integration accomplished over the course of the analytic evolution of such cases is not only the result of a facilitation induced by the analytic relationship, but is also a psychic act that is subjected to the subject's discretion and choices. This is an element that cannot be overlooked, and that explains the impossibility of furthering the analytic working through in those cases of psychosis that find specific secondary gains in the maintenance of an illness state.

The hatred brought to the relationship with the analyst ('You are a shit') demonstrates phenomena ascribable to the negative transference: movements that have the determining function – mediated by analytic reverie – of lowering the pressure of hatred that the patient feels toward himself. The transference movement in this case is especially characterized by the *use of the analyst to de-saturate the vertical body-mind relationship*, when it is exposed to the risk of a paralyzing overload, rather than a relational movement connected to specific dynamic relations. The analyst again fulfils the active function of a mirror and a mental shield for the analysand; lending himself to the containment of these emotional dynamics, he contributes to lightening the impact of the concreteness of emotional pressure – which would risk again petrifying the analysand into an ice crystal – and facilitates, instead, the working through, helping the analysand to master and to 'think' his homicidal hatred against himself. When emotions assume particular intensity, the containing resources of thought are exposed to the risk of being placed in check, so to speak. This is demonstrated to us by the myth of Perseus, in which the *direct vision* of hate, personified by Medusa, becomes a source of annihilation. The analyst contributes to the realization of this *indirect vision* through his reverie, which lightens the concreteness of an 'unbearable heaviness of living' – as Italo Calvino (1988) would say.

The emotions described by Simone as boredom and a desire for death call to mind Freud's (1920) statements about the death instinct as an underhanded force, not easily recognizable – elements that are gradually worked through in the analytic exchange. To actively evoke the *body in the analytic session permits its placement in reality* (Freud 1911) *and brings it within the radius of the mental functioning of attention* ('I should pay more attention. Today I had wet hands . . .'). This body-mind integration becomes an important instrument of containment with respect to the more underhanded and dangerous manifestations of the destructive instinct. Destructivity appears in this way to be more connected to a defect of thinking – or rather, to the difficulty that the patient has in mentalizing – than to an originary death drive. At the same time, we see how the connection with the body catalyzes a connection with the deep unconscious (homicidal self-hatred), coming close to more fragile and undefended aspects of the personality (the homeless man) and a recognition of the role of external objects (the barista who serves cappuccino and a croissant to the homeless man). For the patient, the fully conscious assumption of his experience of madness ('I remember when . . . I was crazy') facilitates a process of integration between the psychotic area and the nonpsychotic one.

Later on, when I assign value to Simone's capacity to take a certain distance from external objects who help him (his father who offers him money, and his analyst in the session) – after which he recognized the importance of this – I attempt to mobilize an elaboration of detachment and solitude ('I was proud that I was alone'). This clinical orientation of mine is born out of the necessity of prioritizing the urgency of accomplishing an internal integration and a strengthening of the analysand's ego – even at the price of risking a slight maniacal decline – rather than emphasizing his dependence on external objects, which would risk promoting regression in a patient already inclined toward passivity and a lack of initiative. With these choices, I try to support the analysand's perception of 'belonging to himself' with which he had begun the session, or rather the recognition of his existence as a separate bodily identity.

Conclusion

Even though our contemporary sensibility leads us to emphasize the subjective and intersubjective dynamics of the analytic relationship more strongly than we have in the past – as a result of which our approach is generally more concentrated on the patient and on the analytic relationship than on theory (cf. Renik 2006) – it is nevertheless very important to utilize our experience in recognizing that the body can be used as a compass for psychoanalytic elaboration. These vignettes are an example of how the absence of memory and desire in the psychoanalytic session (Bion 1970) can meet up with reflections, after the session, on the role of the body in the analytic process, which led me to reconsider some of Freud's powerful intuitions in light of current thinking.

In the course of this clinical presentation, we have witnessed the patient gradually drawing closer to the mental experience of his own body, in parallel with a lessening of paranoid symptomatology and of other threatening disturbances. Emerging from a 'Neverland' of nonexistence, Simone could open himself to a vast range of sensori-emotional experiences: his body, from being cold and mechanical, has been transformed by warmth and liveliness. Changeable new sensations have become tolerable, to the point of his being able to withstand his hatred of limitations and the claustrophobic

113

anxieties connected to living inside his own body. All these experiences have led the analysand toward the gradual definition of a *real subjectivity*, characterized by *real, bodily space – time and by an internal body–mind dialogue*, allowing the emergence, in parallel, of a *growing awareness of intersubjectivity*.

From this material, it emerges that the conditions that make possible the analysand's mental growth do not derive only from a good communicative and empathic capacity in the intersubjective context of the analysis; instead, the activation of a *relationship between the patient and his own body is likewise determinative*, combined with *elaboration of the conflictual and claustrophobic implications* connected to living, feeling, and thinking within the borders of his own real body.

Notes

1 Translation by Gina Atkinson. Previously published as Lombardi, R. (2010). The body emerging from the "neverland" of nothingness. *Psychoanalytic Quarterly*, 79: 879–909.
2 The collaborating psychiatrist-psychoanalyst was Dr Giuseppe Martini, whom I thank for his invaluable contributions.

References

Anzieu, D. (1985). *Le moi-peau*. Paris: Dunod.
Aron, L., & Anderson, F. S. (2003). *Relational perspectives on the body*. New York: Other Press.
Bick, E. (1968). The experience of the skin in early object-relations. *International Journal of Psychoanalysis*, 49: 484–486.
Bion, W. R. (1957). Differentiation of psychotic from the non-psychotic personalities. In *Second thoughts* (pp. 43–64). London: Karnac Books, 1967.
Bion, W. R. (1962a). A theory of thinking. In *Second thoughts*. London: Karnac Books, 1967.
Bion, W. R. (1962b). *Learning from experience*. London: Karnac Books, 1984.
Bion, W. R. (1965). *Transformations*. London: Karnac Books, 1984.
Bion, W. R. (1970). *Attention and interpretation*. London: Karnac Books.
Bion, W.R. (1992). *Cogitations*. London: Karnac Books.
Bria, P., & Lombardi, R. (2008). The logic of turmoil: some epistemological and clinical considerations on emotional experience and the infinite. *International Journal of Psychoanalysis*, 89: 709–726.
Calvino, I. (1988). *Six memos for the next millennium*. Cambridge, MA: Harvard University Press.

Ferrari, A. B. (2004). *From the eclipse of the body to the dawn of thought*. London: Free Association Books.

Freud, S. (1893). Fraulein Elisabeth von R, case histories from *Studies on Hysteria. Standard Edition*, 2.

Freud, S. (1900). The interpretation of dreams. *Standard Edition*, 4–5.

Freud, S. (1911). Formulations on the two principles of mental functioning. *Standard Edition*, 12.

Freud, S. (1915a). The unconscious. *Standard Edition*, 14: 159–215.

Freud, S. (1915b). Instincts and their vicissitudes. *Standard Edition*, 14: 109–140.

Freud, S. (1920). Beyond the pleasure principle. *Standard Edition*, 18.

Freud, S. (1923a). The ego and the id. *Standard Edition*, 19: 1–66.

Freud, S. (1923b). Letter to Fritz Wittels. *Standard Edition*, 19.

Freud, S. (1924). Neurosis and psychosis. *Standard Edition*, 19.

Klein, M. (1936). Weaning. In *Love, guilt and reparation, and other works 1921–1945*. New York: Delta, 1975.

Klein, M. (1952). Some theoretical conclusions regarding the emotional life of the infant. In *Envy and gratitude, and other works 1946–1963*. New York: Delta, 1975.

Joseph, B. (1988). The patient difficult to reach. In E. Bott Spillius (Ed.), *Melanie Klein today*. London: Routledge.

Lieberman, J. (2000). *Body talk. Looking and being looked at in psychotherapy*. New York: Aronson.

Lombardi, R. (2002). Primitive mental states and the body. A personal view of Armando B. Ferrari's concrete original object. *International Journal of Psychoanalysis*, 83: 363–381.

Lombardi, R. (2003a). Catalyzing body-mind dialogue in a psychotic analysand. *Psychoanalytic Quarterly*, 72: 1017–1041.

Lombardi, R. (2003b). Mental models and language registers in the psychoanalysis of psychosis: an overview of a thirteen-year analysis. *International Journal of Psychoanalysis*, 84: 843–863.

Lombardi, R. (2004). Three psychoanalytic sessions. With commentaries by J. Grotstein, V. Bonaminio, J. Greenberg and a response. *Psychoanalytic Quarterly*, 73: 773–814.

Lombardi, R. (2005). On the psychoanalytic treatment of a psychotic breakdown. *Psychoanalytic Quarterly*, 74(4): 1069–1099.

Lombardi, R. (2007a). Shame in relation to the body, sex and death: a clinical exploration of the psychotic levels of shame. *Psychoanalytic Dialogues*, 17(3): 385–399.

Lombardi, R. (2007b). Sull'essere: dispiegamento della simmetrizzazione vita morte. In A. Ginzburg & R. Lombardi (Eds), *L'emozione come esperienza infinita* (pp. 133–149). Milan: Angeli.

Lombardi, R. (2008a). The body in the analytic session: focusing on the body-mind link. *International Journal of Psychoanalysis*, 89: 89–100.

Lombardi, R. (2008b). Time, music and reverie. *Journal of the American Psychoanalytic Association*, 56: 1191–1211.

Lombardi, R. (2009a). Through the eye of the needle: the unfolding of the unconscious body. *Journal of the American Psychoanalytic Association*, 57: 61–94.

Lombardi, R. (2009b). Body, affect, thought: reflections of the work of Matte Blanco and Ferrari. *Psychoanalytic Quarterly*, 78: 126–160.

Lombardi, R. (2009c). Symmetric change and catastrophic change: a consideration of primitive mental states in the wake of Bion and Matte Blanco. *International Journal of Psychoanalysis*, 90: 529–549.

Matte Blanco, I. (1975). *The unconscious as infinite sets*. London: Karnac Books.

Matte Blanco, I. (1988). *Thinking, feeling and being*. London: Routledge.

McDougall, J. (1989). *Theatres of the body*. London: Free Association Books.

Renik, O. (2006). *Practical psychoanalysis for therapists and patients*. New York: Other Press.

Tausk, V. (1933). On the origin of the 'influencing machine' in schizophrenia. *Psychoanalytic Quarterly*, 2: 519–556.

Tustin, F. (1981). *Autistic states in children*. London: Tavistock/Routledge, 1992.

Williams, P. (2007). The body and the mind (including of the analyst) in the treatment of a psychotic state: some reflections. Commentary on paper by Riccardo Lombardi. *Psychoanalytic Dialogues*, 17(3): 401–409.

Winnicott, D. W. (1974). Fear of breakdown. *International Review of Psycho-Analysis*, 1: 103–107.

5

BODY, ADOLESCENCE
AND PSYCHOSIS[1]

In this chapter we shall consider aspects of the clinical development of a male 17-year-old patient brought for a consultation by his parents in the context of an acute psychotic crisis. Psychoanalytic treatment was initiated immediately, starting at six sessions per week in view of the urgency of avoiding hospitalization, which would have reinforced the acute trauma. Medication prescribed by a psychoanalytically trained psychiatrist and family liaison involving a third psychoanalyst commenced at the same time. After some six months, the number of sessions was reduced to four and remained at this level throughout the analysis. The patient's good ego functioning prior to the outbreak of the psychosis suggested that the initiation of psychoanalytic work during an acute psychotic crisis had good prospects, notwithstanding the massive loss of the reality sense, the manifest thought deficiency and the presence of confusion and delusions. Among the various interesting aspects, the clinical progression of this case appears to us to demonstrate the importance of the relationship with the body for the development of the adolescent personality and for definition of the real boundaries of the adolescent ego (Freud, 1914, 1923, 1932; Laufer 1986; Lichtenberg 1978; Mahler & McDevitt 1982). In the clinical material described here, the link with the body and the elaboration of the emotional turmoil of the crisis assisted the patient's emancipation from imitative functioning and the onset of mental growth in the analysis.

Freud (1900, 1915a, 1932) always considered contact with the chaotic world of the unconscious or the id to be a crucial stimulus to growth of the ego functions. In neurosis, while the conflict between

117

the ego and its id impoverishes the ego, it also protects the relationship with external reality and facilitates access to the analyst's interventions. Conversely, in psychosis the ego remains intimately bound to the id; although this obviously makes object relations dangerous and precarious, it also implies a wealth of possibilities stemming from the direct link to the depths of the unconscious.

Where the psychotic tendency is clinically pathological, the ego constructs for itself a new internal and external world on the basis of the wishful impulses of the id; when confronted by the outbreak of the clinical psychosis, the ego can likewise escape the pathological trap if it somehow manages to avoid being torn away completely from reality and to find a way of remaining faithful to the outside world (Freud 1923). Freud's dynamic conception of the internal equilibria involved in psychosis made it possible to see the psychotic part of the personality (Bion 1959/1967) as a stable and structural component of every personality, while also permitting the psychoanalytic treatment of psychotic pathologies.

In *An Outline of Psychoanalysis*, Freud writes that: 'Clinical experience [shows] that the precipitating cause of the outbreak of a psychosis is either that reality has become intolerably painful or that the instincts have become extraordinarily intensified – both of which [. . .] must lead to the same result' (Freud 1940, p. 201). In adolescence, these two aspects are present in tandem: the most obvious intolerable reality is the change in the body, which highlights its subjection to the limiting laws of time and the difference between generations, as well as to the limitations due to the subject's sex. Physical maturation at the same time confronts the subject with an extraordinary intensification of the drives and with the real possibility of procreation. The body and the instincts make their presence urgently felt, thus fuelling a conflict that can assume psychotic proportions, with consequent pressure to dissociate from the body as a source of uncontainable turmoil.

However, if the subject becomes completely detached from his body, he runs the risk of irremediable and permanent loss of the link to reality.

The adolescent catastrophe and the mind–body relationship

A central problem for both adolescents and psychotics is the representation and symbolic organization of an internal world, which is

118

felt to be alien, chaotic and dangerous. As demonstrated by a number of authors (Baranes 1991; Cahn 1991; Laufer, E. 1996; Laufer, M. 1986), psychotic disorders are so common in adolescence that they may be deemed to constitute one of the possible manifestations of the adolescent crisis, in which problems connected with changes in the body and the difficulties of the transition from infancy to adulthood play a prominent part.

In our view, the psychotic manifestations of adolescence can advantageously be linked to the observations of Bion (1970) on catastrophic change, as a model that reflects the explosive nature of internal experience when it is too intense to be contained and expressed. This is because intensity is an inherent characteristic of emotions, which, by virtue of their structural nature, tend towards the infinite (Klein 1932; Matte Blanco 1975), whereas the function of the mind is to provide a notation system allowing the postponement of motor discharge, thus forming a dike that renders emotional experience compatible with the world of reality and the recognition of limits (Bion 1962; Freud 1911). Emotion must therefore find a counterpart in abstract formulations capable of representing it, in order for the mind to be able to contain the emotional magma; in this sense, the mind acts like a container that cools and decompresses the explosive ethological heritage of the affects (Bion 1963; Freud 1923). A functioning mind at the same time constitutes an ongoing source of perceptions and thoughts that confront the subject with elements of uncontrollability and states of impotence, which in turn contribute to the intensification of the emotional response. Considered in these terms, an adolescent can be likened to a thinker waiting to receive new thoughts – thoughts that cannot on any account be cast aside owing to the pressing reality of adolescent change. Bion writes:

> There exist thinkers corresponding to the thoughts awaiting someone or something to think them. The thinkers might be likened to objects sensitive to certain wavelengths of thought, as the eye or radio telescope is sensitive to a particular range of electromagnetic waves. Such thinkers can be impinged upon by thoughts that are too powerful in relation to the sensitivity of the receiving apparatus.
>
> (1992, p. 304)

From this point of view, an adolescent can be regarded as a thinker waiting to think thoughts connected with his or her new adolescent experience – thoughts which, however, sometimes prove, in Bion's words, to be 'too powerful in relation to the sensitivity of the receiving apparatus'.

In the difficult context of adolescent change, the precarious nature of the mental links (Bion 1959/1967) involved in the associated inner turmoil may, almost paradoxically, have two different functions: protection of the mind's stability on the one hand and an attack on the new resources of thought on the other. The protection arises from the fact that the loosening of mental links softens the emotional impact of the new perceptions, which are felt to be potentially catastrophic; while the attacking aspect is due to the weakening of the mind and its containing resources resulting from the damage done to the mental links. Bion (1963, 1970) describes the internal container/contained configuration as a topological model that accounts for both the relational dynamics of the analytic couple at work and the deeper intrasubjective dynamics of the mind on the boundary of the seething cauldron of the id and bodily states. This intrasubjective relationship may prove inadequate in an adolescent, owing either to an insufficiency of the container, which proves to be 'too sensitive', or to excessive pressure of the contained, which becomes 'too powerful' to be managed without manifest destabilization. In this context, the analytic relationship can constitute a relational condition for constructive re-initiation of the container /contained dialectic, thus enabling new perceptions to be integrated and reinforcing emotional containment.

In the wake of Bion's contribution, Ferrari (2004) placed particular emphasis on the problem of the body, the re-emergence of the sensory turmoil and the adolescent's physiological need to act in order to know. This stress on adolescent turmoil as a constitutional condition bound up with the experience of the subject's body helps us to understand the catastrophic vicissitudes of the container /contained relationship in adolescence. After all, whereas the particular intensity of affective life in adolescence inevitably increases the pressure of the emotions and conflicts (and hence of the contained), the container, for its part, may prove to be weak in so far as the subject lacks knowledge of and instruments for representing the problems of the adult internal and external world, as yet inexperienced in his infantile world. A conflict that tends to negate changes and to paralyze adolescent initiative presents an obstacle to the updating needed if an adolescent is to construct new parameters of mental functioning consistent with his or her new experience.

In terms of technique, Ferrari recommends an approach to the adolescent patient involving interventions located on the 'vertical axis' of the mind–body relationship, while leaving the parallel 'horizontal relationship' with the analyst in the background. In this way, at the beginning of the analytic process and especially in acute periods of explosive emotional turmoil, the analysis focuses on a dialogue between body and mind (Lombardi 2002, 2003a). It is then likewise important for the analyst to remain highly attentive and sensitive to his or her young patient's fluctuating emotions, and to make him aware, by way of the emotional tone of his interventions in particular, of the emotional resonance the human involvement that accompanies the relevant experience.

Adolescents must work through mourning for the end of infancy, and must discover linear time as a temporality characterized by irreversibility and limits (see Chapter 6); they must also learn to tolerate the new and the unknown as an essential condition that opens the way to the future development of adulthood. The adolescent subject is faced with limits and the necessity of choice, as well as with that of assuming responsibility – as a necessary condition, Bion (1965) reminds us, for the organization of integrated mental activity capable of performing containing functions. The acceptance of limits and the assumption of responsibility can contribute decisively to the functioning of an internal container, but at the same time compels the individual to confront the violent conflicts resulting from hatred of the limits of reality and the weight of responsibility. This confrontation with limits exposes adolescents to a kind of claustrophobic conflict – between the wish to confront the limits set by growth and the opposing wish to avoid them by negation and lies – thus giving rise to a tension between the opposing centrifugal and centripetal forces, which contributes in turn to the potential catastrophic explosion of the container / contained relationship.

From the bi-logical standpoint, the psychotic adolescent's tendency to negate the body as a source of new stimuli and of change has the consequence that the container / contained relationship becomes symmetrical (Bria 1989). This in turn leads to catastrophic outcomes of non-containment, since the topological subversion of this relationship and the collapse of the container makes it impossible to contain and transform the persecuting infinity that arises in the body (see Chapter 1). In terms of Freud's biblical metaphor from the *Studies on Hysteria* (Breuer & Freud 1893–95), during adolescence the body and the experiential turmoil associated with it must necessarily pass 'through the eye of the needle' of consciousness (see Chapter 3). If, as Freud wrote, 'the ego is first and foremost a body ego', the disappearance of a mental representation of the body firmly anchored in the ego (Freud 1923) threatens the asymmetry that is fundamental to the mind–body relationship, as well as to the functioning of the container/contained relationship. At the same time, the negation of time likewise contributes to the annihilation of spatio-temporal parameters and hence to the symmetricalization of the container / contained relationship.

Again from the viewpoint of bi-logic, it appears necessary to relegate transference interpretations to the margins so as to allow space for the unfolding of the structural unconscious. The aim here is to bring about a more harmonious and vital interweaving of symmetrical and asymmetrical aspects; elaboration of the emotional implications of relational dynamics and of recognition of the analyst's otherness can come later in the analytic process. The clinical material presented below demonstrates that activation of a link to the subject's body, with the associated spatiality and a realistic and linear sense of time, is a key aspect of clinical development towards progressive emancipation from psychosis and the construction of harmonious mental functioning based on containment and consciousness of self.

The symmetrical transference in the psychoanalysis of the adolescent

Given the possibility of analytic work on acute adolescent psychosis, an adolescent overwhelmed by an acute psychotic crisis can be provided with the instruments of analytic reverie (Bion 1962), as a decisive condition for the activation of a functioning container/contained relationship. The analyst facilitates the transformation of the turbulent internal events of the crisis into experience and knowledge, which are crucial to mental growth. As stated, our approach involves deliberately not giving priority to the aspect of transference interpretation, while bearing in mind that the most urgent clinical need is to establish the rudiments of a functioning mental metabolism and of representation and consciousness of self in the patient.

In this way, the analyst seeks to take advantage of the perceptual component and new insights of the adolescent subject – what Bion (1970) would call the 'mystical' aspect of the personality – thus containing the violent and destructive components connected with catastrophic change and, as Grotstein (2007) would say, helping to clear the analysand's 'at-one-ment' with 'O' of the paranoid–schizoid elements that are present on a vast scale in the explosive context of the crisis. Our clinical presentation thus shows the analyst repeatedly emphasizing the patient's emerging perceptions; this choice of technique is far from being a mere redundant echo, but takes account of the need to integrate the new perceptual resources stimulated by the crisis, which are subject to continuous haemorrhagic dispersal owing to the patient's precarious integration during the acute psychosis. A distinction is made between primordial sensory and perceptual levels closer to the unconscious and to dreaming, on the one hand, and, on the other, the more integrated levels of consciousness on which the subject organizes a conscious image of himself and his relationship with the world; however, it may sometimes be impossible to bridge the gap between these two realms because of the powerful link-attacking dynamics that characterize acute psychosis.

The clinical posture of seeking to reinforce the analysand's ego resources arises out of the analyst's capacity to tolerate 'at-one-ment' (Bion 1965) with the psychotic experience, and to accept the associated internal experience of fragmentation and turmoil-related panic. This particular emotional charge enables the analyst, from within an intimately shared experience, to strengthen the perceptual elements appearing on the current horizon of the analytic relationship, which are decisive for adolescent ego growth.

The type of transference observed in these situations is symmetrical (Lombardi 2009c); that is to say, the activity of the logical principle of symmetry (Matte Blanco 1975) – whereby the differences between objects, things and persons are abolished – characterizes the analysand's deep emotional involvement.

Whereas, therefore, the analytic relationship, on the most superficial level of consciousness, involves intersubjective recognition of the two participants in the analytic relationship, so that they are experienced realistically as two separate persons, it follows from the involvement of growing levels of emotion in the relationship that the analyst is plunged into the functional context of an unconscious logic and is therefore seen mainly as the patient's imaginary twin (Bion 1950/1967) rather than as a relational other. Symmetrical transferences occur frequently in difficult patients and are connected with the pressures of the psychotic area of the personality (Bion 1957/1967).

On these primitive levels, the transference is not predominantly a new edition of a past relationship with the parents, but is a new experience whereby the patient begins to have access to himself and to an initial representation of the modes and forms of his internal functioning. Such a transference conforms to parameters already to some extent apprehended by Freud in his first definition of transference (*Übertragung*) in the context of dream functioning (Freud 1900), in which the transfer onto the day's residues allows visibility and representability to be conferred on contents that would otherwise remain unconscious and unrepresentable. By stressing the symmetrical transference in clinical work with difficult patients, one can give priority to the elaboration of a narcissistic area inherent in the patient's link with himself, given that narcissistic love is as yet unable to be directed to the world of external objects (Bion 1965, p. 73), and that confrontation with relational otherness is postponed to a subsequent phase of the analytic process, together with all the triadic dynamics that characterize this more mature level of elaboration.

Elaboration between the concrete and the abstract, and the somatic countertransference

Given the overwhelming presence, in acute psychotic phases, of a sensory catastrophe in effect characterized by an aberrant logic of turmoil (see Chapter 1), the most urgent need is to provide first of all for the spatio-temporal organization of bodily experience, thus facilitating the transition from concrete manifestations to abstraction, with elaboration taking place in the order body–affects–thought (Lombardi 2009b). In other words, the elaborative resources of the analytic relationship should be directed towards confronting the manifestations of the most pressing 'object', which is, precisely, the body. The body's incandescent and chaotic pressure is then relieved by the containment of the analytic reverie, thus encouraging the growth of mental phenomena endowed with a containing function (Bion 1962; Ferrari 2004; Freud 1911). The analyst must therefore move empathically on the same levels as the patient. In so doing, the analyst is directly confronted, not so much with specific mental contents or conflictual areas such as the simple countertransference, as with more complex manifestations such as the 'somatic countertransference' (Lombardi 2003b). In such situations, it is the totality of the analyst's person that is involved, in the sense that the analyst is called upon to contain first and foremost in his or her body the presymbolic and concrete manifestations that 'anticipate' the birth of emotional and mental phenomena (Bion 1979/1987). This creates the conditions for activation of the alpha-function and hence the possibility of generating both conscious and unconscious phenomena (Bion 1962).

The use of the term *somatic countertransference* constitutes a recognition that the concept of countertransference now forms part of an enlarged 'common ground' of psychoanalysis (Gabbard 1995), with specific emphasis on the non-pathological aspects – that is, the physiologically empathic aspects of the analyst's involvement. From this point of view, the counter-transference is consistently aligned with the analysand's emotional dynamics and enables the analyst to keep track of the patient's development step by step. In addition, especially in the most difficult cases and in acute psychotic phases, it is considered that the analyst's participation can become more extensive than a mere contextual reaction to the material of the session; hence the deepest levels of the process of analytic elaboration engage his or her psychophysical subjectivity to a profound and pervasive extent.

Bion (1970) introduced the concept of 'becoming' to draw attention to the need for the analyst to allow his or her personality to develop in step with the development of the analysand, in a context characterized by negative capability and tolerance of the unknown; this work in progress concerns not only containment of the situations projected by the patient, but also a more general dialectical openness to new and unknown potentialities of the analyst's own personality. The role of the analyst's bodily participation and so-called somatic countertransference thus stems from the context of an experience strongly characterized by involvement of the unconscious and its somatic reverberations (Freud 1915b), in which anxiety assumes oceanic proportions (Freud 1930). The elaboration of archaic levels of the personality entails a close approach, on the part of the analyst no less than on that of the patient, to the asymbolic and presymbolic areas of the mind that are deeply embedded in the body and have powerful connotations of non-differentiation and concreteness.

The progress of psychoanalytic elaboration is mediated by the resolution of dramatic mind–body dissociations and entails the activation by the analysand of a transference onto the body (Lombardi 2005), which parallels the establishment of a transference onto the analyst. The counterpart to the activation of the transference onto the analysand's body is a parallel transference of the analyst onto his or her own body, as a necessary condition for the performance of his reverie functions (Bion 1962). Hence the somatic countertransference corresponds to the analyst's transference onto his or her own body, necessarily accompanying the analysand's elaboration of the closer approach to his or her body. This is generally manifested in a range of diverse phenomena, such as an increased perception of one's body weight, particular sensitivity to internal sensory movements, such that certain sensory experiences come to be noticed by the mind as if the relevant sense data were being observed through a magnifying glass, as well as various subjective somatic phenomena (heat, vegetative sensations of different kinds, nausea, vertigo, changes in respiratory rate and the like) and transitory sensations of physical ill-being (pains, muscular contractures, cardiac arrhythmias and so on). These manifestations may be accompanied by temporary reductions in mental cathexis and possibly by limitation of the capacity for abstraction, due to the need to keep energy cathexes available for containing the sensory and emotional experience in the process of becoming organized. An analyst treating severe cases must therefore devote particular attention to the arrangement of his or her life and, in particular, to the need for adequate rest periods, owing to the unusual responsibilities and burdens assumed in such treatments. In other words, in addition to protecting the ability to think, the analyst must cultivate a relationship with the night of non-thought, as a precondition for the dawn of thought: 'Thought is only a flash between two long nights, but this flash is everything' (Henri Poincaré, after Bion 1992).

Familiarity with somatic countertransference experiences enables the analyst to extend the range of bodily perceptions, while also increasing the capacity for sensory and emotional containment and for contact with the 'ineffable' experience of the unconscious (Bion 1965). Particular emphasis is placed on its character as a phenomenon that is progressive rather than regressive, in so far as the extension concerns the analyst's specific capacity for communication and containment in regard to the relationship with the body and the uncertain area of the presymbolic levels and 'unheard melodies' of the mind (see Chapter 7). This generative and creative area should not be confused with the regressive manifestations of the pathological counter-transference due to the presence of blind spots in the analyst resulting from unanalysed conflictual areas, whereby the sensory components of the denied affects are expelled onto the body essentially because their access to symbolization is blocked.

126

These somatic phenomena may be connected with the description given by Bion (1970) of the personal experience of a developing O, which has a specific terrifying and catastrophic character; again, the O of the analysand and that of the analyst are separate, even when they develop 'in unison'.

The profound sensory and emotional tremors that characterize contact with O constitute an agonizing inner experience corresponding to contact with a profound emotional truth. Whereas, on the one hand, the analyst's reference to his or her own body and his or her own deep turmoil confronts the analyst with the need to contain potentially dangerous emotional intensities, on the other, it provides him or her with a decisive basis for asymmetry in his or her own body – an asymmetry that permits unequivocal differentiation of the analyst's identity from that of the patient even at the darkest moments. In this way, the body offers the mind a decisive compass which ensures that the analyst does not lose his or her way among the chaotic manifestations of the symmetrical transference, while at the same time helping him or her not to act out a premature demand for the patient to recognize his or her otherness and separateness by way of the systematic use of transference interpretation.

These aspects of the presymbolic level of elaboration are never detached from the more mature levels of the mind, in the sense that they are accompanied by a constant intention to keep up a functioning verbal dialogue in the analytic relationship. This dialogue constitutes an interaction with the non-psychotic area of the patient's personality (Bion 1957/1967), whereby, even in the most extreme cases of thought deficiency such as acute psychotic episodes, the analyst at all times expects a sensible verbal response of some kind from the analysand as a basis for elaboration (Bion 1955). The analyst is therefore heavily engaged in an onerous task that entails a capacity to alternate continuously between sensory acceptance and symbolic functioning, between concretization and abstraction, while not losing any opportunity to focus on abstract elaboration and to facilitate it by the construction of mental models that can stimulate the patient's self-observation resources (Bion 1962; Lombardi 2003b). With regard to the analyst's verbal communications to the analysand during the initial phases of analysis, the principal technical implications are therefore, as stated, interpretive concentration on the unfolding of the unrepressed unconscious – so as to reduce the paralysing impact of an excess of symmetry – and analysis of the mind–body connection

127

and of the modes and forms of mental disposition used by the analysand (Lombardi 2003a, 2003b, 2005, 2007), rather than of the relational aspect characteristic of transference interpretation.

A key problem with any adolescent psychotic manifestation is that of prognosis; for this reason, as noted by Laufer (1986), psychosis in adolescence can be a prognosis and not a diagnosis. It therefore seems important to consider symptoms of mental disorganization, such as delusions and hallucinations, in the context of the specificity of adolescent mental and relational functioning, and, in particular, to apply a form of psychoanalytic treatment that can tackle the onset of the psychosis from its earliest manifestations. In this way, the psychoanalytic experience makes it possible to initiate the formation of an autonomous mind in the patient and to make use of the anticipations of the future present in the episodes of destabilization, in which old, consolidated parameters swept away by the explosive catastrophe are reconsidered in the light of the newly emerging perceptions of self and the world. Hence the primary task in the psychoanalytic treatment of an acute adolescent crisis is to develop the prerequisites for an opening to change that are contained in the crisis and to avoid reinforcement of the dissociative tendency, which would call for a subsequent highly complex and more prolonged analytic process.

As we have seen, if catastrophic change is regarded as a structural condition of the functioning of the human mind at its deepest and most symmetrical levels (Bion 1974; Lombardi 2009c; Matte Blanco 1975), we shall be more confident about undertaking the psychoanalytic treatment of the most serious adolescent disorders such as that described in the case history presented here. This case takes the form of a contribution from personal experience, showing that the psychotic explosion is grafted onto a situation of arrested growth and that, if the explosive phase is treated appropriately, it can make a decisive contribution to the resumption of growth through the use of the densely woven fabric of perceptions that emerge in the catastrophe. In this way, psychoanalysis accompanies the mobilization initiated by the crisis, makes it containable, and utilizes its positive potential, while avoiding the risk of chronic defensive or delusional manifestations.

A clinical case: Luca

At the beginning of the analytic experience, Luca presented with the typical manifestations of acute psychosis – namely, mental confusion, persecutory delusions, hallucinations, ideas of reference, uncontainable anxieties and insomnia. His thought disorder belonged within a pattern of difficulties that dated back to his infancy. However, we shall not dwell specifically on this point here, both for obvious reasons of confidentiality and because, in this contribution, we wish to concentrate on exploring the modes and forms of internal functioning (Bion 1962), so that consideration of the historical /anamnestic and reconstructive aspects is less important.

The case was initially seen in several consultations with one of us a few days after the onset of the delusional symptoms; with a view to avoiding hospitalization, the patient was referred for psychoanalytic treatment to the second author, who then undertook the analysis on her own account with the assistance of a team of two colleagues, a psychoanalyst responsible for liaising with the family and an analytically trained prescribing psychiatrist.[2]

The psychiatrist diagnosed a schizophreniform disorder, prescribing a daily medium–low dosage of olanzapine 7.5 mg in the acute phase. Psychoses present body-connected biochemical factors which cannot be neglected by the analyst, inasmuch as mental dynamics show an undeniable biologic analogy. For those elements more properly pertaining to the mind, only a psychoanalytic treatment can process the conflictual aspects determining the crisis, mobilize the resources of the ego paralysed by fixation phenomena, face the denial of a psychotic episode often taking over after the remission of acute symptomatology, prevent the relapse of new acute phenomena and avert a degenerative fate toward chronic occurrences.

From now on, the patient's clinical development will be narrated in the first person by the author who undertook the psychoanalytic treatment. Luca was 17 years old and the elder of two children. Prior to the crisis, his character was seemingly gentle and he was intelligent, brilliant both academically and at sports, but with a tendency towards isolation and excessive dependence on his parents. A few months before the outbreak of the psychosis, anxiety symptoms, mood swings, sleep disturbances, anorexia and memory difficulties had appeared, quickly culminating in a breakdown. The symptoms appeared immediately after his first school-trip abroad, which was also his first separation from his family. Upon my first meeting with Luca, I was struck by the fixed look of terror on his face. After looking at me for a few seconds, he turned aside; his facial expression was rigid and his gaunt body lacked muscle tone. He entered the room accompanied by his parents, walking like a robot. His voice was feeble, hardly audible, and he answered my questions in monosyllables.

His first communication, when I asked him to tell me what was happening to him, was: 'I am arrogant and presumptuous. I was a know-all, I thought I could help other people, but I don't know anything at all.' I suggested to Luca that we could take this discovery of his, about not knowing anything, as the basis for the construction of a dialogue between us. He then shut himself off in a prolonged silence and complete bodily immobility and rigidity, punctuated every so often by touching his head and pressing his hands tightly against his temples, as if assailed by unbearable, terrifying thoughts.

I put this into words by directly asking him what he was afraid of. Lifting up his head, he looked me and answered by repeating the same word over and over again: 'Afraid, afraid, afraid . . .'. He then relapsed into his closed-off state, his eyes wandering elsewhere – and the same was true of his mind, because every attempt I made to comment or to ask him to give a name to these fears was lost in the void. Suddenly, however, he spoke:

P: You are a woman.
A: Yes, and you are a man.
P: I am nothing.

I was struck by Luca's drastically negative way of referring to himself: confronted with a difference of sexual identity, he became 'nothing', facilitating the collapse of thought by his disappearance. From the very first exchanges, my countertransference response to the relationship with this patient seemed dramatic: at the end of the session, I was aware of a profound sense of physical and mental fatigue; my body felt paralyzed and my mind was shaken as if it had been bombed.

In the first week of our work, Luca came to his sessions in the company of his parents and appeared completely closed off, silent, moving like an automaton and with his mind totally absent. I had a dream which enabled me to find a place inside myself for the initial experience with this analysand. In the dream, Luca and I were standing beside a wall and could see beyond it an open space with a field that was partly bare of growth and partly green. At our feet were some neatly fashioned baskets containing new-born babies. Luca was silent and calm. I spoke to him, but his mind was far away.

Then, in a sudden paroxysm, he grabbed one of the baskets with a new-born baby inside it and flung it to the ground. With a loud cry, I awoke in terror and was unable to get back to sleep. The dream told me in almost tangible form of the hate, impotence and death anxiety present in Luca, suggesting a possible suicide risk. Having become aware of the dangers of this impasse, I decided to play a more active part in subsequent sessions. For instance, faced with his obstinate silence in one session, I commented:

A: Not speaking is your way of saying 'I don't exist.' Your hate makes you reject what is happening to you. But by negating everything, you can't take care of yourself . . . [Then, as his silence persisted:] Not even an analyst can do very much when faced with a lack of collaboration in such a difficult situation . . . [Luca responded with a gesture, pulling at his head, and casting sad glances at me; then tears poured from his right eye, while his left eye stayed dry. Noting the appearance of emotional involvement in the session, I tried to find words for his nonverbal language, as follows:] When you allow your-self to be emotionally involved in these meetings, as you are doing now, your pain can come out and be expressed in your tears.

Luca listened to me, his eyes seeming to come alive for a few sec-onds; then, lowering his head, he closed himself off again. In the next few sessions, I attempted to activate some form of thinkability on the basis of his body language, by commenting on his gestures, posture and movements, especially those I considered to be tiny signals of openness and communication, saying, for example: 'This rigidity of your body is costing you enormous effort and must be a great strain; you are acting like Samson, pulling down the pillars of the temple and burying yourself into the bargain.' In reply, Luca stretched his arms up into the air, cracking his fingers, but then lapsed back into his closed-off state of immobility and silence.

In a subsequent session, I found myself thinking that Luca was treating himself like a lost file in a computer: he was unable to find himself, even though he knew he was there somewhere. Although aware that this was only a phantasy of mine, I attempted to introduce this metaphor with him:

A: A file can sometimes get lost, but even then it can be recovered. Now you are neither a computer nor a file, but you treat yourself as if you had lost your data. [In response to this comment, Luca unexpectedly rose to his feet, stood in front of me, looked into my eyes.]

P: Yes, that's exactly how I feel. However did you realize that? I've lost my data; I can't even remember my own voice. But if I go on like this, I'll forget that I ever had a voice. Everything has got confused in me; everything got mixed up in me on that trip; I don't feel hungry or thirsty any more, and I can't smell or taste anything. If I don't move, I don't get hungry or thirsty.

A: [I am struck by the fact that Luca was touched by a reference to a mechanical object, a model that obviously corresponded to his feeling like an automaton. At this point, however, the automaton was beginning to recognize the lack of its body and its signals, so I pointed out the following to him:] You are losing your relationship with your needs, as if you didn't have a body.

P: Yes, I even forget to pee.

After a few days, Luca started bringing a little bottle of water along to the sessions, sipping at it every so often, telling me that he did not really feel thirsty, but that he had been told he could get dehydrated; so he tried to drink. After a fortnight of almost complete insomnia, he began to sleep again, although he took a sedative regularly. But waking up was always a source of great anxiety for him. The following sequence shows how I was using simple language, consistent with the patient's level of functioning at the time, in an attempt to keep a line of communication with him open.

P: I slept, but I kept waking up, and didn't know what was happening, where I was, or who I was. Everything has changed, it's like being someone else and not recognizing myself, not recognizing places, not knowing what to do and what has happened. How long have I been like that?

A: For several days you've been so terrified that you've broken off all contact with yourself and with the world. It was terror that made you do that. Now you're starting to notice yourself again.

P: Yes, it's as if everything had disappeared. Now I'm thirsty. Maybe I'm also hungry.

A: What would you like to eat?

P: I don't know.

A: What do you like?

P: Everything and nothing; I don't have any passions. It's like at school: I'm good at everything, but I don't know what I really like. [Then, all of a sudden, as if coming back to life.] Do you know what I'm afraid of? Growing up. Can that be? Before, I never asked myself any questions, I just went on, and that was it.

Reactivation of the biological functions of sleep and hunger went hand in hand with the perception of his lack of interests and passions, and with his fear of growing up. Throughout this first period, Luca was constantly present in my mind; I saw this as an expression of my relational involvement in his catastrophic state and of my reception of his need to find containment in an external mind.

At the end of the first month of analysis, Luca showed that he had recovered his sensory capacity, so that he could explicitly feel and look at his body and bring it into the session.

P: I've never looked at myself very much, but today I noticed I'm very thin. I saw myself in the mirror and my trousers were falling down. I've lost ten kilos; I had stopped eating.

A: You had blotted out your body.

P: When I don't like something, I get rid of it and don't confront it.

From false existence to real existence

After a few more weeks' work, Luca showed signs of improvement; for instance, he could now use the lift by himself and no longer needed to be accompanied up to the consulting room door. He planned to come to his sessions by himself on his moped, but was still terrified of the traffic.

During the sessions in which Luca was most in contact with himself, he was able to talk about what he called his 'crazy thoughts'. The following material is focused on this area.

P: Everything has changed, the state of the roads has changed, from one day to the next everything changes.

A: You are telling me about what you feel has happened to you – about changes connected with your growing up – that your old reference points have changed as you have grown and that you need to find new ones.

133

P: It's very difficult for me to take any initiative. I always say yes so as not to disappoint other people, and I never know what I want: so I stay still and wait.

A: What does saying no involve?

P: If I disappoint other people, they'll think I'm a bad boy who's a fake.

A: The only way not to be a fake is for you to take responsibility for what you are and what you want.

P: That's exactly it: I've always felt myself to be a fake, I've always done everything my family told me to. [Pausing for a moment, he added:] You see, I'm ungrateful too, I'm criticizing them. They've done everything for me.

A: [Becoming aware of the risk that his tendency to imitate might be reinforced through guilt, I try to confront him once again with himself.] It seems to me that what matters is what you can do for yourself, by understanding what your opinions and interests are.

This sequence shows that Luca is disorientated and terrified by change. After all, adolescent change would require Luca to activate personal opinions in an unaccustomed way, having always accepted the opinions and choices made for him by his family. Luca had never used the faculty of saying 'no' – negation (Freud 1925) – as an instrument of self-definition with respect to others. The persecutory anxiety that he might be judged a 'fake' was reminiscent of the use of 'faking' and lies (Bion 1963) as an instrument for copying so as to avoid the responsibility of subjective development of his own. Notwithstanding the analysand's obvious difficulties, the sequence shows Luca attempting a rudimentary form of self-reflection, and seeking to activate an 'observing ego' of his own. My comments were intended to induce him to enter into a relationship with himself, holding back the action of his primitive superego.

Luca was now able to talk to me about the days when he was closed off and about his experience of delusion.

P: I had ended up insane. It all began when I booted up my computer and the family photographs had disappeared. I thought someone was giving me commands remotely just by thinking and that they had killed my family. The television was talking about me, and I stopped watching it. I couldn't leave the house because I was being spied on outside. I only had to blink and the

134

traffic lights would change, making the traffic go mad. There were CCTV cameras everywhere, even in your consulting room. I was convinced that I had to atone for the guilt of having killed all those people. Everyone knew about my crimes. So I stayed still, waiting.

A: Did you hear my words in the sessions?

P: Yes, when you talked about my pain and anxiety, the voices in my head stopped for a bit. Then one day you said something about pain and I felt it intensely in my heart. Perhaps you said: 'You are alive, you are a person, not a computer, and you can express what you are feeling,' and then something opened up.

In revisiting the dramatic moments of the psychotic explosion, Luca was able to begin elaborating the paranoid anxieties about causing the death of his family and the persecutory guilt concerning his phantasy killings, and to continue the elaboration of his disavowed feelings of hate. It was the hate that helped to make the mental traffic go mad, thus contributing to the potentiation of his anxieties about change (the 'change in road conditions' mentioned in an earlier session). It is interesting to note that, when I apprehended his pain (through reverie) and drew his attention to it, he succeeded in owning it and also feeling it physically ('I felt it intensely in my heart'), thus in effect 're-minding the body' (Ogden 2001). When stimulated by me, Luca was able to progress further with his elaboration, and told me at the end of the session:

P: I'm not the perfect child any more; I've disappointed everyone and I'm afraid they could all die because of me. They don't deserve this. We have always been a happy, perfect family, and I let go and destroyed everything.

Simultaneously with his acceptance of the pain experienced in the body, Luca was evidently now tending to give up the perfection anxiety that had turned him into a non-human robot (the perfect child). When Luca arrived for a subsequent session, I noticed the opaque, lost expression in his eyes; however, he came back to life during our encounter, when we were able to work on the 'bizarre thoughts' that were terrifying him.

P: I stopped to buy a little bottle of water as I was thirsty. While sipping it, I suddenly cut off because I felt that the shop assistant had

a murderous look on his face and his voice was telling me not
to drink. Then I also remembered the days when I had stopped
drinking because a voice was telling me that I was taking the
water from everyone else in the world. What a stupid idea, as if
I was guilty of making everyone parched!

A: [Imagining that themes connected with his previously dangerous
anorexia were surfacing.] What do we need water for?

P: The body needs water to live.

A: So, by not giving your body water, you are really acting as if
you didn't exist. By keeping your body parched, you are destructively attacking your body and yourself, as a way of blotting out
your real human needs.

P: Yes, I was a danger to myself. I remember that every electrical device I looked at seemed to me to be a bomb that could
blow up. I felt like an electrical device myself. If I spoke, I could
wreak destruction. So if I were to eat, drink and sleep, I could be
destroyed. Now I know that all this is madness.

Starting from the delusional, persecutory perception of a murderous
look, Luca was gaining a deeper knowledge of his mad world ('Now
I know that all this is madness'). The delusion of the murderous hate
on the shop assistant's face demonstrated that Luca's anorexic symptoms were rooted in a hatred of a body that needed to drink – a body
felt to be responsible for exposing him to the limits set by his physical
needs and by reality (Freud 1911). The anxiety Luca was disavowing
was that of impotence and precariousness (cf. Freud 1926), associated
with his physical existence. Denial of the hate had turned him into
an inanimate electrical device, which was nevertheless filled with his
explosive hate. A little later, he added:

P: But perhaps I was ill even before the trip. I no longer wanted to
study, I was wasting my time, and I was afraid of the passage of
time. At that time [when he had the psychotic breakdown] I felt
as if I was living in another age, I was someone else. [A prolonged
pause.] I had a dream in which I woke up with a long beard and
was an old man.

A: [I was struck by the timelessness whereby instants became years
and he was an old man when he had barely started growing.
I tried to say something to help bring him closer to reality.] The
recognition that you are growing up and that time is passing

makes you very afraid you might end up as an old man right away. So you forget that time passes slowly and is the condition for life.

The hate for a body filled with physical needs was associated with a hatred of time. Luca's fear and hate of time made him want to murder not only his body but also time (Kernberg 2008; Lombardi 2003c), because it was felt to be the source of intolerable limits. The lack of a temporal reference, or of a 'symmetricalization' of time (Matte Blanco 1975), caused him to become depersonalized – 'to feel like someone else in a different age' or to grow old. My comment was intended to introduce a logical, asymmetrical discrimination of time, showing him that days were not decades and that time had a real diachronic duration of its own.

In a later session he was still exhibiting his temporal disorganization, saying: 'Everything is not yet right inside me; I can't very easily put what happened before together with what's happening now that I am feeling better.' I suggested to him that, even if he was afraid that everything might get mixed up, talking about what had happened was also a way of digesting it and burying it once and for all. He replied that what he was afraid that everything would fall apart, as in *V for Vendetta*, a science-fiction film in which a masked male character (a robot) had destructive powers and held sway over everyone, including a beautiful woman. The robot character ultimately fell victim to his own destructiveness and died. I commented that, when he did not recognize himself as a real person and camouflaged himself behind a mask of falsity, he fell victim to his unrecognized hate. In this way I was trying to facilitate his emancipation from the camouflage of a false self (Winnicott 1949), so as to get closer to a real self. Disavowal of a real self rooted in the body was leaving him thoroughly at the mercy of the seductions of a sadistic superego from which there was no escape (Rosenfeld 1952, 1965).

In a subsequent session, Luca suddenly broke off from what he was saying and told me:

P: Can I tell you a phantasy I am having? I'd like to go to an island, like Peter Pan's island that doesn't exist. It's ridiculous, I know.
A: You'd like to stay small for the rest of your days and to halt the passage of time.
P: My ridiculous wish is to stop time, to stay small, and never to die. [Turning to me.] We still have a long way to go!

The island 'that doesn't exist' was reminiscent of Luca's tendency 'not to exist', to hide behind the mask of 'I am nothing' (as in the first communication of his analysis), so as to hold his human needs and limitations in check, and at the same time to embrace a kind of 'Peter Pan syndrome', rejecting time and growth. Time, change and finitude became a recurrent theme which, after the collapse of his omnipotence, permitted the emergence of feelings of impotence and delusionally tinged persecutory hate. As the analysis progressed, Luca gradually acquired the capacity to recognize when his thoughts were crazy or, in his words, 'bizarre' or 'disconnected'.

Opening up to bodily sensations and feelings

In another session, Luca said that, while getting his moped out of the garage to come to analysis, he had thought the attendant was furious with him. I asked him why he might have been furious. He answered: 'No reason, it's an invention of my mind, a disconnected thought.' I suggested that what he called a disconnected thought was actually a way of getting closer to an awareness of the hate present in him, which he deposited in other people, whereas previously he had constantly blotted it out. It is interesting to note that now the hate was no longer 'disconnected', but, through the analytic reverie, 'connected' with the system of mental representation. These communications, in which the hate emerged, were not interpreted in terms of the transference relationship with the analyst, the emphasis instead being placed on elaboration of the hate, without any attempt to reassure the patient with regard to his anxieties.

Following the elaboration of the hate, Luca was able to own his disillusionment with his family and to begin to see its members more realistically: 'But do you realize that I've disturbed the perfect balance of my family? We used to be an "average happy family".' In subsequent sessions, Luca returned to the subject of his 'average happy family', which he now saw as a bogus construction based on disavowal of the hate: 'The "average happy family" is a fiction . . . They're all stressed out. When they quarrel, they do it with a smile. But that's ridiculous. Everything's perfect, but nothing is true. If you're angry, you're angry and that's it; you don't smile!'

In this way, Luca was describing a family system organized on the basis of a mask of appearances and disavowal. This elaboration allowed

Luca to become more confident and autonomous, and from then on he came to his sessions by himself on his moped: 'I left my mother in a state of total dismay. It's her anxiety, but she'll have to learn to handle it, as I am doing here with you.' In a later session, he would say: 'I'm angry with my family, but also with myself. I hate my mother who says with that little smile of hers: "You can't go, you've been so ill since that trip, so you must stay at home."' Owing to the progressive clinical improvement resulting from the intensive psychoanalytic treatment, Luca had in fact become able to plan a short trip away, which then passed off without incident.

The elaboration of the events of the acute psychotic explosion enabled us to draw even nearer to the mind–body relationship, as illustrated by the following fragments.

P: I'm pleased because I had a good tennis lesson. The coach said I had good coordination in my movements.

A: And what do you think of this experience of yours?

P: I felt pleasure in the body, pleasure at feeling my body, and pleasure in moving. When I was ill, I couldn't move, my movements were slow, but now I really want to move. [Touching his face, he went on.] I'm starting to like my beard even though it's not growing very well: it's there in some places and not in others. It was a shock to hear my voice when I was ill: it wasn't mine, it was metallic, the voice of a murderer, the voice of the man in *V for Vendetta*. Now it isn't metallic any more: I'm beginning to like my voice. Now I can recognize myself in the mirror. When I was ill, I looked at myself in the mirror and didn't recognize myself. I was someone else! I'd lost my memory and sense of time. And then I had lots of weird sensations, with terrible smells.

A: What sort of smells?

P: Of death and rotting things. They could have killed me – poisoned me. And if they were my own creations, I was the one doing the killing. Inside my skull, everything was amplified and confused.

The above sequence shows Luca beginning to accept his body ('I experienced pleasure in the body, pleasure at feeling my body, and pleasure in moving'), and this acceptance went hand in hand with his emancipation from the sense of being a computer or machine and with an initial acceptance of his adolescent bodily changes (the beard, which 'was there in some places and not in others'). The recovery of his body and the commencement of a realistic relationship with time enabled Luca to emerge from dissociation ('I was someone else') and to recognize himself in the mirror.

He went on to describe a nightmare he had had at the time of his psychotic breakdown: 'I dreamt that some alien, evil person was getting into the house. I noticed the danger, but couldn't wake up.' I asked him what sort of danger he had in mind. He then told me of a recurring nightmare of his in which invisible creatures first got into the house and then into his body; they were alien creatures over which he had no control and which, if they got out, could do terrible things. 'I don't know if it was imagination or a nightmare, but once', he continued, 'I came home and saw the dismembered bodies of my family on the floor – scattered body parts, and figures escaping through the window.'

We were able to use this material as the starting point for the elaboration of his homicidal hate for his family, and I therefore suggested to him that he was anxious in case he was unable to control the hate and acted it out unconsciously. Luca did not seem unduly worried by this, but was manifestly reassured by the discovery of his hate: now he could at last find his way out of a nightmare from which he had hitherto been unable to wake.

Indeed, a central aspect of his elaboration evidently involved emancipating himself from his inability to wake up from nightmares and to distinguish dreaming from the waking state (Bion 1992) – to tell phantasy from reality.

The introduction of a distinction in these areas enabled him to find a place for his homicidal hate, recognizing it as real and at the same time taking advantage of his capacity to use phantasy to express it. Dreaming of tearing his family to pieces therefore signified a new capacity to represent his hate, which was very different from acting it out in real life. In this sense, the use he made of the existence of his body provided him with a stable reality reference, which he could compare logically with the dimension of phantasy.

With the progressive elaboration of this material, I became increasingly aware of the presence of hate not only in Luca's mind but also in the consulting room: it was a presence I had noticed in highly concrete form from the beginning, but now it was finally taking on symbolic characteristics and actually assuming communicative and verbal substance. The presence of hate at the same time indicated the development of the transference, which was becoming increasingly well-defined and affectively diverse. However, in view of the pressure of confusional elements and the marked tendency towards concrete thought during this phase, I felt that the introduction of any transference interpretation would merely risk intolerably intruding into the still fragile mental fabric that we were laboriously constructing.

In the next session, he returned to the subject of bodily sensations:

P: I've been swimming, I feel tired, I can feel my body. It feels invigorated, strong – a lovely feeling.
A: Feeling your body gives you a sense of mastery, of being yourself.
P: Yes, a full body. When I was ill, it was empty, the very picture of a skeleton. I wasn't master of my body and my mind was all screwed up; I registered everything too strongly and everything was mixed up.
A: As you can see, the mind can register the sensations coming from the body, and that makes it recognize your body as real.
P: Yes, now I can feel without everything getting mixed up in me, and I can look another person in the eye, as I am doing here with you.

It is interesting to note that during the psychotic crisis feeling had taken on extremely confusing, inundatory characteristics; it resembled the oceanic feeling described by Freud (1930). The analytic relationship catalysed the onset of a relationship between the analysand and his body, and at the same time steered Luca's function of attention and perception (Freud 1911) towards internal sensations, thus enabling him to distinguish different kinds of feelings within his experience ('now I can feel without everything getting mixed up inside me') (cf. Matte Blanco 1988). By helping Luca to relate to his body in the context of elaboration in his sessions, the analysis had activated a sensory perception that enabled him to make distinctions within the inchoate magma of his sensations and emotions; this constituted an initial eclipse of a body in turmoil brought about by an internal mental function of registration and containment (Ferrari 2004).

141

Development of affects and an incipient capacity to think

In a later session, Luca pursued his elaboration on the basis of a bodily sensation: red eyes and an itching nose.

P: Did you happen to notice that my eyes are all red? I have an allergy: my nose itches and my eyes are hurting.
A: Are you paying more attention to what is going on in your body?
P: Before, I put up with what I was feeling in silence and tried not to think about it; now I notice much more what I am feeling.

It is interesting to note the appearance of the body and sense data in Luca's communications, whereas previously he 'put up with what he was feeling in silence and tried not to think about it': in that way the patient had eliminated the sensory and bodily element from his thought activity, thus deactivating the latter's containment resources (Freud 1911). We discovered in the course of the session that the allergy was connected with the intense sadness Luca had felt on seeing his grandfather again after a long interval, and finding him in the process of losing his memory.

P: My grandfather doesn't remember anything. It's so awful, so sad ... That brain, that mind, they play such awful tricks. [Then, referring to himself and the experience of his psychotic crisis.] I know myself what a tragedy it is when the mind doesn't work properly. Now I think my grandfather is not only old but also depressed, and that he doesn't want to go on living because he has no future.

He now confessed to having felt paralyzed and afraid of seeing the state his grandfather was in, but had then noticed this and communicated with him in a light-hearted, joking way. This led to fresh associations to his psychotic breakdown, and in particular to how he had shut himself off in silence.

P: If I spoke, I was signing my own death warrant. When you tried to make me speak, I thought a catastrophe would have happened if I had spoken. Now I know it was all due to my sick mind.
A: Now you can accept your sadness at difficult situations that afflict people, without experiencing it as a deadly threat.

142

P: Another ridiculous thing is that I didn't want to wash because I thought I would lose the hair from my body and head. I thought that after losing the election Berlusconi had sent me that shampoo to kill me.

A: Washing is a way of recognizing your body. Even having a body was something you associated with a death threat.

P: When washing, I left the door open because I wanted the cleaning lady to see that I was atoning for my guilt, I was cancelling out my guilt, because she had cleaned up all the blood from my dead bodies with a rag. And when my mother made me close the door, I thought: 'Now they are suffocating me.' Now I think the poor cleaning lady was crying because of the state I was in.

At the end of this dramatic account, he said:

P: I had a terrible pain, it hurt so much, but it's only now that I'm able to feel it. [Touching his heart and weeping for a long time.] When it was happening I wanted my father to kill me, and I asked him to do so, because what I was feeling was unbearable; it's indescribable; everything was absurd.

The realization that I was intensely sharing his emotions came from my painfully pounding heart, which persisted after the end of the session and left me with a profound sense of debilitation for several days. Analytic reverie (Bion 1962) facilitated the catalysis of Luca's process of mentalization on the mind–body boundary: the onset of chest pains indicated that a process of mind–body integration was under way, towards more mature forms of connection between sensations and thought such as emotions (Damasio 1999).

Shortly afterwards, Luca had a dream, which further advanced the process of elaboration leading to his emancipation from psychosis: Luca is at the seaside with his uncle, aunt, and cousin. Together, they are searching for sea shells on the beach. Digging in the sand, he finds a candelabrum. He cleans it and discovers an inscription in ancient Greek which is now virtually obliterated and illegible. His uncle says it must express a wish, and he thinks to himself: 'My wish is to be well, not to lose my mind, to feel alive. I want to be well now that I am 18 years old; I want to feel 18 years old.'

As discussed with Luca in the session, this dream bore witness to his emergence from the ocean of turmoil and mental confusion. By emerging from the formless sea of psychosis, the analysand found himself back on the beach, where he discovered a light-bearing object – the candelabrum – which stood for his capacity to conceive of himself in thought. His emergence from the swamp of psychosis now gave him a sense of well-being at feeling alive and accepting his place in the real time of his 18 years. The dream was therefore a condensation of the progress of the analytic process up to that point, when Luca had found himself confronted with the virtually incomprehensible language of his body (the candelabrum at the seaside with the Greek inscription), so that he could now accept his place within the limits of a real space–time of his own at a specific age, thus overcoming his infantile omnipotence and dissociation from reality.

The patient's progression towards mental phenomena and incipient mind–body integration had its counterpart in myself, in a relaxation of the violent, undifferentiated sensory pressure that had confronted me from the very beginning of the treatment – a somatic counter-transference manifestation which, as stated in the first part of this paper, had more wide-ranging and continuous effects on my experience of life than the more common counter-transference phenomena encountered in everyday psychoanalytic practice.

At the start of our work, when Luca was completely shut off, with his mind remote and his body like a robot, I would sometimes feel that my body and its sensations were uncanny and almost alien; and during the sessions I sometimes heard my voice as if it were about to become independent of myself. On other occasions, I had sudden storms of thermal sensations, alternating between hot and cold. When I noticed that the patient was in the process of absenting himself in a kind of black hole, I sometimes found myself breathing faster, while at the same time feeling that this odd somatic activation was helping me to react to his closed-off state and to prevent him from lapsing into isolation – for example, by directly confronting him with questions about, say, what he was feeling when he told me that he was a robot. At the end of sessions, I often experienced intense physical weakness and muscle pains in my arms and legs, like someone who had been forced to make an enormous physical effort, at the very limit of her resources and capacity.

Once, at the end of a dramatic session, I became aware of an image, or association, that corresponded to my sense of physical destabilization: I felt as if I was holding onto the tiller of a small sailing boat at sea in a storm, buffeted by huge waves. In addition, for the entire

144

period of this analysand's acute phase, as a rule I felt the need to spend some time alone, to help me digest the excessive burden weighing down on me. I therefore got into the habit of taking a slow walk at the end of the day's work, although walking at this pace was normally quite alien to me. At this time, too, I once found myself looking at Caravaggio's paintings in the church of San Luigi dei Francesi in Rome, and in contemplating these artistic creations I had a sense of peace and emancipation from my state of mental fragmentation and bodily exhaustion. It was as if these works of Caravaggio – perhaps not coincidentally a genius who created his masterpieces by giving aesthetic form to his own violent and uncontainable internal emotional disorganization – provided me with a kind of reverie that enabled me to visualize an untranslatable sensory experience of being in contact with the deep unconscious, brought about by the close sharing of my analysand's experiences. So it was, I believe, not by chance that I fully recovered my tranquillity and relational availability as soon as the analysand, in this phase, showed the incipient signs of mental integration and self-containment described here.

Before concluding, let us now consider the acceptance of linear time as an important stage in the consolidation of Luca's emancipation from psychosis.

Elaboration of the passage of time

A particularly significant theme in relation to acceptance of the adolescent experience of change and growth proved to be that of time, which was manifested in different ways. Some examples are given below.

One day, Luca came for his late-afternoon session thoroughly out of breath. I was struck by the animated, happy expression on his face. While still on his feet, he said:

P: On my way here, I saw a fantastic sunset, a ball of fire that was so alive that it absolutely got inside me.

A: [His description moved me intensely.] Now you are paying attention to your emotional experiences, so you are involved and get enthusiastic even about a sunset, as a way of taking a positive view even of experiences that confront you with loss.

P: [As he listened, he looked at me in silence, somewhat astonished.] Yes, that's something new, today I enjoyed the sunset and it didn't frighten me. Now I think I used to see it but didn't see it; today

145

I saw it and it got inside me. I felt the emotion of something big and beautiful. The sunset was life getting inside me.

A: Yes, it's about your being in life and actually living it, taking it in your hands, and not mixing it up or fearing it as you did in the past.

P: The sunset is a day coming to an end, time passing. I used to be afraid of time; I tried to stop time.

A: By maintaining the illusion of stopping time, you only succeeded in damaging your mind.

P: Lowering my eyes, stopping everything, and not living – so I was like a dead person, and I did that so as not to notice the sunset.

A: By abolishing sensations and emotions, you abolish not only time but also life.

P: Do you remember, when I was ill, how I told you that time robs us and we rob time? Now, though, I've understood that if we experience time, we benefit from it: even when time passes, I don't lose everything because I still have the memories of what I experience. Now I understand that, before I fell ill, I was living the life of a dead man, like a zombie in a horror film. And, when I feel I want to turn back, that isn't possible. In the past, it always felt as though I was myself and also another me separate from myself. I never had the feeling of being completely myself before I got ill. I experienced everything differently from today.

In this sequence, the analysand was taking note of the profound change that had taken place in him since the psychotic catastrophe, involving the end of the dissociated state in which Luca was never completely himself, but felt somehow separate from himself. Luca's dissociation was accompanied by his 'theft of time', as a result of which he had never been subject to temporal limits and loss. The experience of the sunset revealed Luca's capacity to reconcile himself to loss (Klein 1936/1975), thus at the same time opening himself up to a new, aesthetic dimension, such as that conveyed by painters who can express the ineffable experience of finitude in impressions of a sunset.

The elaboration of the passage of time brought about by the analysis enabled Luca to relate differently to change and to the passage of his years; in consequence, he was able to celebrate and take pleasure in his last birthday as he had never been able to do before.

P: I really enjoyed this last birthday of mine, in a way that never happened before. The years are mine, the time that is passing is mine,

I am in time and I experience time. I am myself, and I'm with myself. I am here with you, as I am now with my parents or my girlfriend or my new friends at the university. It's an overwhelming emotion that I find it hard to cope with. I don't want to take the risk of going mad again, but now I really exist; before, I didn't exist.

I replied that now he was capable of experiencing real emotions, it might be overwhelming, but that was because of the nature of emotions and not because he was mad; in this way I was trying to help him distinguish better between the intense psychophysical experience of the emotions and the threat of madness. At the same time, the separation of the summer holidays was approaching, with constructive signs of tolerance of change. This the analysand himself confirmed.

P: For the first time in my life, I'm looking forward to the holidays as something positive. I enjoy the time, even when I have to cope with difficult separations. And the fear of separation doesn't seem so intolerable to me as it did in the past.

The analysand's constructive relationship with time enabled him to adopt a new attitude towards his real potential for experience and life, in spite of the price of solitude and emancipation he had to pay. This constituted further proof of his mental growth and of the positive trend of the analytic experience.

With regard to the favourable results of this treatment, the value of a multi-pronged approach to the clinical problem must of course not be underestimated: hence, in its own field, the drug treatment played a by no means negligible part, while the extremely early psychoanalytic intervention and high frequency of sessions from the beginning also proved advantageous. Other positive factors were the patient's keen intelligence and the presence of extensive areas of good ego functioning prior to the outbreak of the crisis. Although it is unclear to what extent each of the individual factors in our clinical approach helped to resolve the acute crisis, it is nevertheless our impression that the choice of concentrating on elaboration of the mind–body relationship greatly facilitated the psychoanalytic progress of this analysand, as we have also found in comparable clinical situations. We therefore felt it worthwhile to present this experience for the attention of our colleagues.

147

Let us end on this note of Luca's emotion in relation to change and his appreciation of his birthday. On account of the crucial changes achieved in the first two years of his analysis, the subsequent course of the process facilitated the consolidation of the analysand's progress and permanently opened the way to mental growth.

Notes

1 Chapter written with Marisa Pola, translated by Philip Slotkin, MA, Cantab. MITI. Previously published as Lombardi, R., & Pola, M. (2010). The body, adolescence and psychosis. *International Journal of Psychoanalysis*, 91: 1419–1444.
2 We would like to thank Dr Giuseppe Martini and Dr Giovanna Mazzoncini for their indispensable support in the handling of this case.

References

Baranes, J.-J. (Ed.). (1991). *La question psychotique a' l'adolescence* [The question of psychosis in adolescence]. Paris: Dunod.

Bion, W. R. (1950). The imaginary twin. In *Second thoughts* (pp. 3–22). London: Karnac Books, 1967.

Bion, W. R. (1955). Language and the schizophrenic. In M. Klein, P. Heimann, & R. Money-Kyrle (Eds.), *New directions in psycho-analysis* (pp. 220–239). London: Tavistock.

Bion, W. R. (1957). Differentiation of psychotic from the non-psychotic personalities. In *Second thoughts* (pp. 43–64). London: Karnac Books, 1967.

Bion, W. R. (1959). Attacks on linking. In *Second thoughts* (pp. 93–109). London: Heinemann, 1967.

Bion, W. R. (1962). *Learning from experience*. London: Karnac Books, 1984.

Bion, W. R. (1963). *Elements of psycho-analysis*. London: Heinemann.

Bion, W. R. (1965). *Transformations*. London: Karnac Books, 1984.

Bion, W. R. (1970). *Attention and interpretation*. London: Karnac Books.

Bion, W. R. (1974). *Il cambiamento catastrofico* [*Catastrophic change*]. Florence: Loescher. (Italian compilation)

Bion, W. R. (1979). Making the best of a bad job. In F. Bion (Ed.), *Clinical seminars and other works*. Abingdon: Fleetwood, 1987.

Bion, W. R. (1992). *Cogitations* (F. Bion, Ed.). London: Karnac Books.

Breuer, J. & Freud, S. (1893–95). Studies on hysteria. *Standard Edition*, 2: 1–306.

Bria, P. (1989). Il cambiamento catastrofico come struttura astratta bi-logica [Catastrophic change as an abstract bi-logical structure]. In *Il pensiero e l'infinito* [*Thought and the infinite*]. Castrovillari: Teda.

Cahn, R. (1991). *Adolescence et folie* [*Adolescence and madness*]. Paris: Presses Universitaires de France.

Damasio, A. (1999). *The feeling of what happens: Body and emotion in the making of consciousness*. New York: Harcourt Brace.

Ferrari, A. B. (2004). *From the eclipse of the body to the dawn of thought*. London: Free Association Books.

Freud, S. (1900). The interpretation of dreams. *Standard Edition*, 4–5.

Freud, S. (1911). Formulations on the two principles of mental functioning. *Standard Edition*, 12: 213–226.

Freud, S. (1914). On narcissism: an introduction. *Standard Edition*, 14: 67–102.

Freud, S. (1915a). Instincts and their vicissitudes. *Standard Edition*, 14: 109–140.

Freud, S. (1915b). The unconscious. *Standard Edition*, 14: 159–215.

Freud, S. (1923). The ego and the id. *Standard Edition*, 19: 1–66.

Freud, S. (1925). Negation. *Standard Edition*, 19: 233–240.

Freud, S. (1926). Inhibitions, symptoms and anxiety. *Standard Edition*, 20: 75–176.

Freud, S. (1930). Civilization and its discontents. *Standard Edition*, 21: 57–146.

Freud, S. (1932). New introductory lectures on psycho-analysis. *Standard Edition*, 22: 1–182.

Freud, S. (1940). An outline of psycho-analysis. *Standard Edition*, 23: 139–208.

Gabbard, G. O. (1995). Countertransference: the emerging common ground. *International Journal of Psychoanalysis*, 76: 475–485.

Grotstein, J. (2007). *A beam of intense darkness*. London: Karnac Books.

Kernberg, O. (2008). The destruction of time in pathological narcissism. *International Journal of Psychoanalysis*, 89: 299–312.

Klein, M. (1932). *The psycho-analysis of children*. London: Hogarth Press.

Klein, M. (1936). Weaning. In *Love, guilt and reparation and other works 1921–1945* (pp. 290–305). London: Hogarth Press, 1975.

Laufer, E. (1996). The role of passivity in the relationship to the body during adolescence. *Psychoanalytic Study of the Child*, 51: 348–364.

Laufer, M. (1986). Adolescence and psychosis. *International Journal of Psychoanalysis*, 67: 367–372.

Lichtenberg, J. (1978). The testing of reality from the standpoint of the body self. *Journal of the American Psychoanalytic Association*, 26: 357–385.

Lombardi, R. (2002). Primitive mental states and the body. A personal view of Armando B. Ferrari's concrete original object. *International Journal of Psychoanalysis*, 83: 363–381.

Lombardi, R. (2003a). Catalyzing the dialogue between the body and the mind in a psychotic analysand. *Psychoanalytic Quarterly*, 72: 1017–1041.

Lombardi, R. (2003b). Mental models and language registers in the psycho-analysis of psychosis. An overview of a thirteen-year analysis. *International Journal of Psychoanalysis*, 84: 843–863.

Lombardi, R. (2003c). Knowledge and experience of time in primitive mental states. *International Journal of Psychoanalysis*, 84: 1531–1549.

Lombardi, R. (2005). On the psychoanalytic treatment of a psychotic break-down. *Psychoanalytic Quarterly*, 74: 1069–1099.

Lombardi, R. (2007). Shame in relation to the body, sex, and death: a clinical exploration of the psychotic levels of shame. *Psychoanalytic Dialogues* 17(3): 385–399.

Lombardi, R. (2008). Time, music, and reverie. *Journal of the American Psychoanalytic Association*, 56: 1191–1211.

Lombardi, R. (2009a). Through the eye of the needle: The unfolding of the unconscious body. *Journal of the American Psychoanalytic Association*, 57: 61–94.

Lombardi, R. (2009b). Body, affect, thought: Reflections on the work of Matte Blanco and Ferrari. *Psychoanalytic Quarterly*, 78: 123–160.

Lombardi, R. (2009c). Symmetric frenzy and catastrophic change: a consideration of primitive mental states in the wake of Bion and Matte Blanco. *International Journal of Psychoanalysis*, 90: 529–549.

Mahler, M., & McDevitt, J. (1982). Thoughts on the emergence self, with particular emphasis on the body self. *Journal of the American Psychoanalytic Association*, 33: 827–848.

Matte Blanco, I. (1975). *The unconscious as infinite sets.* London: Karnac Books.

Matte Blanco, I. (1988). *Thinking, feeling and being.* London: Routledge.

Ogden, T. (2001). *Conversations at the frontiers of dreaming.* Northvale, NJ: Aronson.

Rosenfeld, H. (1952). Notes on the psycho-analysis of the superego conflict of an acute schizophrenic patient. In *Psychotic states* (pp. 63–103). London: Hogarth Press, 1965.

Rosenfeld, H. (1965). *Psychotic states.* London: Hogarth Press.

Winnicott, D.W. (1949). Mind and its relation to the psyche-soma. In *Through paediatrics to psycho-analysis* (pp. 243–254). London: Tavistock, 1975.

TIME IN PRIMITIVE MENTAL STATES[1]

Ho studiato un metodo	[I devised a method
per far diventare gli anni	to make years
corti come giorni.	as short as days.
E con la scusa di aspettarti	And with the excuse of waiting for you
mi cullo in un dolce non vivere	I rock myself in a sweet non–living]
(Nora).	
E il tempo passa.	[And time goes by.
(. . .) La vita che sembrava	(. . .) Life which seemed
vasta è più breve del tuo fazzoletto	vast is briefer than your handkerchief]

(Eugenio Montale, Mottetti II, Le occasioni, 1928–39)

Sometimes our patients show a special skill in putting the experience of their inner worlds into words, as is the case with Nora, the author of the above lines of poetry which express in such a transparent fashion a relationship with time founded on the foolish desire to shorten it to the point of annihilating it. Montale's poem, on the other hand, bitterly contemplates the existence of time and the boundaries of existence and seems therefore to be in contrast with Nora's wish for timelessness. I believe that the conflictual area where denial and acceptance of time come to confront each other is particularly worthy of our attention, in so far as it regularly surfaces in the context of our analysands' inner functioning. This is an area corresponding to a level of the mind also represented, and this is not a coincidence, in mythical thought.

151

Uranus, before dying, had prophesized to Cronus that one of his children would dethrone him. Cronus then decided to devour his children as soon as they were born from Hera (Hesiod, *Theogony*, 453–67 [ca. 700 BC/1973, p. 38]). To swallow children as they are delivered is an omnipotent attempt to deny time as it produces something new: one of the founding myths of our civilization represents in Cronus the conflict of man faced with the flowing of time, which involves the dimension of all that is relative, of boundaries and of loss.

Using in my clinical work a psychoanalytic focus on the mental functions utilized in the process of learning from experience (Bion 1962b), the theme of temporality and its related conflicts seems to me to be an often relevant catalyst in the development of those many difficult cases which create powerful hurdles to progression and change. I can state on the basis of several clinical experiences that giving prominence to the subject's relation to temporality can facilitate change as a goal of the psychoanalytic process (Bion 1966; Caper 2001; Jacobs 2001) and bring about alterations to the ways affects are experienced: not by acting directly upon them, but by working instead on the formal parameters which organize the mind, that is primarily on its spatio-temporal organization.

A theoretical note

This chapter is not attempting to provide a general theorization of temporality in psychoanalysis. The only purpose of this note is to summarize some of the theoretical elements in line with my own perspective.

The theme of temporality has been for centuries the domain of philosophical speculations (pre-Socratic philosophers, Augustine, Husserl, Heidegger, Sartre, Ricoeur, etc.). An interesting outcome of such philosophical studies could be these authors' conviction about the ultimate impossibility of defining time (Garroni 1998). Philosophical ideas about temporality have been linked to clinical practice through phenomenological and existential psychiatry (Straus, Gebsattel, Minkowski, Binswanger, etc.), which has explored various modalities of temporalization, both in sane individuals and in those with serious psychotic conditions (see Cargnello 1966). After Binswanger's famous letter of 1926, when he distanced himself from Freud, the relationships between existential analysis and psychoanalysis have remained characterized by a sort of 'mutual neutrality' (Galimberti

1979, p. 210). Once we have recognized the brilliant insights on the different temporal configurations in the domain of subjectivity, it must be said that phenomenological psychiatry uses a language that cannot easily be translated into a psychoanalytic one. Despite the availability of such authors as Fornari (1971, p. 86), the phenomenological contribution has failed to have a direct impact on psychoanalytic thinking (with a few notable exceptions, e.g. Resnik 2001).

The knowledge of time I have referred to in the title of this chapter does not therefore involve the aspect of time distortion (indeed, a primary concern of phenomenology), nor its more openly psychological features (Fraisse 1957), but rather the more immediate empirical significance of time as it manifests itself to our common sense. This concept will become clearer as I develop my arguments, but for the time being we could start to imagine it, for example, as being intuitively represented by the time indicated by clocks, in so far as house clocks are among the strictest educators of the child (Bonaparte 1940, p. 428), or in so far as 'we had better bow to our little watches' (Bion 1990, p. 102). In other words, I look at time from a psychoanalytic perspective as an aspect of reality testing which does not involve a philosophical conception on the nature of reality but implies instead a capacity to distinguish between what is objective and what is subjective (Hartmann 1956), as well as to differentiate between representations derived from the external world, on the one hand, and from mental life (itself characterized by a tendency to phantasize and by primary process functioning), on the other (Arlow 1969).

Freud's description of the mental levels located in an area bordering with somatic processes is particularly topical here, if one considers the growing attention psychoanalysis is currently paying to primitive mental states. Here it becomes necessary to provide a sensory matter, in itself chaotic, undifferentiated and by its very nature alienated from thought, with both organization and 'thinkability'.

Freud writes:

> We approach the id with analogies, we call it a chaos, a cauldron full of seething excitations. We picture it as being open at its end to somatic influences, and as there taking up into itself instinctual needs . . . The logical laws of thought do not apply in the id, and this is true above all of the law of contradiction . . . and we perceive with surprise an exception to the philosophical theorem that space and time are necessary forms of our mental acts. There

is nothing in the id that corresponds to the idea of time; there is no recognition of the passage of time, and – a thing that is most remarkable and awaits consideration in philosophical thought – no alteration in its mental processes is produced by the passage of time.

(1932, pp. 73–74)

The id's lack of connections to a spatio–temporal structure leads Freud (1924) to anchor the idea of time to the discontinuity in the functioning of the Perceptual-Conscious system. The 'alternation' deriving from it would be a major contributing factor to the establishment of the idea of time. Analogously, when Freud (1911) attributes to thinking the primary function of restraining motor discharge, time can be seen in relation to the activation of a consciousness linked to the sense organs.

Freud (1917), however, reserves a special place for the importance of time in the working through of emotions, in particular those concerning mourning. The drive tends to create stable, that is timeless, links with the objects it invests: for this reason mental operations related to mourning are especially complex and require the active contribution of the conscious system in order to acknowledge the changes brought about by the loss of the loved objects.

Connected to the flowing of time, the theme of 'transience' (*Vergaenglichkeit*) is dealt with by Freud in a brief essay where he refers to what he had learned, mainly from his research on mourning, about the meaning of boundaries. 'Transience value is scarcity value in time. Limitation in the possibility of an enjoyment raises the value of the enjoyment' (1916, p. 305). In parallel with this view, Freud also considers the opposite 'demand for immortality' and human beings' 'revolt in their minds against mourning' when facing the ephemeral quality of beauty: an attitude mostly determined by their inborn tendency to avoid pain. Although time is conceptually related to boundaries, to transience and to death, Freud emphasizes that we should not neglect its fundamental links with life and with the doors it can open toward experience (see also Lachmann 1985).

Freud's clinical researches on the Unconscious have found a significant development in Klein's explorations of the child's phantasy world. Compared with Freud, Klein considers time from her characteristic relational perspective, speculating that 'the change from intra-uterine to extra-uterine existence, as the prototype of

154

all periodicity, is one of the roots of the concepts of time and of orientation in time' (1923/1977, p. 99). Furthermore, it is obvious from a Kleinian point of view that not unlike symbolization, also 'the sense of time originates in the absence, and from the absence, of the breast: . . . if the painful experience lasts too long, the baby feels lost yet again in a timeless anxiety (where, that is, the sense of time is yet again lost)' (Meotti 1980, p. 47).

The child has his/her own specific context, shaken from within by violent and most intense drives and emotions (greed, envy, jealousy). Such impulses tend to jeopardize the spatio–temporal organization of the mind at the very time when the mind, through growing, is desperately trying to assert itself. During child analyses the awareness of time and the building/internalization of the parameters provided by the calendar offer, at times of separation, a kind of realistic control over the moment when the analyst comes back. In this way the presence of time contributes to a significant extent to the establishment of a mental apparatus featuring spatio–temporal structures and functioning as a container (Lombardi 1983).

Bion (1962a/1967), developing Klein's original ideas, observes that the prominence of projective identification leads to a confusional state where the acknowledgment of space and time is attacked, thus removing the conditions for the building of concepts and abstractions. Bion brings to our attention that kind of mental disposition whereby time never passes, as is the case in the Mad Hatter's tea party described in *Alice in Wonderland*, where the clock is forever stuck on four in the afternoon. Expanding Freud's notion of the Unconscious, Bion suggested that '"Unconscious" can at times be replaced by "obvious, but not noticed"' (1992, p. 318). In this perspective the psychoanalytic work on temporality can allow us to observe and comprehend an 'obviousness' which will reveal itself to be far from obvious. An object that tends to avoid our awareness of it, as well as becoming a source of mental working through, can fulfil instead an important role in mental metabolization. Such a perception could introduce a 'caesura' (Bion 1987, p. 306) which will be of crucial importance in providing access to the mind and allowing, in certain instances, a true foundation to the opportunity of learning from experience (Bion 1962b). '[The] non–psychotic personality must be capable of . . . frustration, and hence awareness of temporality' (Bion 1992, p. 1). It then seems to me that promoting the awareness of temporality is equivalent to that aspect of the work on K (Knowledge) that facilitates tolerance to

155

frustration and acts as a catalyst for the functioning and growth of the non-psychotic part of the personality.

It is also worth remembering that the importance Bion attributes to abstaining from memory and desire means that 'the analysis itself is made in the present. It cannot be done in anything else whatever' (1990, p. 8). And again, 'nostalgia or anticipation are important because they exist in the present' (p. 8). In this perspective the idea of a 'timelessness' encouraged by the repetitiveness of the sessions and functional to the patient's 'regression' (e.g. Sabbadini 1989) is turned upside down to emphasize instead a 'progressive' perspective where what is of central importance is the directionality of the time's arrow. Sabbadini, emphasizing the need of 'timelessness' to access analyzability, quotes Greenson, for whom 'in order to approximate free association the patient must be able to regress in his thinking, to let things come up passively, to give up control of his thoughts and feelings, and to partially renounce his reality testing' (1989, p. 310). In the primitive mental states I refer to, the situation is quite different in so far as the lack of temporal parameters is a specific aspect of the patient's disturbance. It is for this reason that I stress the activation of reality testing rather than its renunciation. Furthermore, while Sabbadini emphasizes that 'the analytic relationship follows the pace dictated by the analyst's clock and by his calendar' (p. 306), and therefore the dependence on the analyst, I am more interested in the relation with time as a link to mental activity. I am, however, in agreement with Sabbadini when he emphasizes the links between time and space (p. 306). In my perspective, though, what is central is the relation of time not just to the space of the setting (Lombardi 2002b), but also to the body space (Lombardi 2002a).

Time and depth levels of the mind

Recent research demonstrates that at birth a child can already perceive time and the duration of his/her own and a partner's behaviour (Beebe, Lachmann & Jaffe 1997). This level, however, would seem to relate to what Gaddini described as 'use of the time' (1978, p. 401), to be differentiated from an awareness of time mediated through secondary process. I would agree with Terr's (1984) distinction between a 'sense of time', as 'the subjective feelings and meanings connected with the perception of time passage', which develops very early in life, and a 'perception of time' as 'the conscious sensory experience

156

of time', which is a level of temporality closer to what I have been exploring in this chapter.

In the context of contemporary psychoanalysis, the author who has placed most emphasis on the formal features of the Unconscious, including its timelessness, is Matte Blanco (1975, 1988) with his theories on the Unrepressed Unconscious. He describes an aspect of being, alien to logic and to difference, by introducing a conceptualization of an aberrant logic that he calls *symmetrical logic*. '"When" and "where" we apply the principle of symmetry, space, time and all differentiation between the whole and its parts, between the individual and his class, and among individual things disappear; and, with it, disappears the principle of contradiction' (Matte Blanco, quoted in Bria 1981, p. 35).

So-called difficult cases of psychopathology are dominated by such a symmetrical logic and by a weakening of the temporal parameter. Under conditions of impasse in particular, the activation of the asymmetrical function of thinking through the utilization of time has been most helpful in facilitating the analytic process (Fink 1993). In this context, interpretation has as its primary function the allowing of an 'unfolding' of the symmetrical configurations or of the infinite number of qualities which characterize mental functioning in the presence of emotions. In this respect, Matte Blanco's suggestions are close to Bion's in so far as here the interpretative emphasis is on the dynamic aspects of experience and on the differentiation between finite and infinite (Bion 1965, p. 46).

Following on from Bion's approach, Ferrari (1992) has postulated a Concrete Original Object (COO) which is the body as a total source of sensations and ethological manifestations, as well as of anatomo-functional potentials for perception and mental recording (see Lombardi 2002a). The original body has 'marasmic' connotations, as indifferent to discrimination and logic as Freud's id or Matte Blanco's indivisible mode (Lombardi 2000). The body as ethological object constantly offers stimuli which require parameters to organize and structure them. In this perspective, the introduction of time and of the mental operations that derive from it is particularly important, for it allows a reorganization of the primary process (Freud 1900) in relation to sensory experiences.

According to Matte Blanco and Ferrari, then, the perception of time becomes meaningful in all those clinical conditions chaotically dominated by sensory phenomena and where the capacity to discriminate, to test reality and to acknowledge others is impaired.

It must be pointed out that these authors' approach to interpretation is mediated by analytical propositions (Ferrari 1986) or by an unfolding-translating function (Matte Blanco 1975), which leave ample room to the analyst's interventions while renouncing those expectations of completeness and articulation which characterize other more classical approaches to interpretation. This is a view that keeps into account, among other things, Bion's approach: such an approach, by emphasizing how to pass 'to "being" that which is "real"' (1965, p. 148) as clearly different from a mere knowledge of phenomena, demands the analysand's responsibility in his/her way of acknowledging the analyst's.

My approach is therefore quite distinct from the intersubjective view of the problem of time (Priel 1997): not because it excludes such a dimension, which in the psychoanalytic context is always present and relevant, but because it concerns the patients' needs in their most primitive levels of mental functioning, with their strong connotations of concreteness, which affect the individual being 'in its original aspects, unrelated to the world and to introjective processes' (Ferrari 1998, p. 112). The activation of discrimination within the original sensory marasmus can take place thanks to the mediation of an object capable of reverie (Bion 1962b; Bon de Matte 1988). Intersubjectivity, like temporality, is a prominent component of the analytic relationship, itself endowed with its own original and 'specific constructivity' (Ferrari & Garroni 1987, p. 41). Priel establishes a kind of watershed between a conception of time as a subjective phenomenon deriving 'from a viewpoint that focuses on the workings of an isolated mind', and an intersubjective perspective understood 'as a mutually construed organizational principal characteristic of mother–infant interactional patterns' (1997, p. 435). Such a viewpoint, in my opinion, creates an unnecessary conflict that might undermine the psychoanalytic contribution to our understanding of time.

According to Matte Blanco, the deepest layer of mental functioning is the basic matrix, where any distinction between people and things, between subject and external world, and the thought's space-time disappear (1988, p. 194). Here, infinity is in the present, whereby movement and time disappear, as in Zeno's paradoxes where Achilles never succeeds in overtaking the tortoise (Bria 1981, p. 40). The introduction of the temporal parameter creates here a sort of containing and discriminating film which allows the mind to find its way in the space-time and to circumscribe 'an infinite within finite limits' (Matte Blanco 1988, p. 171). This kind of intervention, ultimately centered on the patient's relationship to him/herself, concerns a 'vertical relation' (Ferrari 1992), in parallel to the 'horizontal relation' to the analyst, and allows progress in the working through, even without those interpretations that make direct reference to the transference.

It will be clear now that I refer to a view of interpretations in primitive mental states that does not directly hinge on the transference. From a technical point of view my approach utilizes the mental models proposed by Bion (1962a/1967) as suitable tools to promote abstraction because that is the most urgent requirement in those clinical situations characterized by lack of thinking (Lombardi 2003).

From the perspective of mental models, this chapter is also an attempt to formulate in a more general sense a number of situations which, on several occasions, have been useful to me (Bion 1962b, p. 80). Twenty years ago I was already aware of the importance of time, as can be seen in a case of child analysis I published at that time, where I described the structuring effect of the experiences of analytic separation on the patient's mental functioning (Lombardi 1983). In my clinical research on psychosis, I later became aware of various intrapsychic factors in relation to temporality. These involved the foundations themselves of the patient's inner organization and its relationship to death (Lombardi 1986). It became clear to me that in primitive mental states 'the physical measurement of time was experienced as the prime representative of the reality of loss, i.e. of the limits that reality imposed on the limitless demands of the patient' (Lombardi 2003, p. 853).

I will now move on to consider some vignettes from three analytical cases. An interesting scenario will emerge from the observation of the different situations I shall describe, where each analysand presented a specific kind of link to temporality. An element in common to these patients, otherwise very different from each other, was the primitive level of their mental functioning, as well as the high risk of impasse in their clinical progress. My selection of the material is deliberately focused on certain aspects that could illustrate my topic. In the case of Giorgia, the reader interested in a wider perspective and on the multiple levels of my analytic work with her could find them published elsewhere (Lombardi 2003).

Nora

Nora is a young woman of nearly 30 years of age, in four-times-a-week analysis for a panic crisis and a 'block' in her studies. An inadequate working through of her developmental issues in adolescence makes her look physically like a teenager. As in the other cases I shall describe below, this patient had difficulties in sticking to the temporal parameters of the sessions, often being extremely late and remaining indifferent to all my attempts to interpret them in a transferential context. I must add that her literary and lyrical sensitivity, which allowed her to write verse (including the poem quoted at the beginning of this chapter), was an important ally to our analytic work.

One day Nora starts a session by saying that she feels sucked out of her own body, and immediately associates to this: 'I feel out of time, I can't put my feet down on the ground. I feel I am a little girl, other times a 13-year-old, even if I am 28.' Her experience of lacking temporal references seems then to be linked to a strong tendency to depersonalization. When the psychotic aspect of the personality (Bion 1957/1967) takes over, I can see in front of my very eyes the fragmentation of her spatio-temporal coordinates. A very careful analytic reverie becomes necessary in order to follow the sudden appearance of violent anxiety states and to help her put into words those experiences which, before her analysis, used to devastate her in a very concrete way by throwing her into a blind and unrepresentable state of suffering. I shall now describe brief sequences of sessions characterized by the emergence of the issue of time.

One day Nora tells me that when she happens to feel alive she has a vision of a graveyard. While saying this, she looks most upset and conveys to me, in a very direct way, her fear of going mad. I feel it is important to help her extricate herself from her confusion and I tell her she is expressing a thought about the passing of time and death. Nora then tells me that death appears to her as if it were to take place immediately. I reply that, if it is true that we die, it is also true that before death we have a whole lifetime. Nora replies, 'When I think of death I feel time has stopped and life does not exist any more.' Then she becomes silent and, feeling her anxiety spreading, I also remain quiet. 'Recently', she adds after a pause, 'I have noticed that I find it easier to tolerate this anxiety. I have discovered that looking at my watch and at the moving hand of the seconds gives me a sense that life is going on, that life is moving forward. At that point I feel alive, no longer paralyzed.'

This material shows an evolution toward the abstraction of a near-hallucinatory visual image. The analytic dialogue deals here with the absence of time and the state of psychic death experienced by the patient. Then, in the here-and-now of the session, time stops: by sharing with me her internal catastrophe, terror melts away and mental time starts flowing again like the moving hand of her watch. From the graveyard to the moving watch: two meaningful images open and shut this fragment – a functioning by images, close to unconscious functioning, very characteristic of the mentalizing style of this analysand.

But let us look now at a fragment from another session. After a long silence, Nora reports she feels she is being 'pulled away'. She does not feel any longer inside her skin and she feels that the objects in my room, the flowerpot and the picture, are the same as those in her childhood bedroom. I feel her slipping away toward an almost hallucinatory state. In the transference Nora had the tendency to experience herself as a child in front of her parent, but in the past my attempts to interpret at this level had only increased her confusion. I kept wondering how to intervene, feeling myself in a state of confusion. Suddenly Nora tells me, 'I think we should differentiate longing from regret.' I am intrigued by her differentiation and ask her for the meaning of her words. She replies, 'Longing is the acknowledgment of time past, while regret is the absolute demand to go back and relive the past. When I am under the spell of regret I lose the sense of time.' While listening to her words I could see Nora changing in front of my eyes and emerging from her confusion. This is an instance of what also happened in other sessions when Nora came out of a state of almost psychotic confusion, through perceptions or differentiations which provided the session with a structure. In these contexts, my contribution could be limited to my taking on her paralyzing anxiety, helping her to move toward a solution rather than offering her one myself.

Let us move now to another clinical vignette where we can find again some material on time. It is a session from the end of September and Nora starts it with a question: 'Are you cold? Because my hands are frozen!' I noticed that I was aware the temperature had gone down and I told her so. I felt, however, that this sensation of hers was but the tip of the iceberg of a developing emotion. And, indeed, Nora starts telling me of her difficulties in accepting seasonal changes. Then: 'It's a problem of my relationship to time. It's difficult for me to accept changes, but the only way is to accept that changes occur.' She then connects her facing of changes to a fear of unknown situations and of going mad. She had thought that the only way to protect herself from it was to eliminate time. I object by saying that if she eliminated time she could end up not protecting herself at all, but helping madness. In the associations that follow Nora talks of the return of her periods, which had ceased for several weeks 'due to her excessive anxiety'. She has also decided that she will go away for a short trip. These associations indicated to me that Nora was entering into time – the time of her body (the menstrual cycle) and the time of her experience of the world (the trip). These moments of working through brought me some relief, also because they came after times of intense suffering when the patient seemed almost shut inside a shell.

The entrance of this analysand into temporality occurs in her next session's opening statement: 'Coming in here today I looked at the sky and thought that when I come out again it will be completely dark. I felt the need to make an experience of this session.' Statements such as this left me surprised and moved for their clarity and affective intensity. It is her having to face the boundaries of the beginning and end of the session that stimulates Nora to value the relevant temporal domain as an important experiential opportunity. I also felt that perceiving the session's boundaries was for Nora the expression of a more general acceptance of the spatio-temporal boundaries of any real experience.

As the end of her analysis approached, the experience of separating from me for the holidays became for Nora affectively more intense. On one occasion I was struck by her reference to some lines by Montale, where the poet expresses his sense of absence following his wife's death:

> Ho sceso, dandoti il braccio, almeno un milione di scale
> e ora che non ci sei è il vuoto ad ogni gradino
> [I have gone down, holding your arm, at least one million stairs
> and now that you are not here the void is in each step].
> (Xenia II, 5, *Satura*, 1962–70)

I felt that, in those lines, the movement of going downstairs had an almost musical rhythm, whereby the feeling of the flowing of time, shared within our relationship, became almost tangible. Two profoundly beautiful lines which were a sign of both her gratitude and the internal achievement of a time that can't be stopped, a time that continues to flow with all its vitality even when facing a major separation.

Giorgia

I will now move to a more serious phenomenological typology, characterized by major thought disturbances. I will present a fragment from Giorgia's analysis, a patient in her 40s, who in the initial stages needed six weekly sessions in order to overcome a dramatic psychotic crisis. Through several months of intense work, during which she moved restlessly around the room, we had gradually built the conditions allowing Giorgia to lie on the couch. I remember in particular a session when her frequent lying down and getting up from the couch had become the main focus of our attention. I asked her then, quite directly, what it was she was trying to do. She replied, 'I go backward and forward in time,' a statement that made me connect her lack of containment of motor discharge (Freud 1911) to her missing temporal boundaries.

But let us move now to some more extended clinical material and observe in detail what happened in one session. That day, as Giorgia enters the consulting room, I have the impression that she is less confused than usual. As soon as she lies on the couch, she starts:

P: The difficulty of talking here is that it does not continue. [Pause.] I have made many mistakes; I cannot start all over again.
A: [I feel almost paralyzed and frightened by the persecutory atmosphere Giorgia activates against herself. I feel quite instinctively the need to modulate my voice in order to produce a calming effect.] You interpret everything as your mistakes, as your fault, even the breaks between a session and the next. To end and to start new experiences, however, is necessary in life.

I believe that in this sequence the analysand was showing a realistic perception of the beginning of the session. The outcome of this approach is a perception of temporality characterized by discontinuity and the resulting emotional 'difficulty' to work this through, whereby the atmosphere tends straight away to take on persecutory connotations. Giorgia interprets the beginning of each new session as a 'starting all over again', because the previous experience has been destroyed as a result of her own mistakes. More than by a hatred for separation, this analysand seems overwhelmed by her guilt ('I have made many mistakes').

I then considered that the most urgent priority was to help Giorgia extricate herself from the confusion concerning the new beginning as mistake/fault, by differentiating it from the need for change as a necessary condition to access new experiences. In this way I considered the deficiency in her capacity to think to be more relevant than her attacks on thinking.

Giorgia remains quiet for a while and seems to register somehow my statement. Then she adds:

P: It's my birthday, today. Forty-five years ago I was born and I screamed. Perhaps I must scream here too.
A: [I notice all the concreteness in her communication. I place myself on her wavelength and, at the same time, I search for a more symbolic register.] By suggesting you should scream, you acknowledge that your hatred and your suffering are ways of feeling that you have been born and that you are now alive.

With this comment I offer her a link between the feeling of hatred/ suffering and an access to life, suggesting a connection among these emotions and the potential 'birthday-birth' experience that she can register in the here-and-now of the session. In my formulation I understand 'time' as an element that the analysand could fruitfully use to become mentally present to herself, following on what I had already suggested at the beginning of the session. If I dared to use here a philosophical terminology, I would say that in both sequences I value 'time' as a sort of *transcendental parameter* (Kant) that stimulates access to thinkability of what is experienced in the present.

Let us now jump forward and look at the material emerging toward the end of that session. Indeed, as the session moves to the end, I start to notice a slowing down in our dialogue and a sense of heaviness. After a longer than usual pause, Giorgia tells me, without any apparent connection to what we have been talking about:

P: When I go out of town I don't take the watch with me. There, at the seaside, I spoke with some people but it was boring: time was stuck, it never passed.

164

A: [I link this bit of her communication to the impression of distancing and heaviness that I had felt earlier.] When you leave here you throw away your internal clock, your capacity to think, in order not to have to notice the boundaries of the session. But then you realize you have heavy and boring feelings which seem never to end.

P: Well, you seem to say that one starts again even if one stops! [In a more serious tone of voice] What's this nonsense about past and present?

A: [Noticing the patient's effort to remain in a state of integration when faced with her own realization] You are always the same, in the past as in the present. It's this that allows you to have continuity, to end today's session and to come back for tomorrow's.

As I get up at the end, I notice that the patient seems to be more 'in touch' and, on her way out, she meets my eyes, as she had done on other occasions when there had been some form of shared communication.

The theme of 'time' has then re-emerged toward the end of the session, revealing this time the attack against the link with time through her rejection of the watch. Giorgia's communication also portrays the transferential shifts in the here-and-now of the session, whereby when it is time to finish she would tend to place herself in a timeless dimension where time does not move, consistently with her phantasy of never becoming separate from me. I interpret and work with her tendency to deny time in this sequence, in order to actively contrast her attitude to get stuck on primary process timelessness (Freud 1900): a very dangerous timelessness which could reinforce the omnipotence of the psychotic area (Bion 1957/1967).

Roberta

I shall conclude this clinical section by briefly reporting the case of Roberta, a 20-year-old woman whom I was seeing four times a week. Her motivation to come to see me was a difficulty in working through her grief following her father's death. She was also suffering from major irregularities in her menstrual cycle, which had required detailed medical investigation. Her relationship to the analytic setting was extremely precarious and this precariousness would become dramatic at times of separation, revealing the patient's tendency to introduce an element of chaos that would conceal the events surrounding the end of the holidays and the return to her analysis.

Roberta brought me a dream where she met some flying insects with a strange circular shape which, if one looked carefully, were, in fact, pocket watches shaped like onions[2] with little, transparent wings. At this point the patient, having become very curious, grabbed one of those odd insects and brought it to her mouth as if it were an object that could be eaten. In her experience during the dream it was as if she was eating a candy. Her way of telling this story conveyed to me a sense of almost sweet tenderness, which was unusual in relation to such a rigidly defended and intellectualizing patient. She gave me the impression that something important was changing inside her. In her associations Roberta linked the flying watches to the passing time, and in particular to that time which is marked by the onset of periods. These had lately stopped, but she added that on that same day, after her dream, her period had started again. Furthermore, those watches were related to certain pocket watches belonging to her father's family, thus pointing toward a link to her introjected paternal figure.

A few sessions later Roberta brought a new dream: 'I was asleep in bed with an elderly couple. She wore a wig and he slept in his underpants. I moved away and went to sleep in a bed of my own. I was very pleased to be able to be more comfortable.' While telling this dream, my patient conveyed a sense of relief, of space opening up. Immediately after, Roberta commented, 'I am cold!' I felt her emotionally close and I thought her feeling cold was not due to her distancing herself from me but to her emotional involvement. I asked her what she thought of the dream and she said, 'It feels closely connected to my becoming more autonomous . . . But I'd like to make better sense of why an elderly couple. I don't understand.' I asked her what that couple made her think of. The patient remained quiet for a long time before saying, 'I think it is the past. I'm separating from my past.' At this point I commented on her associations, emphasizing her relation to the internal parental couple and her chance to grow by creating a space where she could separate from her parents – a space that was becoming increasingly noticeable also in her external everyday life.

I think what is most relevant in the context of this chapter are the patient's spontaneous associations to her two dreams, which bring to the fore the link to temporality. The passing time is concretized by the dream images in the shape of flying insects, which then get eaten up. The patient must then overcome her phobic reaction that would make her think of time as something repulsive and disgusting, and therefore impossible to introject. When she succeeds in overcoming her resistance, the insects in the shape of pocket watches turn out to be not at all unpleasant, as they remind her of candies. The choice of the 'onions', as I pointed out to the patient, was probably related to their well-known characteristics of bringing tears to the eyes of those who slice them and of taking on a sweet flavour when cooked: two aspects which are symbolic of the painful and melancholic feeling evoked by her relation to time. The reference to food in the first dream, as well as the cold sensation associated with the second one, highlighted her bodily involvement with the mental working through, and also the patient's important overcoming of her defensive body–mind dissociation. The tears, made less painful by a certain melancholic sweetness associated to the passing of time, also proved to be consistent with Roberta's new capacity to think of herself as separate from me, as well as from the parental couple, as an expression of a successful growth process. After this phase, Roberta became significantly more respectful of time and of her sessions.

Discussion

The emergence of the theme of time in the course of analytic work, as it manifests itself in various ways in the clinical examples I have reported here, has a strong stimulating effect on the functioning of the ego, consistently with Freud's (1924) intuition on the connections between temporality and consciousness. The theoretical shift introduced by Bion (1962b) emphasizing the importance of the alpha function makes us review today with renewed interest some of Freud's (1911) considerations on the modalities activating the functioning of the conscious system. Patients with serious conditions are usually characterized by a predominance of unconscious features, among them in particular an indifference to temporal parameters, and they require analytic intervention in order to activate mental functioning. This is, in these cases, much more important than the overcoming of repression.

Those life changes mark in particular the emergence of an awareness of temporality. It is not a coincidence that Klein (1923/1977) had associated the discovery of temporality to the theme of childbirth. Special importance, then, also goes to adolescence, in so far as the changes brought about by the stage of puberty are experienced by the individual as a kind of second birth (Ferrari 1994; Bon de Matte 1998). Among the various authors who have studied adolescence, Laufer and Laufer (1991) have emphasized the adolescent's difficulty in accepting changes in the body image and in metabolizing the loss of an 'idealized prepubertal body image', to the point of forming a 'psychotic core'. This, if not worked through in adolescence, could later explode at any age. Nora's and Roberta's clinical material shows the impact of a failure in the working through of temporality and change in analysis, with themes strictly connected to adolescence.

In the case of Nora, what is relevant is the activation of the non-psychotic aspect of her personality, whereby important perceptions, made possible by analytic reverie, can resonate in counterpoint to drastic operations of dissociation and denial. In particular, the elements which could be assimilated and confused had to be discriminated through the asymmetrizing activity of thinking (Matte Blanco 1975), as is the case in the distinction between real death and perception of death, or between longing and regret. The perception of life appears for Nora to be indistinguishable from the acknowledgment of death, with a strong symmetrical relation to it (Matte Blanco 1975). This reminds us of what Freud (1910) had noticed as a coincidence of opposites in the meaning of primal words. The perception of the watch's hand as a means to come out from a paralyzing state of anxiety shows the importance of activating the system Perceptual-Conscious, when emotional intensity creates inappropriate correspondences.

In many of the adolescent patients I have worked with, I have come across a tendency to experience the new adult temporality, in contrast with the fantastic timelessness of childhood, as a catastrophic event involving old age and death, which appear to them as being imminent. This experience is also accurately portrayed in the narrative imagination of Francis Ford Coppola's film *Jack* (1996) where an adolescent, due to a pathological cause, falls precociously into old age. A significant outcome in Nora's working through was her appreciation of the session time when faced with temporal boundaries ('I felt the need to make an experience of this session'). This reminds us of the appreciation, referred to by Freud (1916), of the 'smiling countryside' made more precious by our knowledge of its transience.

As I have hinted at earlier, the understanding of time in psychosis is upset by the patient's mental disposition, which itself is an expression both of a thinking deficiency and of attacks on linking (Bion 1959/1967). The loss of the time parameter, therefore, is related to the fragmentation of the spatio-temporal parameters of thinkability due to a saturation caused by primitive emotions. This creates obstacles to the proper functioning of the mental faculties delegated to representation and awareness. Conversely, at times the denial of time emerges as a way to express hatred toward boundaries, in relation to the self and the object. In Giorgia's clinical material the beginning and the end of sessions are moments when her relation to time becomes more visible, revealing dynamics connected to deficiency and attacks. I have noted how it was necessary to point out to the patient either one or the other of her internal tendencies, depending on the context. The urgent task forced on me by the patient's clinical condition was the building of an intrapsychic conception of 'boundaries' through a deliberate perception of temporality. In this sense it does not seem to me, as Sabbadini suggests, that for the beginning and the end of a session 'the darkest and the lightest areas of shading should never be at the edges of a drawing' (1989, p. 310), but that, on the contrary, we should leave space to the 'contrasts' emerging in this area: a specific construction of the drawing's 'framework'.

Also emerging from the material presented here is the realization that the anxiety connected to temporality can at times take on ontological connotations, thus showing its relation to the boundaries of birth and death.

Searles (1961), among others, has demonstrated the central place occupied by death anxiety in the genesis of psychosis. Recently Rossi (2000) has described a psychotic case where the perception of temporality emerged in the shape of dreams of one's own death.[3] Furthermore, with reference to the work of Aulagnier, Rossi stresses how 'the entrance of the subject into temporality' is a specific alternative to psychosis. Jackson, in a case presented in detail, has emphasized the role of the link with time in psychosis, writing that,

> time was the great enemy, to be defeated by his belief in his omnipotent power of controlling it in order to achieve everlasting life. In a rare moment of thoughtful self-reflection he had remarked: 'Time does not exist. Time brings age, and age brings death. I'm not a man, I'm a little boy.'
>
> (2001, p. 130)

An interesting element emerging from Giorgia's material is that the boundaries of temporality appear to have been shaped also by her emotional attitude to birth – an observation that sends us back to Klein's (1923/1977) important suggestions. Childbirth forces on Giorgia the boundaries that generate hatred and lays the conditions for a sense of existential continuity which she feels is under threat.[4] Beside the themes of birth and death, the theme of temporality is obviously connected to the end of analysis, which makes patients feel in a most tangible way the limitations of time (De Simone 1997). This, however, is a different topic, which I do not explore in this chapter.[5]

In the last case, that of Roberta, we have come across in her dream of the clocks a libidinal orality which is in contrast to the sadistic and destructive orality of the Cronus myth, which inverts the arrow of time through an incorporation that denies birth. Such a libidinal orality allows for the introjection of the spatio–temporal parameters as well as of an internal father who can help her tolerate the limitations of reality. 'The idea of time comes to represent the father . . . The demands of time, as part of reality, conflict with the pleasure principle' (Lewin 1952, p. 309). This has a specific correlation, within the analytic relation, to the acquisition of a respect for the boundaries of the setting. The analysand's progress later showed how our work had anticipated reality, for Roberta later gave birth to a child and thus became a mother.

Conclusion

It is likely that some readers, by considering my presentation as a whole, will have the impression that my clinical perspective may excessively neglect the relational dynamics of the analytic couple and the analyst's own subjectivity. I think this is in part the expression of a theoretical choice of mine, whereby – within the complementary swinging of analytical phenomena between subjectivity and objectivity (Gabbard 1997) – I tend on this occasion to prioritize a research focused on objective phenomena. By doing so, I value a relation to temporality which, because of its connections with the setting, could help us counterbalance certain 'subjective influences that distort or hamper the psychoanalytic process' (Louw & Pitman 2001, p. 762).

On the other hand, I could also state, almost paradoxically, that all that I take into account in this chapter is also the countertransference, in the meaning which is commonly attributed to this term (that is, not as a form of resistance). In order to clarify this statement I would like to recall the television interview given by Cesare Musatti, one of the founding fathers of Italian psychoanalysis, not long before he died. He indicated on that occasion that, under pressure from the passing of years and by the worsening of his physical health, at times he found himself caught by the terror of dying. With the ironic wit that characterized him, Musatti said that on one such occasion, having stopped to reflect on it, he had addressed himself by saying, 'You are not expecting to be immortal, by any chance!?' With this episode I would like to indicate that this chapter suggests that our link to time, and to the limitations stemming from it, belongs to the personal mental work that, more or less consciously, we carry out as analysts throughout our clinical experience; for it cannot be denied that the reference to death is always somewhat implicit in the theme of temporality (Bonaparte 1940; Hartocollis 1972; Arlow 1984). As Lasky has very appropriately noticed, 'an analyst who has never contemplated his mortality . . . is engaging in a form of denial' (1990, p. 456). The working through of time, as can be seen in the example from Musatti, is unsaturable in so far as it is conditioned by the limitation itself of the ethological dimension to which we belong. This means we can never offer a definitive answer to the request for containing the anxieties characteristic of our temporally bound nature.

Sanft wird der Mensch.	[Sweet becomes man.
Er sieht die Sonne sinken,	He watches the sun set,
Er ahnt des Lebens wie des	And anticipates the end
Jahres Schluss.	of life and of the year.
Feucht wird das Aug',	Wet get his eyes,
Doch in der Träne Blinken	But in the twinkle of his tears
Erströemt des Herzens seligster	Flows the brightest
Erguss.	outpouring of the heart.]

(J. Brahms 1889: *Im Erbst*. Op.104, n.5
with text by K. Groth)

Notes

1 Translated by Andrea Sabbadini. Previously published as Lombardi, R. (2003). Knowledge and experience of time in primitive mental states. *International Journal of Psychoanalysis*, 84: 1531–1549.

2 Translator's note: The Italian expression is *orologio a cipolla*, which literally means 'a watch in the shape of an onion'.

3 For the theme of death as a representation of borderline time in relation to the end of analysis, see Ferraro and Garella (1997).

4 From a philosophical viewpoint, Garroni (1998) moves the Heideggerian perspective of the 'being-for-death' to the 'not being-already-since-always' linked to birth.

5 Each analysis, through the experience of its end, creates the conditions for a working through of time. The problem of impasse in many serious clinical cases, however, presents itself before the completion of the analytic process which eventually opens up the analysis. If it is true that many interrupted analyses are caused by unconscious separation anxiety, I believe that the hypotheses about time which we have here considered could be usefully applied to that notoriously problematic aspect of our work.

References

Arlow, J. (1969). Fantasy, memory and reality testing. *Psychoanalytic Quarterly*, 38: 28–51.

Arlow, J. (1984). Disturbances of the sense of time – With special reference to the experience of timelessness. *Psychoanalytic Quarterly*, 53: 13–37.

Beebe, B., Lachmann, F., & Jaffe, J. (1997). Mother–infant interaction structures and presymbolic self-and object representations. *Psychoanalytic Dialogues*, 7: 133–182.

Bion, W. R. (1957). Differentiation of psychotic from the non-psychotic personalities. In *Second thoughts* (pp. 43–64). London: Karnac Books, 1967.

Bion, W. R. (1959). Attacks on linking. In *Second thoughts* (pp. 93–109). London: Karnac Books, 1967.

Bion, W. R. (1962a). A theory of thinking. In *Second thoughts*. London: Karnac Books, 1967.

Bion, W. R. (1962b). *Learning from experience*. London: Karnac Books, 1984.

Bion, W. R. (1965). *Transformations*. London: Karnac Books, 1984.

Bion, W. R. (1966). Catastrophic change. *Bulletin of the British Psychological Society*, 5: 13–25.

Bion, W. R. (1987). *Clinical seminars and other works*. London: Karnac Books.

Bion, W. R. (1990). *Brazilian lectures*. London: Karnac Books.

Bion, W. R. (1992). *Cogitations* (F. Bion, Ed.). London: Karnac Books.

Bonaparte, M. (1940). Time and the unconscious. *International Journal of Psychoanalysis*, 21: 427–468.

Bon de Matte, L. (1988). An account of Melanie Klein's conception of projective identification. In I. Matte Blanco (Ed.), *Thinking, feeling and being* (pp. 319–330). London: Routledge.

Bon de Matte, L. (1998). L'età dell'inquietudine. *MicroMega*, 3: 209–217.

Brahms, J. (1889). *Fünf Gesänge, Op. 104*. Berlin: Simrock.

Bria, P. (1981). Pensiero, mondo e problemi di fondazione [Thought, world, and problems of 'foundation']. In I. Matte Blanco, *L'inconscio come insiemi infiniti* [*The unconscious as infinite sets*] (pp. 1–107). Turin: Einaudi.

Caper, R. (2001). The goals of clinical psychoanalysis: notes on interpretation and psychological development. *Psychoanalytic Quarterly*, 70: 99–116.

Cargnello, D. (1966). *Alterità e alienità*. Milan: Feltrinelli.

De Simone, G. (1997). *Ending analysis. Theory and technique*. London: Karnac Books.

Ferrari, A. B. (1986). La proposizione analitica. In *L'interpretazione psicoanalitica*. Rome: Bulzoni.

Ferrari, A. B. (1992). *L'eclissi del corpo*. Rome: Borla.

Ferrari, A. B. (1994). *Adolescenza. La seconda sfida*. Rome: Borla.

Ferrari, A. B. (1998). La rete di contatto: Ipotesi. In A. B. Ferrari & A. Stella, *L'alba del pensiero* (pp. 96–119). Rome: Borla.

Ferrari, A. B., & Garroni, E. (1987). La narrazione originaria. La temporalità nella relazione analitica e nel racconto. In *Psicoanalisi e narrazione* (pp. 33–54). Ancona: Il Lavoro Editoriale.

Ferraro, F., & Garella, A. (1997). Niveaux temporels dans le processus de la fin analyse. *Revue Française de Psychanalyse*, 61: 1803–1820.

Fink, K. (1993). The bi-logic perception of time. *International Journal of Psychoanalysis*, 74: 303–312.

Fornari, F. (1971). *La vita affettiva originaria del bambino*. Milan: Feltrinelli.

Fraisse, P. (1957). *Psychologie du temps*. Paris: Presses Universitaires de France.

Freud, S. (1900). The interpretation of dreams. *Standard Edition*, 5.

Freud, S. (1910). The antithetical meaning of primal words. *Standard Edition*, 11.

Freud, S. (1911). Formulation on the two principles of mental functioning. *Standard Edition*, 12: 213–226.

Freud, S. (1916). On transience. *Standard Edition*, 14.

Freud, S. (1917). Mourning and melancholia. *Standard Edition*, 14.

Freud, S. (1924). A note upon the 'mystic writing-pad'. *Standard Edition*, 19: 227–232.

Freud, S. (1932). New introductory lectures on psycho-analysis. *Standard Edition*, 22: 1–182.

Gabbard, G. (1997). A reconsideration of objectivity in the analyst. *International Journal of Psychoanalysis*, 78: 15–26.

Gaddini, E. (1978). L'invenzione dello spazio in psicoanalisi. In A. Mascagni, A. Gaddini, R. De Benedetti, & E. Gaddini (Eds.), *Scritti* (pp. 387–404). Milan: Cortina.

Galimberti, U. (1979). *Psichiatria e fenomenologia*. Milan: Feltrinelli.

Garroni, E. (1998). Temporalità e periodo di latenza. *Psicoterapia e Istituzioni*, 4: 45–59.

Hartmann, H. (1956). Notes on the reality principle. *Psychoanalytic Study of the Child*, 11: 31–53.

Hartocollis, P. (1972). Time as a dimension of affects. *Journal of the American Psychoanalytic Association*, 20: 92–108.

Hesiod. (ca. 700 BC). *Theogony*. (D. Wender, Trans.). Harmondsworth: Penguin, 1973.

Jackson, M. (2001). *Weathering the storm. Psychotherapy for psychosis*. London: Karnac Books.

Jacobs, T. J. (2001). Reflections on the goals of psychoanalysis, the psychoanalytic process and the process of change. *Psychoanalytic Quarterly*, 70: 149–182.

Klein, M. (1923). Early analysis. In *Love, guilt and reparation*. New York: Delta, 1977.

Lachmann, F. (1985). On transience and the sense of temporal continuity. *Contemporary Psychoanalysis*, 21: 193–200.

Lasky, R. (1990). Catastrophic illness in the analyst and the analyst's emotional reactions to it. *International Journal of Psychoanalysis*, 71: 455–473.

Laufer, M., & Laufer, E. (1991). Body image, sexuality and the psychotic core. *International Journal of Psychoanalysis*, 72: 63–71.

Lewin, B. (1952). Phobic symptoms and dream interpretation. *Psychoanalytic Quarterly*, 21: 295–322.

Lombardi, R. (1983). Separazione e strutturazione spazio-temporale. Aspetti di un caso clinico. *Neuropsichiatria Infantile*, 266–7: 523–532.

Lombardi, R. (1986). Lutto e psicosi: nota clinica. In S. De Risio, F. Ferro, & H. Orlandelli (Eds.), *La psicosi e la maschera* (pp. 303–311). Rome: IES Mercuri.

Lombardi, R. (2000). Corpo, affetti, pensieri. Riflessioni su alcune ipotesi di I. Matte Blanco e A.B. Ferrari [Body, feelings, thoughts. Reflections on some of the theories of I. Matte Blanco and A.B. Ferrari]. *Rivista di Psicoanalisi*, 46: 683–706.

Lombardi, R. (2002a). Primitive mental states and the body. A personal view of Armando B. Ferrari's concrete original object. *International Journal of Psychoanalysis*, 83: 363–381.

Lombardi, R. (2002b). *Setting e temporalità*. Relaz. 12 Congr. Naz. SPI, Trieste. Unpublished manuscript.

Lombardi, R. (2003). Mental models and language registers in the psychoanalysis of psychosis. An overview of a thirteen-year analysis. *International Journal of Psychoanalysis*, 84: 843–863.

Louw, F., & Pitman, M. (2001). Irreducible subjectivity and interactionism: A critique. *International Journal of Psychoanalysis*, 82: 747–764.

Matte Blanco, I. (1975). *The unconscious as infinite sets*. London: Karnac Books.

Matte Blanco, I. (1988). *Thinking, feeling and being*. London: Routledge.

Meotti, F. (1980). Contributo alla riflessione psicoanalitica sul tempo. *Rivista di Psicoanalisi*, 26: 43–52.

Montale, E. (1928–39). Le occasioni. *In Tutte le poesie* (pp. 135–228). Milan: Mondatori, 1977.

Montale, E. (1962–70). Satura. In *Tutte le poesie* (pp. 323–468). Milan: Mondadori, 1977.

Priel, B. (1997). Time and self: On the intersubjective construction of time. *Psychoanalytic Dialogues*, 7: 431–450.

Resnik, S. (2001). *The delusional person: bodily feeling in psychosis*. London: Karnac Books.

Rossi, P. (2000). Vedere e non vedere. Considerazioni sull'autismo e la regola fondamentale. *Rivista di Psicoanalisi*, 46: 465–662.

Sabbadini, A. (1989). Boundaries of timelessness. Some thoughts about the temporal dimension of the psychoanalytic space. *International Journal of Psychoanalysis*, 70: 305–313.

Searles, H. F. (1961). Schizophrenia and the inevitability of death. *Psychiatric Quarterly*, 35: 361–365.

Terr, L. (1984). Time and trauma. *Psychoanalytic Study of the Child*, 39: 633–665.

7

TIME, MUSIC AND REVERIE[1]

'In these rooms there's always some slight noise, like the rustling of a curtain, a woodworm, or a fly bumping against a window-pane. You notice it only later, in your memory. [. . .] In your memory you discover that you had *heard* it constantly without attaching importance to it. But it's later that this detail becomes important.'

These words are spoken in a famous sequence of Luchino Visconti's film *Senso* (1954), during which the two lovers, Franz and Livia, converse, in the privacy of their room, about separation and memory, and become aware, prompted by their imminent separation, of an auditory world which is a direct emanation from their own inner worlds and from the emotional experience of their relationship. The ability to tune in to 'slight noises' would here seem to represent the intimate and impalpable world of feelings in the context of a mental functioning which an intense and saturating passion threatens to disrupt. And the affective significance of the auditory dimension is made, so to speak, 'tangible' in the film by the soundtrack with the splendid Adagio from Anton Bruckner's *Seventh Symphony*: a work which the Austrian composer wrote to commemorate the death of Richard Wagner, his teacher and inspiration. The extremely evocative nature of this music – in the exemplary interpretation by the great conductor Franco Ferrara – plays a fundamental role in creating the atmosphere of the film, offering a musical correlative to the verbally expressed recognition of the importance of auditory experience. Indeed the audible world seems an expression of the ability to organize an amorphous sensory magma, which would have risked to be lost in the adimensionality of the unconscious (Freud 1900), within the boundaries of the evocative forms of music. This 'philomusical' orientation seems established from the beginning of the film, which

176

opens on the finale of the third act of Giuseppe Verdi's *Il Trovatore* at the Teatro La Fenice in Venice and later goes on to present – as background to the start of the actual narrative – the 'Miserere' from the beginning of Act IV. The music and the libretto of *Il Trovatore* conjure up the dread of annihilation, harrowing separation and depressive and suicidal grief in the face of loss, providing a condensed foretaste of the tragic enslavement to passion recounted by *Senso*. And these are, not by chance, the same emotional reverberations that are developed in a purely symphonic manner by the Bruckner Adagio. In *Senso*, Visconti emphasizes, perhaps more completely than in his other masterpieces, the musical register that supports the filmic-visual-narrative dimension. And the ear catches – by means of the sensory condensation inherent in the primary process (Freud 1900) – the dialectic of feelings and intuits the dramatic developments of the plot.

This scene from *Senso* thus summons up two of the meanings of the verb *sentire*, to hear and to feel, and also the film, by means of its elegant and apposite use of the soundtrack, in a more general way exalts its background music in relation to its visual, linguistic, symbolic and narrative components. So *Senso* seems an appropriate introduction to the subject I mean to consider in this chapter, i.e. the importance of the auditory dimension in the more general context of sensory (visual, olfactory, coenesthetic, etc.) and symbolic experience that takes place in the analytic relationship. The importance of the acoustic dimension is in contrast to its relegation to an insignificant background position: *hearing* 'without attaching importance to it'. If instead we recognize our more intimate and significant relationship with 'hearing', however, sounds such as 'the rustling of a curtain, a woodworm, or a fly bumping against a window-pane' can represent the 'noises' that populate the analytic office, as an external reflection of the impalpable harmonies of our internal world. The most common fate of this motley and fluctuating auditory landscape is to make way for other more obvious and objectifiable manifestations of affects and thought that emerge in the context of intersubjective exchanges and of the working through: a fate which may in some part be the result of Freud's well-known disregard for music, which had caused him to declare that 'a rational or perhaps analytic temperament sets me against letting myself be moved without knowing why or by what' (1913, p. 299). More recently, on the other hand, Feder, Karmel and Pollock, in their collection of pieces about the relationship between music and psychoanalysis, observed that 'acoustic-musical experience and expression occupy an exceptional position in relation to other sensory modalities. Consequently, musical creations may be a primary source for insights into certain aspects of psychic functioning' (1990, pp. xiv–xv). So I shall focus my attention on the relationship between the development of the patient's awareness of time and the replaying of music in the analyst's mind, in accordance with the notion that music is 'time made audible' (Langer 1953).

Musical experience is just one example taken from a vast selection of internal events that hinge on the functioning of the specialized sense organs (hearing, sight, smell, taste, touch, etc.), a specific area where the activation of the sense organs (Freud 1911) contribute to the construction of *alpha elements* (Bion 1962), catalyzing the access to consciousness and thinking. (Bion 1962, 1966).

To exemplify the internal transformative processes that the *alpha function* gives rise to, Bion generally used visual elements, but he could equally well have chosen other senses, including hearing. 'The totality of that moment of experience', he writes (1992, p. 180), 'is being perceived sensorially by me and converted into an image. [. . .] I am sure that much more takes place than I am aware of. But the transformation of my sense impressions into this visual image is part of a process of mental assimilation. [. . .] By contrast, the patient might have the same experience, the same sense impressions, and yet be unable to transform the experience so that he can store it mentally.'

What I propose here about music should accordingly not be misunderstood as implicitly claiming uniqueness in this regard for the sense of hearing, but is instead a 'model' (Bion 1962) which can be applied to other senses such as sight, touch and taste. Musical experience is just one example taken from a vast selection of internal events that hinge on the functioning of the specialized sense organs (hearing, sight, smell, taste, touch), a specific area in which the activation of the sense organs (Freud 1911) contributes to achieving access to consciousness and thinking. According to Freud (1920), the sense organs function as a 'protective shield' (*Reizschutz*) that makes it possible to construct elements that are thinkable in 'small doses': thus sense experience and its 'distillation' in the internal world make a decisive contribution to the passage from the atemporal character of the unconscious, which is unrepresentable, to an experience that fits within the limits of some form of representability. Thanks to the distillation of sense experience in the internal world, the spaces occupied by silence during sessions can, like rests in music, be a medium of communication and exchange at a preverbal level. As Bion wrote, 'the psychoanalyst can employ silences. He, like the painter or musician, can communicate non-verbal material' (1970, p. 15). In Matteblanchian terms, the internal music of shared affects seems located at the crossroads of symmetry and asymmetry in the analytic relation and acts as an organizing stimulus to mental growth.

While Freud (1900, 1915) recognized atemporality as a distinguishing feature of the unconscious, emancipation from the primary process and access to representation and discrimination must perforce proceed by way of the asymmetries that the temporalization of experience introduces, without which there would be nothing but the undifferentiated state of primordial chaos, with no recognizable ordered element. So when I speak of the objective component of consciousness of time, I am referring to the fact that, from Kant onwards, time has been seen as essential to mental functioning. Those authors who, like Matte Blanco (1975, 1988), have stressed the importance of the unrepressed unconscious in psychoanalysis, recognize that the acquisition of spatiotemporal elements – in relation to the disorganized context of profound emotions – plays a decisive role in the growth and integration of mental functioning: the relational context of the analytic situation makes it possible, through the experience of *at-one-ment* (Bion 1965) between analyst and analysand, to construct shared experiences in which emotions that had been infinite and unthinkable begin to take on a spatiotemporal framework which makes them recognizable and thinkable.

Sabbadini (1979), using philosophical terms, underlines the contrast between the Kantian view of time as pre-established, a priori, capable of organizing consciousness, and Locke's empirical view which, at the end of the 17th century, already regarded it as derived from sense experience. This Lockean notion of time is of particular interest to psychoanalysts, because it helps them understand the clinical problems and need for growth of those analysands who seem unconnected to temporality, and hence to any authentic form of mental activity that is open to change and novelty (Bion 1966), a condition that leads to a serious impasse (cf., e.g. Jacobs 2001).

In the course of this chapter I shall be emphasizing the affective experience and the intersubjective exchanges on the basis of which a knowledge of time is constructed; I shall thus be creating a sort of counterpoint to the scrutiny of more 'objective' phenomena – like the discovery of the existence of watches and of the different concrete manifestations of the passing of time – bound up with the perception of time during the analytic sessions, which I explored on an earlier occasion. This is not, of course, a contradiction, but two complementary aspects, like two sides of the same coin, which however can to be treated separately. A psychoanalytic examination of time involves specifically *intrapsychic elements*, which are comparable, in philosophical terms, to Kant's transcendental parameter, and, at the same time, an *intersubjective side*, understood as a context which has been created mutually according to interactive parameters. Hence my intention to consider the two *complementary modalities* for regarding the psychoanalytic significance of time separately: on the one hand the realm of conflictuality and thought defect (Bion 1962), which is found on the intrapsychic level in relation to time, and, on the other – and the focus of this chapter – the side of the more nuanced and 'ineffable' (Bion 1965) relational dynamics, as well as the specific quality of the analyst's participation in the clinical context where perception of time is activated, as an occasion for constructing a sort of structural *relay* for the passage from the primary to the secondary principle (Freud 1900).

Here I shall be training my sights on the sensory phenomena that surface in a session and within the analyst, in contexts where the emergence of a perception of time in the patient's mind is central. I shall consider the internal auditory experience of brief musical sequences, associated with visual and gustatory aspects, among others, as well as with associative sequences of a verbal nature. The involvement of only minimally organized psycho-sensory levels, similar as they in some ways are to dream *flashes*, have been noticed by various authors, who report a specific *reaction pattern on the part of the analyst at the protosensory level*, where the provisional activation of the sense organs becomes a critical precursor of abstract thought (Gardner 1983; Norman 1989; Schust-Briat 1996; Ferro & Basile 2004). On the other hand, in this chapter I shall not explore the specifics of the relationship of time with the professional practice of music or with sublimational processes (for which see, e.g. Boyer 1992).

So in connecting time with the experience of music and with *reverie*, I seek to build a bridge between the objective awareness of time and the subjective context of experience, by attempting to describe components of temporality as indissolubly both cognitive and emotional, i.e. woven of elements of the perception of reality and the 'unheard melodies' (Keats) of feelings.

Affects and temporal limits

Affects are by nature linked to the primary process (Freud 1900), and tend to be isolated from reality testing, which is connected with perception of time (Bonaparte 1940; Hartmann 1939/1958), as well as with the spatiotemporally organized aspects of mental functioning. This means that affects naturally have an intensity which is impervious to moderation and limits. Klein (1932), in particular, connected unconscious emotions with the intense emotions of small children; Matte Blanco wrote of the presence of the infinite in the mind, a presence which disregards the differentiating and dividing parameters of thought.

My conception of time in relation to affects diverges from the view of those authors who stress the importance of the *quality* of the distortion of time, so that 'the ego's particular orientation in time provides an essential element in the qualification of a particular affective experience' (Hartocollis 1972, p. 106). Instead I consider it more useful in terms of clinical psychoanalysis to emphasize *activating a perception of linear time* in the patient's mind in the interests of reappraising the sense of infiniteness and uncontainability presented by the affects (Matte Blanco 1975, 1988), particularly in primitive states in which emotions are hardly integrated at all with perceptual functions. 'One of the terrors of patients suffering from psychosis, melancholia, or similar conditions', Grotstein writes (2000, p. 98), 'is that they cannot endure time gaps (e.g. those between analytic sessions), either because they cannot partition time without dissociating or splitting off from it or because they cannot represent it symbolically in terms of object faith and trust.'

In the child's mental world, not unlike all clinical contexts in which the psychotic aspects of the personality have the upper hand (Bion 1957/1967), awareness of time as a representative of limits is very labile, as Sybille Yates succinctly demonstrates in this simple but telling example: 'Adults can say when they have acute tonsillitis "the doctor says in three days it will be better"; this makes the present pass more quickly than it would were it not lightened by hope. The very small child, on the contrary, does often feel that the pain *will go on for ever* like this' (Yates 1935, p. 342, my italics). She goes on to observe that this way of functioning exposes the child, particularly if it is not protected by sufficient parental support, to 'its earliest experience of annihilation'; so, to escape from these first experiences of anxiety

181

'perhaps the most drastic way is to break all contact, make oneself independent of time by *putting oneself temporarily outside of time*. There is *a loss* of the sense of reality and *of awareness of the passage of time.*' (Ibid., p. 343, my italics). Yates particularly highlights the relationship between a disordered time sense and bodily participation, which, by means of the rhythms of excretory functions, contributes decisively to the construction of a sense of time. Thus getting to know the limits of the body interacts with the infinitization of intense emotions, fostering deinfinitization and mental containment (Bion 1965; Matte Blanco 1975).

Some aspects of the interrelation between *reverie* and music

The concept of *reverie*, introduced into psychoanalysis by Bion (1962), indicates a mother's receptivity towards her child's projective identifications. This concept was recently expanded by Ogden 'to refer not only to those psychological states that clearly reflect the analyst's active receptivity to the analysand, but also to a motley collection of psychological states that seem to reflect the analyst's narcissistic self-absorption, obsessional rumination, day-dreaming, sexual fantasising, and so on' (1994, p. 9). For Ogden, *reverie* is seen 'as simultaneously a personal/private event and an intersubjective one. As is the case with our other highly personal emotional experiences, we do not often speak with the analysand directly about these experiences but attempt to speak to the analysand *from* what we are thinking and feeling. That is, we attempt to inform what we say by our awareness of and groundedness in our emotional experience with the patient' (1997, p. 568). And Ogden points out the contribution somatic participation makes to the events of the analytic process, to the point where the development of certain phases of analysis can actually depend 'on the analyst's capacity to recognise and make use of a form of intersubjective clinical fact manifested largely through bodily sensation/fantasy' (1994, p. 13).

In this chapter I shall take Ogden's suggestions into account as I explore some of the implications of the occurrence, in the analyst, of sensations, hence all closely related to the body but at the same time an original construction of the analyst's and the response to a certain type of primary emotional need of the patient. Various authors (e.g. Niedlander 1958; Boyer 1992) have seen a link between music and concrete thought, connecting it to physical contact: 'many, if not all, of music's essential processes', Blacking writes (quoted by Storr 1997, p. 24), 'can be found in the constitution of the human body and in patterns of interaction of bodies in society'.

Music, of course, is not significant exclusively intrasubjectively: it also has an important function 'by virtue of its relationship to an archaic emotional form of communication' (Kohut 1957, p. 407); 'music brings about similar physical responses in different people at the same time,' Storr notes (1997, p. 24). 'This is why it is able to draw groups together and create a sense of unity. [. . .] They will certainly be sharing some aspects of the same physical experience at the same moment as well as sharing the emotions.' As a specific application to psychoanalytic practice, Di Benedetto (2000) in particular discusses a musical mode of thinking that can transfer imagery into sounds which are able to function as precursors of verbal language, and to play a role in communication in analysis: thus music can contribute to the creative orientation which is necessary for making some of the most difficult clinical situations advance. The idea that music can actively foster progress in thought formation is in line with the orientation of those authors who consider artistic expression in terms of its specific contribution to 'transforming the unthinkable into the possibly expressible' in analysis (Ginzburg 2001), or those who have studied the correlation between the 'musical dimension' of the transference and the primitive mental states involved in the so-called implicit memory (Mancia 2003, 2007).

Empirical research and presymbolic interactions

A last point we should briefly consider concerns the realm of empirical research correlatable with what I have suggested earlier about clinical and conceptual research. Neuroscientific experiments have demonstrated the connection between music and the body and also the vegetative functions of the emotions (Harrer & Harrer 1978), as well as the role of music in organizing the spatiotemporal activities of the brain (Gooddy 1978). Research into the early mother-child relationship has been particularly important, showing, on the whole, a great sensitivity on the part of the new-born baby in grasping temporal and musical material (e.g. in differentiating between very similar linguistic sounds and between changing maternal moods) all of which suggests that the voice and body language convey a particular musicality in the context of the interpersonal relationship (Trevarthen 1977; Stern 1985; Eisemberg 1989). We are dealing here, of course, with a primitive use of time, as Gaddini did well to point out (1978), which is to be distinguished from a real awareness of time fostered by the secondary process: factors which, while they must be differentiated, should nevertheless be recognized as parts of a continuum. So infant research emphasizes the importance of 'temporal patterns' and a 'coordination of interpersonal timing' (Beebe & Jaffe 1992), as a result of which experiences of synchrony and rhythm and, at the same time, the presence of non-synchronic events in fact encourage the development of a sense of time as a *dyadic phenomenon*, which cannot be described as based solely on a single participant, and which can foster the gradual differentiation between the self and the other, as well as the acquisition of a sense of personal identity (Priel 1997; Sabbadini 1988).

In the new-born infant there exists, in point of fact, an inchoate capacity to perceive time (Lewkowicz 1989), and the new-born's interactive ability is fostered by the temporal perception of its own behaviour and of external stimuli (Allen et al. 1977). At birth it already possesses an 'Auditory Discrimination of Self' (Butterworth, quoted by Beebe et al. 1997), and early mother–infant dialogue contains a temporal scansion based on the baby's ability to place the duration of events in time (Beebe et al. 1997). Infants also show a particular capacity for 'cross-modal perception' which allows them to translate flashes of light into an auditory rhythmic sequence (Lewkowicz & Turkewitz 1980), and gustatory information into visual information (Meltzoff & Borton 1979). Cross-modal perception enables the infant to deduce a coherent model from stimuli to its various senses, thus promoting internal sense-perceptive integration and the development of object relations. The pre-symbolic categorization which comes into being by means of an early ability to abstract common forms from different kinds of sensory experience contributes to the development of the infant's capacity for abstraction, forming the first foundation for the development of symbolism in the form of language (Bornstein 1985).

Thus the study of infancy provides a scientific background for those subtle exchanges to be found in the analytic relationship, which make it possible to reconstruct a 'missing side' of pre-symbolic interaction: it is lodged in the depths of the unconscious and symbolic interpretation does not often succeed in getting at the essence of these levels.

Similarly, pre-symbolic categorization reveals an element of continuity between the abstract dimension of words and the nonsymbolic concreteness of music, providing a scientific basis for the so-called synaesthesias which Plato intuited in his *Cratylus* when he spoke of the principle of onomatopoeia, or imitative sounds, as a result of which the acoustic impressions made by a word can be translated into visual impressions.

This principle was no secret to composers of 'impressionistic' music, such as Debussy, who attempted to represent visual impressions by means of sounds produced on a piano, and it is related to the spirit of those Romantic composers who believed in the possibility of a creative relationship between music and landscape: Beethoven evoked both acoustic and visual elements in his Sixth or Pastoral Symphony, although he explicitly cautioned against a too literal identification (in fact one finds, at the beginning of the score, '*Mehr Ausdruck der Empfindungen als Malerei*' – 'an expression of feelings rather than the painting of a picture'); Wagner, particularly in certain passages of the *Ring*, did not shy away from the attempt to reproduce the mysterious sounds of nature; Brahms compared the spirit of his Third Symphony to a view of the alpine glaciers of the Jungfrau, while Mahler, who had introduced definite rural evocations into his scores, said quite explicitly to the young Bruno Walter, who was lingering in admiration of the mountain scenery, 'Come along, it's all in my Symphony' (Mila 1985, pp. 140–143). Similarly some painters, such as Whistler, Kandinsky and Mondrian, attempted to represent acoustical experiences in a visual language (Gombrich 1959/1960, p. 446 et seq.).

This kind of participation and sensory interchange can re-emerge in particularly intense emotional passages of the analytic exchange, helping to establish a plan of working through that refers back to the profound levels of mental functioning that Freud (1929) called 'oceanic feeling', i.e. to those aspects of the primitive Ego that precede the differentiation between subject and object (for the correlation between oceanic feeling and temporality cf. Loewald 1980/1999, p. 121ff).

Clinical section

It is my hope that what I have presented in concise form will make it easier to understand the hypothesis of this chapter, that the surfacing of known musical passages, or of other forms of sense experience, in the analyst's mind can in certain circumstances facilitate the perception of time and, concurrently, the organization of primitive emotions in the analysand, thus offering a chance of proceeding towards more spatiotemporally organized mental functioning, as well as contributing to the conscious and unconscious communicative processes of the analytic couple.

The difference between this and free association or interpretation, both mediated by verbal thought, consists in the specific immediacy of the connection that sound and music maintain with sensation. Hence musical association is not just a cognitive act, but is one of the impalpable sensory events that inhabit the analyst's subjectivity, like what Bion called alpha-elements: 'the alpha-elements may be presumed to be mental and individual, subjective, to a high degree personal, particular, and unequivocally belonging to the domain of epistemology in a particular person [...] [and] to the lowest level of empirically verifiable data' (Bion 1992, p. 181).

In our more difficult patients we often find that the passage from the world of sensation to words and thought expands disturbingly to the point where it becomes unbridgeable, a dramatic state due to serious forms of dissociation in which symbolic communication tends to remain essentially alien to the subject's intimate and corporeal core. This problem has been described in the literature in a variety of ways, e.g. in terms of representational deficits (Green 1990), defects of thought (Bion 1962; Marty 1980) and mind-body dissociation (Winnicott 1949/1958; Gaddini 1980; McDougall 1989; Ferrari 2004). The advantage of music is that it is equally linked to the world of subjective sensation and to that of external reality, since it is part of a complex cultural system: hence it is an important transitional phenomenon (Winnicott 1953/1958) which can keep the internal and external worlds connected. Musical association can thus bridge the gap between the concrete and the abstract, body and mind, the non-symbolic and the symbolic, as well as between the internal and the external.

I shall now consider two clinical cases in which the analysand's achievement of time perception was intertwined with musical aspects of the analytic *reverie*. I shall, as far as I can, omit case-specific information, both for reasons of privacy and because I do not mean to get involved here in a reconstructive perspective, but prefer instead to focus on the internal and relational events that accompanied psychoanalytic development. These clinical examples show specific

186

moments of the evolution and should not be mistaken for an illustration of technical methods, to be used exclusively, of carrying the analytic process forward. Thus they do not imply a rather limited notion of the use of the countertransference, nor do they entail neglecting other more symbolic levels such as those involved in transference interpretation. The choices I made in the contexts that follow took into account the most primitive needs brought to analysis by the patients, and also the opportunity to encourage the organization of experience on a pre-symbolic level.

Arianna

Arianna, a middle-aged woman, came for three sessions a week since (for practical reasons I shall not go into) it was impossible to add a fourth session. This arrangement was, in the event, sufficient for the development of her analysis. A person of great sensitivity and a decidedly artistic temperament, she had often felt the urge to try analysis, but had always found some reason to put it off. The initial phase was particularly difficult because of her lack of trust, which made her very distant and unable to bring in subjects which, I felt, might involve her inner emotional life. Analytic exploration revealed, even in this first period, the trouble she had staying in touch with her emotions and her use of drastic splitting mechanisms, so that she would generally oscillate between a frightened, defenceless level, devoid of all resources, on the one hand, and a flaunted self-confidence, the result of the elimination of every form of internal contact, on the other. This state of affairs had, not by chance, caused the failure of every relationship she had entered into in the course of her life.

I shall describe a session which I found significant. A. told me about a horror film she had seen on television the previous evening, in which there was a murderer who killed women and a police inspector who was working on the case. She had felt both attracted and frightened by the film, the name of which she had forgotten: without having even determined whether she wanted to see it or not, she found herself watching it, changing the channel when it became too violent. At the end of the film, A. realized with horror that she was alone in the house and she had begun to be afraid that burglars could get in. She started obsessively to check and recheck the windows and doors, but she only felt her fear increasing, to the point where she was in a state of panic. As she recounted all this she seemed to be talking of feelings she had by no means overcome or relegated to the past, even the recent past of the night before: instead she seemed to be speaking about emotional situations that were still going on even as she recounted them. She passed her anxiety on to me in very concrete form, so that I began to feel a sense of physical oppression in my chest. At a certain point I heard in my mind an associated musical passage. I shall take a little time to explain this connection, which was almost instantaneous during the session and which took auditory form within me.

The anxiety produced by suffering that does not pass is the essence of the chorale from Felix Mendelssohn's Symphony in B flat minor, *Lobgesang* (1840), a work composed of three movements for orchestra and a choral movement which features some biblical texts. In the last-mentioned we hear a question ring out three times in a row: '*Hüter, wird die Nacht bald hin?*' ('Watchman, will the night soon pass?'). The music conveys growing tension, reinforced by the watchman's dramatic response, which seems to confirm the unresolvability of anxiety: 'The morning cometh, but also the night.' At the end the tension is resolved in the majestic chorale: 'The night is far spent, the day is at hand. Let us therefore cast off the works of darkness and let us put on the armour of light.' This is a song of praise which (above and beyond any formal programmatic purpose to write a work, it would seem, to commemorate the inventing of printing) represents in emotional and symbolic terms the culmination of the working through accomplished by means of *coming to terms with waiting and tolerance for time*. The end of the night is the equivalent of achieving an emotional working through and a release from a paralyzingly blocked condition.

So it was the musical setting of 'will the night soon pass?' that was running through my head, a passage that voiced the oppressive anxiety that had my patient and me in thrall. Although it was broad daylight, our feelings had transported us to the dark of night and a solitude where anxiety held sway. After taking stock of my feelings, I realized that my patient was going on to tell me about the outcome of the events of the preceding evening: she had gone to bed and, for what she said was the first time, she had allowed herself to be alone with her fear. Thus she had discovered, to her great surprise, that after a while her fear had started to subside. In the wake of my musical association, to which I did not allude directly, I told her that, when she was willing to be alone with her anxiety, she was also setting in motion *trust in time*, with the consequent belief that 'the night of *anxiety cannot be unending* and just as time passes, so anxiety passes too.' In this way I underlined the *creative discovery of the passage of time* which had emerged from her experience of emotions she had actually accepted and lived through.

A. answered by telling me about the astonishment she had felt at seeing her anxiety dissipate, anxiety she had previously felt to be paralyzing and infinite: she felt like 'admitting defeat', but instead she had found an unforeseen solution. At that point I could indicate the counterproductive effect of *control*, which she used concretely, for example on windows and doors, or by changing TV channels: control that had only increased her anxiety. On the contrary, *granting inner space to her emotions* had enabled her to discover unsuspected resources.

A. was then reminded that at the cinema, when there were powerfully emotional scenes, she was unable to stay in her seat and had to get up and leave. It occurred to me that her claustrophobia had to do not only with the actual physical cinema but also, more generally, with every form of contact with emotions. A. went on to say that whenever she became aware of anxiety she first tried to cancel the anxious imagery, replacing it with gratifying images: for example by recalling some other film which, by contrast, she had liked. When she realized, however, that this was not working, she would resort to flight as a last defence. At this point, with what I considered significant intuition, A. added that the cinema should be regarded not only as the scenes that one sees on the screen, but also as the *internal film*, or rather the emotions the film awakens in the spectator. I felt sudden anger at the loss of contact with her inner world that A. had brought about. Following in the path of my affective response I said that she, out of fear of being exposed to her emotions, was continually in danger of losing this internal film, of whose existence and importance she appeared to be aware. A. was silent; she seemed to be feeling the effect of my intentional provocation, by which I sought to show her how, where her internal emotions were concerned, she sacrificed that very dimension that she valued so highly in external artistic manifestations. After a few seconds she said that she had been reminded of *The Hours* (S. Daldry 2002), which she had considered a good film, because she had felt that it allowed her space to be with herself.

I asked her how it was that she was telling me about a film that was concerned with time, and was called, of all things, *The Hours*, when we had just been talking about waiting for a few minutes when faced with anxiety. A. added that the film was very distressing, but that she had managed to watch it despite its containing three suicides in three different situations. I noticed that there was nothing artificial about the way A. was expressing herself, and that her feelings of sadness seemed to be surfacing. I spoke about the change she was bringing about inside herself: as she got herself used to bearing minutes of anxiety, these minutes could turn into 'hours', as was the case with her *hours of analysis,* in which we could share minutes or *hours of anxiety* and so discover that one is not annihilated by them, that in fact they can help one to face one's authentic emotions with confidence.

At this point A. spoke about her childhood, which had been, because of certain events, very dramatic, and during which she had grown used to *using images as a way of escaping from difficult situations.* Then, as time passed, she added, she had realized that *she no longer felt anything,* and that whatever happened, it meant absolutely nothing to her. She had her world of images and that was her world.

I was very struck by this association, which revealed the autistic aspects of this analysand: with images she had constructed a private world as an alternative to reality, and it gave her the illusion of being protected against the precariousness of emotions and the absence of external help. This dimension had in a certain sense played a positive role in that it fostered her artistic sublimations, but at the same time it had laid her open to the loss of connection with her own real feelings. With her feelings frozen, A. had not been able to gain experience from her real-life emotions, or to become acquainted with the *time frame of emotions*: instead she was left with the terror of infinite anxiety.

In the context of this session I felt that my emotional response – which made use of music, in the form of a passage in which music and words together create convergent meanings – was significant: concurrently the patient had begun to re-establish a link between her *mental images* and her *emotional states*, overcoming the dissociation that had pitted thoughts against sensations. My way of communicating affectively with her had summoned up a musical memory, rather than thoughts or images, as if music were more capable than abstract thought of summoning, in a session, the presence of that very ability to 'feel' that she had done away with by getting used to 'not feeling' as regarded her intimate, private emotions.

I should like to mention incidentally that this moment of working through turned out to herald a subsequent phase of A.'s analysis, in which music played an explicit part in our dialogue, becoming an important element of communication between us. Indeed our shared passion for music greatly strengthened our shared participation in the work at hand. Far from being a form of collusion, this allowed us to approach subjects which were critical to the internal and relational functioning of a patient whose commitment to analysis, as I suggested earlier, had been, at the outset, very shaky.

Giacomo

I shall now consider Giacomo, an almost 40-year-old man with very strong defences, including intellectualization and anorexic symptoms, whom I saw four times a week. For the whole initial phase of his analysis, G. had shown no reaction of any kind to any temporal discontinuity in his sessions (Grunberger 1971/1998): it was, quite simply, as if, for him, time did not exist. G.'s denial of time seemed consistent with his general tendency to live mechanically and repetitively, avoiding anything new by assuring himself that 'he'd get around to it later.'

The development I am about to describe appeared altogether quite unexpectedly in a session of the fourth year of his analysis. In the thick of the intensely obsessive atmosphere that characterized G.'s communications, he suddenly fell silent. When he started to speak again, he told me that there had appeared before him *the image of a woman in a hat*, with her hair gathered up beneath it, and that he saw her from behind and at an angle, so that the concave curve of her eye socket and the roundness of her cheek were fairly clearly visible. On a few rare occasions G. had presented other such almost hallucinatory experiences, which had then turned out to be the harbingers of important development. It was as if in these circumstances an extremely significant affective nucleus had succeeded in emerging from his unconscious: as if these images were fragments of an undreamt dream that managed to surface during a session.

The unforeseen and hallucinatory quality of his utterance had transmitted a certain disquiet and fear. As I attempted to bring the image G. had described into focus, I saw before my eyes the image of a woman in a hat which was, I recalled, on the cover of an old LP of Mozart's Piano Concerto n. 21 in C Major. I was struck by the fact that my association was immediately transformed into music for me: I could hear, in my mind, the slow movement, that hauntingly expressive Andante.

Meanwhile the patient told me that the image reminded him of a kind of drawing he always used to make when he was in the sixth grade. This was followed by his account of a series of events that took place when he was 11: the beginning of his mother's serious chronic illness, from which she never recovered, and other sad happenings. I sensed great pain and emotional distress that G. had never conveyed before. Once again I could hear in my mind the Mozart slow movement. At a certain point the patient interrupted himself to say, 'The image of that woman has reappeared. Her hair is ruffling. The wind is blowing.' This unexpected remark made me shiver. I too felt at the mercy of the winds of emotion with a patient who until that moment had always seemed like someone in a straitjacket. Before I could get down to anything more definite there ran through my mind the musical phrase '*Soave sia il vento, tranquillo sia l'onda*' ('May the winds be gentle and the waves calm'), that extraordinary moment from Mozart's opera *Così fan tutte*, in which the regularity of the quadruplets in the strings assuages the consuming emotion expressed by the voices, and which seems to me to express everything that can be *felt* about a separation.

'I just felt something inside me,' the patient said softly, 'I don't know what to call it . . . maybe nostalgia.' I continued to shiver with emotion joined with astonishment. The drawing of a woman's profile, Mozart's music, the movement of the wind, the farewell trio – it was as if the patient's experience and mine had constructed a fine-spun web, an intertwining of inner melodies, as a consequence of which the patient was now able gradually to settle on a word: *nostalgia*, a word that seemed not so much a symbolic abstraction as an object to which his very emotion had given birth, and which was dripping with fluid, as it seemed to me, like an infant just at the moment of birth.

Later, as the session was about to finish, G. said, 'Shortly after those things I told you about that happened when I was 11, my father's father died too. It was the only time I ever saw my father cry. Before and after that he never did. Afterwards, he brought my sister and me to a café and bought us a bar of chocolate: he never did things like that. I can taste it as if it were now, that sweet taste of the chocolate.'

This session explicitly marked the birth of feelings which had previously been foreign to G.'s antiseptic world. The experience was striking in the way it was accompanied by complementary sensory experiences: to a visual image of G.'s a corresponding auditory memory of mine had corresponded. Lastly, a gustatory sensation had made its appearance. In these 'at-one-ment' moments of the analytic couple, as Bion called them, differences in identity seem to disappear, converging instead on that undifferentiated level that forms the 'basic matrix' where projections and introjections originate (Matte Blanco 1988, p 193). So the intersection of sensations pertains to the analytic couple just as it does to a single subject whose sense experiences shift by turns from one sensory modality to another (Rayner 1992).

The image of the woman and her ruffling hair seem to mark, among other things, the patient's retrieval of a 'feminine' or, more specifically, affective and corporeal aspect, which had been buried since his early adolescence. As the session developed, these feminine aspects combined with masculine ones, enabling G. to give a name to and find a symbol that corresponded to the sensory level in question.

Let us look, in conclusion, at some elements from a session that followed a break for vacation.

As soon as G. had stretched out on the couch he noted that 'there are changes': the antimacassar was missing from the couch, and there was a new computer. I was struck by his ability to place himself perceptually in the analytic office. He spoke of his feeling for his girl-friend, his desire to live with her, the difficult decision he had at last made to introduce her to his daughter. Then he told me about a dream: 'I dreamt that I was waking up and I realized that by sleeping I had missed my sister's funeral – my younger sister. I spoke about it with my other sister, the middle one. Then I went to my grand-mother's and I lay down with my head on her lap and told her how sorry I was about my sister's death, especially after my mother and my father had died.' I asked what he thought about it, and he commented on his difficulty with painful situations, which made him prefer to sleep through them. I mentioned that this was particularly true of occasions of separation. Although I was well aware of it, I made no comment about his having failed to work through our separation before the vacation, nor did I allude to his reference to the trans-ference, with his picturing me as his welcoming grandmother who enabled him to allow internal space for his pain: I preferred to make a general observation without going into specifics.

The patient, apparently relaxed and calm, fell silent, while I became aware of a sense of relaxation and began to feel my body growing heavier and heavier. After a while G. said that he had come to under-stand that in analysis one makes an 'enormous physical effort' and that 'the greatest effort consists in realizing that a thought comes to an end and then something else happens which one doesn't yet know anything about: sometimes it's a sensation, sometimes an image, other times it's another thought.' This was the first time G. had made a comment that revealed a capacity to contain the continuity between body, affects and thoughts (Lombardi 2009). I commented that the passages he was talking about were like his sister's death as represented in his dream: something that he often missed, because he preferred to go to sleep, i.e. to be emotionally absent rather than run the risk of being at a funeral. And the funeral, here in our session, was also for a thought that had come to an end. G. answered that previously he just hadn't been able to follow these changes, but that now, just when he realized what an effort he was making, he felt that *things were changing inside him*, and that *things were appearing* that he would never have been able to predict.

Discussion

At this point I should like to return briefly to the clinical material, and to what it implies. In the case of Arianna, it was apparent that I tend in general not to interpret transference and countertransference manifestations directly, despite their importance in terms of affective participation, as I prefer instead to stress the *development* that impact with the analytic relationship produces, together with its consequences as regards learning from experience (Bion 1962). Thus I make use of the events of the session, on the one hand, to *work out their affective implications* by means of the reverberation of musical associations stirred up within me and, on the other hand, to *distil a by-product of abstraction* of the experience itself, i.e. *the perception of time* as a prerequisite for the digestion of anxiety. In this manner I try to foster a binocular vision (Bion) in which the *affective working through and its cognitive implications are, as much as possible, combined*.[2]

My participation in A.'s feelings paved the way, in the course of the session, to a *negative capacity*, which allowed the patient to approach an unknown dimension of her internal world (Bion 1970). Contact with O gives rise also to a relationship with *time*: a parameter of knowledge which is essential to activating the inner resources of *trust* and *patience*. One needs, in fact, a spatiotemporal framework – which can never be taken for granted in mental activity – in order for new experiences to be created.

The clinical orientation sequence characterized by the analyst's frame of mind should also be seen as related to the subject of time: indeed at first I sought to support a certain *indefiniteness* in the analysand's experience by not introducing exact references to the distinction between 'yesterday' and 'today'. I was thereby attempting to foster the circulation of affects in the here and now of the analytic relationship. By contrast, I later introduced a reference to time as a *generalized and abstract element*, destined to be combined with precisely that *concrete and atemporal level* of sensations, which are thrown into disorder by anxiety. I was thus suggesting a form of knowledge (*K*), or rather time as a differentiating element capable of functioning as an organizer on the *less structured levels* of experience, i.e. on the levels of formless terrors which know neither space nor time.

Turning to the case of Giacomo, the session that featured the image of a woman wearing a hat seems important because it reveals for the first time the patient's unsuspected ability to enter into contact with fluid or unforeseen emotions, which take the form, initially, of images, and then, more clearly, of memories and affects. In this context I feel that the analyst's musical participation plays a significant role in encouraging a transformation that opens the door to emotions that were previously feared to be uncontainable. So in the course of the session we witness the associative activity of the analytic couple, which has a *generative function in affective and representational terms*: an associative activity, which proceeds logically and freely, in accordance with methods comparable to what we find in poetry. In the case at hand the expressive modes do not necessarily utilize the abstract functions involved in poetic language, but they do make use of the sense organs of sight and hearing as creative thought-organizers (Freud 1911), catalyzed by an alpha function constructed conjointly in the environment of the analytic relationship (Bion 1962).

Lastly, the session to which G. brought the dream about his sister's funeral began with his perception of changes in my office after the vacation. Time and change, as Aristotle noted, are indissolubly complementary. You can't have one without the other. In G.'s recounting of the dream we find the theme of mourning and his difficulty in coping with it: in the mourning process (Freud 1917), a feminine sensibility, which this patient had kept buried ever since his adolescence, may play a role. The setting in which G.'s working through took place on the transference level was evidently connected to the working through of our summer separation. Here too I opted to

195

leave some mental space unsaturated (Bion 1970), so as to allow G. the chance to approach deeper levels. He spoke of the effort and the drama of the end of a thought: this drama may seem minimal, but actually it reveals a level of working through which is deeply connected with tolerance for the unknown and for the appearance of change as a catastrophe that can be contained (Bion 1966), thus making a critical contribution to mental growth, if it is true that 'without a sense of catastrophe there would be no self and without a self no sense of catastrophe' (Eigen 1985, p. 324).

In confronting the end of a thought, G.'s mind finds itself face to face with the dizzying spectacle of an unknown universe waiting to be explored, the product of an analytic orientation at some remove from the realm of reconstructive preoccupations, favouring instead the here and now of the intersubjective relationship and the construction of experience which is capable of organizing mental growth (Bion 1962). And here the working through of the question of time is seen to be connected to the ability to open oneself to the inexhaustible world of the unconscious which is *before* us, in the future (Bion 1975/1990).

Doch uns ist gegeben	[But it is our fate
Auf keiner Stätte zu ruhn,	To know repose nowhere,
Es schwinden, es fallen	They fail, they fall,
Die leidenden Menschen	Suffering mankind,
Blindlings von einer	Blindly from one
Stunde zur anderen,	Hour to the next,
Wie Wasser von Klippe	Like water cast from rock ledge
Zu Klippe geworfen	To rock ledge
Jahrlang ins Ungewisse herab.	Year after year, down into uncertainty.]

(Friedrich Hölderlin – Johannes Brahms:
Schicksalslied, op. 54)

Notes

1   A different version of this chapter was published as Lombardi, R. (2008). Time, music, and reverie. *Journal of the American Psychoanalytic Association*, 56: 1191–1211.

2   An association between the Bionian insight of binocular vision and neuroscientific discoveries about the different functions of the two cerebral hemispheres might lead one to think that in this kind of concurrent

cognitive and musical participation, the rational, verbal and abstract thinking that takes place in the left hemisphere is co-opted by the right hemisphere for its work both in emotional expression and, very specifically, in perception and musical expression (cf. Damasio & Damasio 1978).

References

Allen, T., Walker, K., Symonds, L., & Marcell, M. (1977). Intrasensory and intersensory perception of temporal sequences during infancy. *Developmental Psychology*, 13: 225–229.

Beebe, B., & Jaffe, J. (1992, May). Mother–infant vocal dialogue. *Infant Behavior and Development*, 15 (ICIS Abstracts Issue): 48.

Beebe, B., Lachmann, F.M., & Jaffe, J. (1997). Mother–infant interaction structures and presymbolic self- and object representations. *Psychoanalytic Dialogues*, 7: 133–182.

Bion, W. R. (1957). Differentiation of the psychotic from the non–psychotic personalities. In *Second thoughts* (pp. 43–64). London: Karnac Books, 1967.

Bion, W. R. (1962). *Learning from experience*. London: Karnac Books, 1984.

Bion, W. R. (1965). *Transformations*. London: Karnac Books.

Bion, W.R. (1966). The catastrophic change. *Bulletin of the Psychoanalytic Society*, 5.

Bion, W. R. (1970). *Attention and interpretation*. London: Karnac Books.

Bion, W. R. (1975). *A memoir of the future. Book one: the dream*. London: Karnac Books, 1990.

Bion, W. R. (1992). *Cogitations* (F. Bion, Ed.). London: Karnac Books.

Bonaparte, M. (1940). Time and the unconscious. *International Journal of Psychoanalysis*, 21: 427–468.

Bornstein, M. (1985). Infant into adult: unity to diversity in the development of visual categorization. In J. Mehler & R. Fox (Eds.), *Neonate cognition* (pp. 115–138). Hillsdale, NJ: Lawrence Erlbaum Associates.

Boyer, L. (1992). Roles played by music as revealed during countertransference facilitated transference regression. *International Journal of Psychoanalysis*, 73: 55–70.

Daldry, S. (Director). (2002). *The Hours* [Motion picture]. United States: Paramount Pictures.

Damasio, A., & Damasio, H. (1978). Capacità musicale e dominanza cerebrale. In M. Critchley & R. A. Henson (Eds.), *La musica e il cervello* [*Music and the brain*]. Padua: Piccin.

Di Benedetto, A. (2000). *Prima della parola: l'ascolto psicoanalitico del non detto attraverso le forme dell'arte*. Milan: Angeli.

Eigen, M. (1985). Toward Bion's starting point: between catastrophe and faith. *International Journal of Psychoanalysis*, 66: 321–330.

Eisemberg, R.B. (1989). Stimulus significance as a determinant of infant responses to sound. In E.B. Thoman (Ed.), *Origins of the infant's social responsiveness* (pp. 1–32). Hillsdale, NJ: Lawrence Erlbaum Associates.

Feder, S., Karmel, R.L., & Pollock, G.H. (Eds.). (1990). *Psychoanalytical explorations in music*. New York: International Universities Press.

Ferrari, A. B. (2004). *From the eclipse of the body to the dawn of thought*. London: Free Association Books.

Ferro, A., & Basile, R. (2004). The psychoanalyst as individual: self-analysis and gradients of functioning. *Psychoanalytic Quarterly*, 73: 659–682.

Freud, S. (1900). The interpretation of dreams. *Standard Edition*, 5.

Freud, S. (1911). Formulations on the two principles of mental functioning. *Standard Edition*, 12: 213–226.

Freud, S. (1913). Moses. *Standard Edition*, 13.

Freud, S. (1915). The unconscious. *Standard Edition*, 14: 159–215.

Freud, S. (1917). Mourning and melancholia. *Standard Edition*, 14.

Freud, S. (1920). Beyond the pleasure principle. *Standard Edition*, 18: 7–64.

Freud, S. (1929). Civilization and its discontents. *Standard Edition*, 21.

Gaddini, E. (1978). L'invenzione dello spazio in psicoanalisi. In A. Mascagni, A. Gaddini, & R. De Benedetti Gaddini (Eds.), *Scritti* (pp. 387–404). Milan: Cortina.

Gaddini, E. (1981). Note sul problema mente-corpo. *Rivista di Psicoanalisi*, 27: 3–29.

Gardner, M. R. (1983). *Self Inquiry*. Boston, MA: Little, Brown.

Ginzburg, A. (2001). Un castello grande come il mondo. *Rivista di Psicoanalisi*, 47(1), 129–144.

Gombrich, E. H. (1959). *Arte e illusione*. Turin: Boringhieri, 1960.

Gooddy, W. (1978). Il timing e il tempo dei musicisti. In M. Critchley & R.A. Henson (Eds.), *La musica e il cervello* [*Music and the brain*]. London: Heinemann.

Green, A. (1990). *La folie privée*. Paris: Gallimard.

Grotstein, J. S. (2000). *Who is the dreamer who dreams the dreams?* Hillsdale, NJ: Analytic Press.

Grunberger, B. (1971). *Il narcisismo*. Turin: Einaudi, 1998.

Harrer, G., & Harrer, H. (1978). Musica, emozioni e funzioni vegetative. In M. Critchley & R.A. Henson (Eds.), *La musica e il cervello* [*Music and the brain*]. London: Heinemann.

Hartmann, H. (1939). *Ego psychology and the problem of adaptation*. New York: International Universities Press, 1958.

Hartocollis, P. (1972). Time as a dimension of affects. *Journal of the American Psychoanalytic Association*, 20: 92–108.

Jacobs, T. J. (2001). Reflections on the goals of psychoanalysis, the psychoanalytic process and the process of change. *Psychoanalytic Quarterly*, 70: 149–182.

Klein, M. (1932). *The psychoanalysis of children*. New York: Delta.

Kohut, H. (1957). Observations on the psychological functions of music. *Journal of the American Psychoanalytic Association*, 5: 389–407.

Langer, S. (1953). *Feeling and form*. New York: Scribner.

Lewkowicz, D. (1989). The role of temporal factors in infant behaviour and development. In I. Levin & D. Zakay (Eds.), *Time and human cognition*. Amsterdam: North-Holland.

Lewkowicz, D., & Turkewitz, G. (1980). Cross-modal equivalence in early infancy: audiovisual intensity matching. *Developmental Psychology*, 16: 597–607.

Loewald, H. W. (1980). *Papers on psychoanalysis*. Milan: Masson, 1999.

Lombardi, R. (2003). Mental models and language registers in the psychoanalysis of psychosis. An overview of a thirteen-year analysis. *International Journal of Psychoanalysis*, 84: 843–863.

Lombardi, R. (2009). Body, affect, thought. Reflections on some of Matte Blanco's and Ferrari's hypotheses. *Psychoanalytic Quarterly*, 78(1): 123–160.

Mancia, M. (2003). Dream actors in the theatre of memory: their role in the psychoanalytic process. *International Journal of Psychoanalysis*, 84: 945–952.

Mancia, M. (2007). *Feeling the words: neuropsychoanalytic understanding of memory and the unconscious*. London: Routledge.

Marty, P. (1980). *Les mouvements individuelles de vie et de morts: Vol. 2. L'ordre psychosomatique*. Paris: Payot.

Matte Blanco, I. (1975). *The unconscious as infinite sets*. London: Karnac Books.

Matte Blanco, I. (1988). *Thinking, feeling and being*. London: Routledge.

McDougall, J. (1989). *Theatres of the body: a psychoanalytic approach to psychosomatic illness*. London: Free Association Books.

Meltzoff, A., & Borton, R. (1979). Intermodal matching by human neonates. *Nature*, 282: 403–404.

Mila, M. (1985). *36 articoli di Massimo Mila*. Turin: La Stampa.

Niederland, W. (1958). Early auditory experiences, beating fantasies, and primal scene. *Psychoanalytic Study of the Child*, 13: 471–504.

Norman, J. (1989). The analyst's visual images and the child analyst's trap. *Psychoanalytic Study of the Child*, 44: 117–135.

Ogden, T.H. (1994). The analytic third: working with intersubjective clinical facts. *International Journal of Psychoanalysis*, 75: 3–19.

Ogden, T.H. (1997). Reverie and interpretation. *Psychoanalytic Quarterly*, 66: 567–595.

Priel, B. (1997). Time and self: on the intersubjective construction of time. *Psychoanalytic Dialogues*, 7: 431–450.

Rayner, E. (1992). Matching, attunement and the psychoanalytic dialogue. *International Journal of Psychoanalysis*, 73: 39–54.

Sabbadini, A. (1979). *Il tempo in psicoanalisi*. Milan: Feltrinelli.

Sabbadini, A. (1988). Tempo e identità: alcune considerazioni psicoanalit-iche. In P. Reale (Ed.), *Tempo e Identità*. Milan: Franco Angeli.

Schust-Briat, G. (1996). Considerations on visual phenomena in the ana-lyst's mind at work. *Psychoanalytic Inquiry*, 16: 376–389.

Stern, D. (1985). *The interpersonal world of the infant*. New York: Basic Books.

Storr, A. (1997). *Music and the mind*. London: HarperCollins.

Trevarthen, C. (1977). Descriptive analyses of infant communicative behav-ior. In H.R. Schaffer (Ed.), *Studies in mother-infant interaction* (pp. 227–270). London: Academic Press.

Winnicott, D.W. (1949). Mind and its relation to the psyche-soma. In *Col-lected papers: through paediatrics to psycho-analysis*. London: Tavistock, 1958.

Winnicott, D.W. (1953). Transitional objects and transitional phenomena – a study of the first not-me possession. In *Collected papers: through paediatrics to psycho-analysis*. London: Tavistock, 1958.

Yates, S. (1935). Some aspects of time difficulties and their relation to music. *International Journal of Psychoanalysis*, 16: 341–354.

8

ON DEATH-LIFE SYMMETRIZATION
Stubborn silences as 'playing dead'[1]

Antonio was sent to me by a colleague to whom he had applied to start a new analysis. The patient felt he was in increasingly desperate shape and on the point of committing suicide. My colleague had been greatly struck by the lack of emotional resonance in the patient, who seemed as if made of stone, despite being fully aware that his life was in danger. This was why my colleague considered the patient unsuitable for analysis, at least by him. Knowing of my experience with extreme situations, he had asked me if I would be willing to see the patient at least once for a consultation so I could form a first-hand impression.

In my first encounter with Antonio I found myself facing a massive and athletic person who projected a distinct sense of remoteness and emotional frigidity. He spoke very softly and even when he looked directly at me he seemed to be somewhere else.

Indeed Antonio seemed as if made of marble, such was the sense of rigidity and impassivity he projected. He complained of an uncontrollable urge to gamble, with disastrous financial results, said he found it difficult to feel alive and was generally without emotions, which condition had been exacerbated when, some months before, he had ended his second analysis after six years of four sessions a week. This end had come about, according to the analysand, since nothing of any real significance to him had taken place during that experience, leaving him prey to a sense of emptiness and to intense suicidal urges. Hence the need for a third analysis. Although all of these particulars confirmed my colleague's impression, I was nevertheless struck by Antonio's determination to seek analytic help and by his eagerness to protect his relations with his family: he had a little son of whom he said he was very fond and a wife who had already threatened to divorce him several times. It was as if, somewhere inside Antonio, there still existed a belief in the possibility of being helped by psychoanalysis, despite his unsatisfactory previous experiences.

Considerable difficulties arose, however, in organizing our work, and Antonio could not be induced to start with more than two sessions a week. His preceding analysis had, it seemed, also left him at the mercy of a deep scepticism about analysis in general, so that he gave the impression of taking care in advance to stand aloof from what promised to be one more failure.

Antonio's childhood had been, he reported, traumatic because of the coldness and absence of emotional resonance in the relational context: it was characterized, in his words, by 'the dehumanizing atmosphere of a death camp'. His past relational experiences, viewed reconstructively, had been the focus of his two previous analyses, but without any therapeutic benefit whatever.

During the initial phases of his analysis Antonio displayed two different modes of participating in the analytic situation. On the one hand he would constantly return to situations from his childhood, flooding his analysis with repetitive stories about his past. On the other hand he would, in some sessions, tend to keep silent, not responding to any of my comments or attempts to stimulate his participation. When asked directly, he claimed that he felt nothing and thought nothing. After a while he also tended to arrive late and to skip sessions. This kind of behaviour had apparently been a constant in his last analysis.

What was common to these apparently contradictory situations was the fact that in both of them I felt that Antonio was far away – because of his silence, but equally because of the lack of any apparent correlation between his stories, which were treated like human interest items on a television news program, and his own involvement in them. At the same time I began to note Antonio's extraordinary ability to convey violent hatred which I found it very hard to contain. Especially his silence, far from being the silence of self-acceptance and peace, conveyed such a strong sense of unpleasantness and violence that I noticed that *I tended to absent myself from emotional feeling.* Perhaps this was precisely the solution that Antonio had long used for managing his hatred: absenting himself mentally. The fact that I did not give in to the blandishments of absence and silence was, I believe, an important element in catalyzing development.

When my comments were aimed at indicating his hatred for me in the analytic relation, they seemed either to meet with rigidity as a response, or to be totally rejected. His reaction seemed more constructive, on the other hand, when I spoke of hatred in general, and of his propensity for ignoring it and the ways it manifested itself. This was apparently consistent with *a need to focus on a working through at the level of the analysand's relation to himself* (Bion 1987) – or, more precisely, on the axis of the body-mind relationship – rather than on the traditional transference interpretation, which, in a case like Antonio's, would just risk increasing the patient's confusion and dissociation.

My method of proceeding, at this point, focused increasingly on spurring Antonio to observe his way of relating to hatred, and I generally emphasized his hatred for himself and his tendency to leave it concretized in his acting out, rather than highlighting his hatred for his analyst. At the same time I tried to call his attention to the mechanical way he talked about his childhood experiences and also to the utter pointlessness of continuing to discuss subjects that he had already considered and tackled from a variety of perspectives, and which, in the context of our relationship, served only to cut him off from his present situation, i.e. from the thoughts and emotional states that might crop up spontaneously.

Emphasizing the analysand's own mental functions and responsibilities towards himself so as to enhance his subjectivity

This way of proceeding left more room for discussing his tendency to squander his money by gambling. It emerged that he had a strong sense of guilt about this, which seemed to hamstring every form of apparent working through in this area. I observed, in fact, that every time the subject of gambling came up, Antonio seemed more rigid and tense as he lay on the couch, so I suggested that he consider more carefully what he expected from me, and more particularly his expectation that I would judge him harshly and condemn him. This relational situation corresponded to *his intrapsychic difficulty in keeping the sphere of knowledge separate from that of morality*, which meant that every apparent analytic working through was actually of no use because for him it was like a judgment passed on him from outside himself. One consequence was that he could never really observe his behaviour and compare it with the actual expectations and desires he had regarding himself. At the same time it emerged that *Antonio had delegated to me the expectation of a 'cure'*, so that, paradoxically, *'being better' had become*, for him, a way of being accepted by me, and hence *a way of losing himself*, rather than the realization of a project of his own.

This passage marked a development, in that it made it possible to consider his behaviour in a less obvious way. While it might at first have seemed self-evident to relate gambling to a kind of addictive behaviour with distinct self- and other-destructive components, we discovered that gambling had a specific mental function: it was not only destructive behaviour, but was also a form of acting out that *allowed Antonio to feel* in some way excited, and hence *alive. Analyzing the dead and alive contradictoriness* of his behaviour seemed to help the analysand to free himself from a blind tendency to feel guilty and to live as though he were a complete mistake.

Differentiating between knowledge and morality, recognizing whose business it is to feel motivated to proceed with analytic treatment, and distinguishing between the dead and alive components of his addictive gambling are examples of the need to introduce mental differentiations in Antonio's potentially paralyzed mind. Matte Blanco (1975, 1988) stressed the unconscious destructuring action of symmetry, as a result of which distinctions disappear, and how *essential* it is that the analyst *introduce asymmetrizations* (i.e. differentiations) so as to foster the development of realistic thinking in the patient. We shall shortly see other examples of symmetrization and the consequent need for the analyst to activate an unfolding, during the session, towards asymmetrical forms that are compatible with the reality principle.

Working through these aspects made possible a reduction of the compulsive aspect of his gambling. At the same time he began to evince some actual participation in the events of analysis, to the point that he spontaneously spoke of his need to add a third weekly session, which we introduced after the first long break for summer vacation. The new three-session rhythm seemed more in keeping with his needs, and it remained our pattern for the rest of his analysis.

This change seemed indicative of the different way in which Antonio was beginning to relate to the analytic context: whereas, in his past analytic experiences, the number of weekly sessions had been decided by the analyst and the patient had felt he had to comply with this external requirement, in his relationship with me we had started with the rhythm that he himself had felt was most appropriate, and when we increased the number of sessions it was at his specific request. This helped him feel that his current analysis was constructed on the basis of his actual needs, instead of being built on the analyst's ideological assumptions. This state of affairs also meant, importantly, that he could begin a de-idealization of his analysis, no longer regarding it as *an external object that had to be swallowed whole* in order to find a remedy for his insufficient self-esteem, but instead as *an experience whose starting-point was himself* as a real person whom he might begin to accept as such.

It should be noted here that the danger of insisting on a strictly prescribed technique is that one may provoke a kind of compliance in the analysand, which becomes the equivalent of what Winnicott (1960) called 'false Self'. This 'pseudo-compliance' turns into a powerful negative boomerang when the analyst attempts to direct the analysand towards an independent subjectivity. Seligman (2007), among others, stressed the risks of proceeding according to a 'standard psychoanalytic technique' as the only way of gaining access to a supposed 'complete form of mentalization', so that 'this "technical" way of going about things leads to (at least) a detour rather than a more authentic or integrative process' (p. 379). In addition to bearing in mind that the precedence of the clinical response over preconceived assumptions is what particularly distinguishes an empirical science, there should always be room for *epistemological self-questioning* about the reasons why the so-called psychoanalytic frame should make sense – a sense which cannot but be, each time, specific to the case at hand – as a consequence of the spatiotemporal implications of an approach based on the unconscious, which has deep levels that are structurally nonspatial and atemporal (Freud 1900; Matte Blanco 1975).

Constructing the analytic relationship through dialogue and authenticity

The problems connected with his silence, in particular, did, however, continue to come up, a spur to carrying on with our working through. Antonio's use of silence seemed to fit nicely with his tendency to keep himself emotionally absent. He used silence in part to reject perception of the space-time of the session. Through silence, this spatiotemporal experience was nullified and, together with it, the spatiotemporal categories of experience and thought. At the same time it seemed that a certain amount of his silence served to defend a healthy autistic space, by means of which he protected himself against the risk of what he perceived as possible invasion. It was, for me, rather like navigating between Scylla and Charybdis, given the risk of blocking development if silence was abused.

I believe that cases like Antonio's reveal the limits of regarding the analytic process exclusively from the symbolic–interpretive angle. Indeed clinical psychoanalytic evidence demonstrates that where a patient's subjectivity does not yet have distinct bodily roots and the ego resources are weak, verbal interpretation has no transformative power. It is no accident that Bion (1963) placed the basic levels of his grid in the sphere of the pre–symbolic transformative processes and that he emphasized the role of the analytic relationship in creating internal container/contained configurations capable of generating experience and thought (especially the symbiotic type of container/contained relationship, which involves mutual benefit for the two participants in the analytic relationship). In keeping with Freud's insight that the ego takes on structure in contact with the disorganized and incandescent manifestations of the id, Bion stresses the leading role, in terms of mental growth, played by an orientation that favours thinking in the presence of emotions. Thus we can think of the therapeutic action of psychoanalysis today as of something that passes mainly through the construction of an analytic relationship which highlights the role of the analysand who, faced with the challenges of living, makes use of his or her ability to activate containment and thought. Hence psychoanalysis can be seen as an experience oriented primarily towards 'navigating' the sea of experience and 'making the best of a bad job' (Bion 1979/1987) in the presence of sensations and primitive emotions of a chaotic nature, rather than systematically making the patient aware of specific complexes, conflicts and defences and of a recapitulation-reconstruction of individual development within the transference.

A basic aspect of this analytic process was my decision to interact in a variety of ways with the analysand, not letting him seal himself off, but prodding him to participate actively by means of my verbalizations, thus curbing his tendency towards paralysis. Also, *my comments were not oriented primarily towards interpreting, but rather towards interacting and maintaining a dialogue with him.* At certain moments it did not matter about what we spoke: the essential thing was keeping the dialogue going, thus keeping open a channel of communication which would make it possible to develop a relationship and to evolve a way of thinking based on reality (common sense). Despite this orientation of mine, his tendency towards silence and paralysis returned in massive form with the approach of the first long interruption of analysis. It thus became apparent that Antonio was by no means so indifferent to his analyst's relational contribution as he persisted in pretending.

At this point I intensified my perceptible presence in the session and actively and often reminded the analysand that he could express what was happening to him in the here and now of his experience, both in terms of his sensations and of the thoughts that passed through his mind. Working in this way meant, for me, facing my own violent participation in his hatred, which I felt quite tangibly in the form of strong physical sensations, culminating in intense and inexplicable nausea. What I was experiencing in my own person was that Antonio's tendency to absent himself mentally was the expression of a tendency to keep himself at a distance from his hatred by eliminating the instrument that would have perceived it, i.e. his mind. And the obliteration of affect (feeling) was not less determinative than the obliteration of the limits suggested by the spatiotemporal coordinates of separation (thinking).

I believed, however, that *what I was experiencing was a matter of mine*, although it had indeed been brought on in the context of my relationship with the analysand, so *I neither considered nor interpreted his hatred as directed principally at me*, but instead understood it as a signal of his approach to sharing an area which until that moment had been dissociated and acted out. In psychoanalysis two subjects with their own emotional lives interact, with reciprocal influence that activates a specific experience in each of them. Bion would have spoken of two distinct *evolving* Os, the analysand's and the analyst's, such that the analyst's capacity for containing his or her own emotional life performs a decisive *reverie* function for the analysand's development and capacity for emotional contact. Thus Antonio's experience of hatred in the session was, I felt, evidence of *some progress towards the world of emotions*, and not an attack upon the analytic relationship. If it is, in fact, true that the subject's mental development is formed by starting with his or her concrete original body (Ferrari 2004), it would seem decisive, in terms of technique, to consider the usefulness of fostering the development of the subject's primitive sensations towards progressively more articulate forms of emotions and feelings, which can then generate the capacity for the abstraction of thought (Bion 1963; Damasio 1999).

Meanwhile, during our sessions Antonio's customary defensive imperviousness seemed proof against all my attempts to break through it. Neither did the patience with which I faced his silence result in any apparent development. It seemed instead as though the analysand interpreted my joining in the silence as the expression of an aloofness which was every bit as impervious as the aloofness he was employing.

During a session for which Antonio had arrived 20 minutes late, only to spend a good part of the rest of the hour in silence, I decided to follow the course of my feelings and to lose my patience quite openly. Without attempting to disguise the obvious anger in the tone of my voice, I told him that he was showing a disregard for his own time which I found incompatible with his presumed motivation for analysis; this was apparent in both his repeated lateness and the paralysis of the rest of the session that he caused with his silence. Indeed, I said, it seemed to me that an analysis implied *at least some form of confrontation at the verbal level* and some discussion of what he felt was his internal condition, so that if it was his intention to continue to use his sessions in that manner – or rather not to use them – perhaps it would be best if he gave some serious thought to spending his time and money in some other way or with other people, rather than continuing to come to me for analysis so unproductively. I added that while he had complained to me that his last analysis was a failure and that the rigidity of his last analyst had contributed to its failure, I, for my part, faced with his way of proceeding, disclaimed all responsibility for what became of his current analysis.

Confronted with the recognition of my powerlessness to change his attitude and with my avowal of the limits of my tolerance, as well as the patent hatred I was acting out in the session by getting angry, the patient reacted with obvious embarrassment. Although he did not express it with any specific verbal response on that occasion, an emotional participation that was far from his customary flaunted frigidity was nonetheless unmistakable.

Considerably further along in his analysis Antonio referred to this episode as a *moment of revelation* for him of the humanity of his interlocutor and *of the responsibility that devolved upon him personally for the outcome of his analytic experience.* Seeing with his own eyes the exasperation that his defensive reticence gave rise to in me, he dis-covered who his actual interlocutor was – in terms of intolerance no less than of the tolerance I had shown up to that point. If until then he could have mistaken my reception of his silence for a parallel form of emotional impermeability, from that moment forth such a mistake was no longer even remotely possible.

From that day on it was at any rate the case that his systematic lateness simply disappeared and his silences became less drastic and impenetrable; most notably, no session finished without our having the chance to carry out some sort of working through and exchange.

Experiencing mental boundaries and the limits imposed by reality within the psychoanalytic session

Thus as we came to the date when our sessions were to be sus-pended for the long summer break, we had an analysand with some sort of sense of himself as a real participant in the analysis, and for whom the arrival of the spatiotemporal caesura of interruption did not sink into an undifferentiated void. Not letting Antonio have his mental presence founder in the context of his sessions, but encourag-ing him instead to be present and to experience the temporal limits determined by the approach of a separation was particularly useful in avoiding the disappearance of an awareness of himself in which a place could be found for hatred and pain – both current pain and the pain he had been carrying about with him all his life.

It did not seem incidental that, starting with this phase of his anal-ysis, Antonio showed what appeared to be a certain sensitivity to the temporal course of his sessions (Lombardi 2003), manifested by some new and quite noticeable events. Indeed the approach of the end of a session sometimes caused the emergence of phenomena that seemed to signify that his icy armour was beginning to melt away. In a most sudden and unexpected manner Antonio would start to let out des-perate howls, which rained upon me like the gusts of a hurricane; the howls were followed by wailing sobs – in the course of which he seemed on the point of suffocating – only to be succeeded at once by inconsolable weeping of an equally extreme acoustic quality. The sense of catastrophic pain that Antonio managed to communi-cate at those moments left no room for doubt about the authentic-ity of what he was going through: despite the externality of these expressions I did not feel that there was anything about them of empty pretence or hysteria. Instead I felt they were a sort of externalization of something that had been long buried and that needed to enter into life in that explosive way in order to be digested in the present and really buried in the past for good and all. The experience of being alive thanks to contact with infinite-level emotions (Ginzburg & Lombardi 2007) remained foreign to verbalizing thought in this first stage.

Thus the intellectual reconstructive viewpoint was sidelined in favour of a focus on experiencing the here and now, which made possible the surfacing of affects that, experienced unconditionally, caused the emergence of 'memories in feelings' (Klein 1957) without any specific connection to past events. The appearance of the affects of hatred and sorrow, infinitized in lacerating volcanic explosiveness, came to have the important function of connecting Antonio to himself and to his authentic emotional experience of himself (for a discussion of infinite-level feelings in relation to 'remembering in feelings' see Matte Blanco 1988).

From this point of view the evolution of this case, in keeping with other observations I have made in the course of my practice, seems to suggest that the analyst's expectation of working through a past traumatic situation (such as Antonio's childhood in fact was) by means of the intellectual and reconstructive working through of memories, just risks reinforcing the patient's dissociation from the explosive world of his deep affects. However, a working through focused on the absence of memory and desire (Bion 1970), which fosters the emergence, in the course of the session, of unorganized sensori-emotional levels of subjective experience – as an expression of a *progressive orientation* towards integrating the personality and *not* of a therapeutic regression – leads to a confrontation with undifferentiated affects that surface from the analysand's oceanic depths during the session, like flotsam from past shipwrecks. They become actually buriable once and for all precisely because what had not been really lived through is faced in the actual present of the relational experience of analysis, rather than simply considered on an abstract level. In other words, *if there is a past trauma to work through*, it should be encountered as one *moves towards the future*, as a situation to be worked through while one proceeds towards development and change: a perspective which is consistent with the complex temporality involved in unconscious affects (Freud 1900; Matte Blanco 1988).

Exploring the analysand's deepest anxieties and defences: stubborn silences as 'playing dead'

Only later on could we verbally approach the experience of his primitive anxieties – particularly those that were connected to the fear of death which motivated his tendency to absent himself or disappear – and analyze some elements linked to the defective thinking of his internal theories. I am now going to present a short but telling clinical sequence that should give an idea of the dimension of Antonio's anguish and of the defences he mobilized, in which the confusion between life and death, and hence the lack of differentiation between them, played a prominent role.

The sequence is from a session further along in Antonio's analysis than what I have described so far, at a point where the reduced danger of the clinical situation gave me some scope to let Antonio face his silence in analysis more directly, without my having to worry about its leading to the same paralyzing impasse he had experienced in his earlier analyses. The decreased danger of Antonio's silences was the consequence of a series of experiences which had come about in the analytic relationship through interactions in which I had been called upon to exercise a complex and protean responsiveness, attuned in each instance to the patient's current needs and intended first of all to keep him realistically anchored to his subjective presence and involved in the mental events that emerged in the course of the session. His tendency to hide behind imitative manoeuvres and to use both the rejection of responsibility and mental absence in relation to his experience had required a series of continual specific adjustments, which could not be formalized on the basis of any sort of pre-established technique. In this context of evolution in the quality of our analytic interaction his experience of silence seemed to take on the quality of a springboard for exploring some of his own internal theories.

After about 25 minutes of silence I note that half the session has now gone by, so I adopt a more active mode and ask Antonio what he's thinking about. He answers:

PATIENT: The usual things. [There's a pause, and then, with the same muted and inexpressive tone of voice]: Always the usual things.

ANALYST: [I take in his defeatist orientation with its tendency to nullify the temporal duration of the session, making everything 'usual', the same, and denying the specificity of the experience of the here and now he is living through. Hence I seek a wording that can expose the sense of pre-determination he attributes to events, a wording capable of making him feel responsible for the use he makes of his time. So I say:] Not so usual, because half the session has passed. [Then, changing my tone of voice to emphasize a certain disappointment:] And what you throw away, you can't really ever retrieve.

PATIENT: [with a less expressionless tone of voice:] If I'm not alive, at least I don't feel afraid of dying.

ANALYST: [I note with pleased surprise that Antonio is allowing me a glimpse of an anxiety of his – fear of dying – which he has so often denied by 'playing dead'. I try, however, to find a way of expressing myself that does not stop at welcoming his recognition of this anxiety, but can show him the damage he does to himself by pursuing the illusory possibility of sparing himself contact with anxiety. So I suggest:] If you're not living, you don't avoid anxiety about dying; instead you bring on yourself at once, by your own hand, the very death you're so afraid of and long to avoid.

PATIENT: [apparently somewhat revitalized:] Well, even if I'm not living, at least I'm biologically alive.

ANALYST: [I sense that this last verbalization has brought to the surface an important core lie that Antonio uses in relating to himself, i.e. that he can afford to treat himself as if he were dead, thus avoiding the fear of dying that a living person might have, since after all there is still the biological fact of his being alive to rescue him from actual death. This illusion of being rescued through biological life, without mentally confronting his anguish about and hatred of death, seemed to play a central role in his tendency towards silence in analysis. By means of his silence he affirmed his life on the biological level – since he was physically present – without, however, dealing with his psychological life, meanwhile imbuing his analysis with a sort of mental death. This way of relating to analysis – going to it and paying for it without actually making any use of it, indeed without paying the emotional and mental price for it – seemed to correspond to his parasitic way of relating to life generally, with the illusion of not paying the price of anxiety. So I observe:] The fact of being biologically alive doesn't save you, since your keeping yourself mentally dead has damaging consequences for your life itself, not the least of which is the danger of your killing yourself with your own hands in a moment of acute despair: the danger of suicide.

This sequence shows us the confusion – what Matte Blanco (1988) called a 'symmetrization' – of life and death which was leading the analysand to pursue a biological life that in fact corresponded to psychic death: life and death were thus rendered indistinguishable. Death was not recognized perceptionally on a realistic level, but the patient's tendency was also to obliterate the anxiety that might be produced by the discovery of it. As a consequence the perception of death was replaced by *acting out death against himself* – concrete thinking – *by keeping himself mentally dead, with the ultimate danger of acting out in suicide.*

In a subsequent session Antonio returned to some complementary aspects of these theories, highlighting his relationship with his corporeal space, when he declared: 'If we didn't have stomachs we'd live much better.' (After a moment he added, by way of self-correction) 'But actually I hadn't thought that if there's no stomach there's no life.'

The basically psychotic statement, and the corrective response from the non-psychotic part of his personality (Bion 1957/1967) are evidence of the evolution that our work in analysis had brought about, so that the analysand was now capable of maintaining an internal dialogue with his psychosis.

His statement correlating the absence of a vital organ with an absence of life is of interest because it seizes upon different elements which are inextricably related. Death, represented as the absence of a stomach, is treated – symmetrically – as if it were life, thus leading to the paradoxical conclusion that without a stomach, and hence without life, we would really live better. Since the stomach is an essential part of the body, Antonio's proposition could also be understood as: *If I didn't have a body I would live better.* But given that the body and life are indissolubly connected, Antonio could assert: *If I were not alive I would live better.* Or, in more general terms: *When one is dead one lives better, because one is not subject to the anxieties and dangers of life.*

Although these theories represent a glaring assault on common sense, they appear repeatedly in so-called difficult patients. One need but think of the importance such a theory can have in cases of ano-rexia, for instance, to the point where it supports the fundamental perversion whereby the most radical way of asserting one's desire to live is by dying of hunger. See, for example, the case of anorexia quoted in the chapter on emotional experience and infinity.

Working through the mental models and theories (Bion 1962; Lombardi 2003) involved in Antonio's life-denying orientation was a high point in the evolution of Antonio's analysis, which led to important changes in his life, such as a substantial reduction of anxiety and the disappearance of all references to the temptation of suicide, the total cessation of any form of gambling, as well as – on a more concrete level – the purchase of an apartment for himself and his family with the attendant exhausting move into the new apartment, which opened up new horizons for him. This was seconded, some-what later, by a greater commitment to his profession and a career advancement. In all, the analysis was completed in three and a half years, leaving the patient satisfied by the experience we had faced together in the course of that period.

Concluding remarks

As I reconsider some aspects that helped bring about a development in the case of Antonio, I am struck by the importance of forgoing a reconstructive perspective. The reconstruction of the past had been central to his previous analyses, but this had fostered an atemporal crystallization and a sterile repetition of emotional discharge. In his new experience with me, the patient was able to enter temporal real-ity and, by experiencing the present (Bion 1973/1990), to face him-self and the other realistically.

It also seemed significant that I did not let the patient abandon himself to a regressive state, thus avoiding, particularly during his silent periods, setting up a condition of isolation. For my part, I supported *a progressive orientation* rather than a regressive one, by actively stimulat-ing Antonio's interventions and associations. The psychoanalytic ideas that hinge on regression as the key to entering the atemporality of the unconscious levels (Freud 1900) strike me as captive to a century-old theoretical bias, without taking any account of the clinical evidence that a tendency towards regression and atemporality is part of the patient's disorder; neither do they bespeak any familiarity with the evidence that the unconscious plays a part, to a varying extent, in

214

every single mental act of ours (Matte Blanco 1975). Hence I consider the clinical validity of psychoanalysis to be connected primarily to its relationship with the reality principle (Freud 1911), which implies a linear conception of time, for which regression is not an option.

As regards content, the full *recognition of hatred*, and self-hatred in particular, gave an important boost to the development of the analysis. Antonio's denial of hatred, in fact, dangerously reinforced the thought defect related to his life-challenging theories. Perceiving hatred made it possible to reintegrate the sadistic components of his tyrannical and punitive superego into his ego, thereby modifying the serious weakness of his personality.

The exploitation of hatred as a structural element of his personality – what Bion would have called element *H* (1963) – also made it possible to effect a positive utilization of gambling, which was seen as evidence *not* of a destructive orientation *tout court*, but essentially, instead, of the patient's urgent need to prove to himself that he was alive through the excitement of gambling. A conventional and condemnatory interpretation of his hatred could easily have fostered a proliferation of guilt: a mechanism such as 'I am guilty of aggression, so I must continue to attack myself in order to atone for it.' The more we progressed in our analysis of his life-defying orientation, the more his compulsion to gamble diminished, until finally it disappeared altogether.

In the course of my clinical narrative I have especially stressed the importance of the analyst's *emotional participation*, or what Bion (1962) called the *reverie* function. My participation, by allowing glimpses of my affective life, steered clear of introducing the *rigid and artificial barrier of analytic neutrality*. Choosing neutrality would, in my opinion, have endorsed this analysand's defensive impermeability to emotions, thus blocking his evolution towards life and relational participation.

We have seen that when his silences appeared particularly rigid and immutable *I gave him some indication of the actual limits of my tolerance, reminding him of his responsibility* towards the analytic relationship and towards what would eventually become of his analysis. In such contexts I consider it important for the analyst to be willing to be oneself, as an amalgam of emotion and thought, allowing one's thought to be coloured by emotion and subjectivity. Thus I made use of my capacity *to think in the presence of emotions* (Bion 1962) as an important communicative and empathic bridge with the analysand.

This experience also contributed significantly – and we were able to talk about it together – to dispelling his fantasy that entering analysis implied a sort of protection offered by a psychoanalytic tutelary deity who facilitated the solving of one's problems simply by one's entering into contact with this numinous being, instead of regarding analysis, realistically, as an encounter with an actual person, requiring all the patient's resources of active collaboration in order to gain the experience of being part of a couple (the analytic couple) which is focused on facing and understanding the troubles that have led the patient to enter analysis.

It would seem that Bion, when faced with a silent patient, had recourse to irony, addressing his analysand in three different languages (cf. Grotstein 2007). Since I am not Bion, I found my own communicative style for this context, which took account of the problems introduced by the analysand's tendency to petrify, and which could instead lead him towards a *'non-mechanical', living participation in our intersubjective experience.* And indeed my comments on this occasion intentionally revealed my countertransference – as a conscious physiological response to interaction with the patient – thus using my emotions to strengthen the communicative impact of my analytic suggestions.

This experience appears to suggest that a carefully dosed amount of pressure from the analyst is connected to the very structure of psychoanalysis, which requires the use of thought as an instrument for activating mental growth – thought that involves 'spending' psychic energy, since it is based on the contents of a motor discharge (Freud 1911) – and connected as well to the very real need for the patient to set in motion a rescue operation on his or her ego functions in order to bring about some development. As Bion wrote, 'One is really putting pressure on the patient to grow up, not to remain a baby or a patient or a neurotic or a psychotic forever. *The analyst expects something from the patient besides just punctuality, fees and so on: he expects some improvement*' (1987, p. 5, my italics). I find this statement quite accurate, and strikingly in line with my own impression that a traditional neutral psychoanalytic approach may involve the danger of heading towards an interpretive dead end which is an end in itself. Psychoanalysis of this sort leads to fostering the severing of thought from action and from real life, with the inevitable result of either an impasse or interminable analysis. Whereas *what seems to me to be important in analysis is change*: emotional and symbolic working through is a fundamental springboard to catalyzing a real change which bears witness – concretely as well – to the resources of thought and the mental growth activated by the work done during sessions.

In the case of Antonio there was, in addition, a certain autistic element that tended to be strengthened by his resistance, to the point where he was in danger of creating the same impasse that had undermined his previous analyses. In the cases of adult patients who use autistic barriers, Tustin (1981) has stressed the importance of pre-verbal sensory pairs such as *hard* and *soft* in the context of analysis. I have repeatedly observed in my own experience that, particularly when primitive autistic levels are to the fore, the analyst is called upon to operate between extreme sensory opposites and must go to and fro, according to the context, between a 'soft' or rather sensitive and impalpable sensory participation and 'hard', or rather more taut and turbulent moments of communication, which pull the patient towards a recognition of the uncomfortable real perceptions which are surfacing in the session (cf. Lombardi 2003). Instead of floating on the cadences of Boccherini or Haydn, the analytic relationship makes its way across complex musical landscapes, passing through a dissonant and atonal emotional world more reminiscent of, for example, Mahler's symphonies.

Finally, in the clinical presentation we have seen how the careful and repeated *analysis of Antonio's internal theories*, as they related to his way of resorting to an internal deadness in order to escape from his anxieties, was decisive in bringing about a development related to his thinking defect (Bion 1962). By means of his personal system he would distil and reapply the modes he had had to resort to in the course of his difficult childhood. These modes, however, introduced damage that was greater than the damage he was trying to overcome, such as when he 'played dead/deadened himself' so as to avoid death anxiety: in this way he was, by his own hand, bringing about what he most feared, i.e. his death. This was indeed just a psychological death, but it ran the risk of becoming actual physical death when the spectre of suicide loomed.

My perspective takes into account the importance Bion (1962) attributes to the thought defect, so that it is not so much a blind death instinct that pushes the patient towards suicide as instead a primally self-protective instinct, although mediated by dangerously unrealistic and life-threatening theories. In a context of this sort, clinging to primitive modes of functioning leads to a state of non-differentiation in which a perilous confusion between life and death takes place (Lombardi 2007).

The unfolding of the non-repressed unconscious we met in the working-though with Antonio shows us that a living psychoanalysis needs to reinvent itself constantly if it is to stand up to the challenge of thought and existence and not succumb to the trap of a formalism that offers neither containment functions nor a vital thrust towards change.

Note

1   A wider version was published as Lombardi, R. (2010). Flexibility of the psychoanalytic approach in the treatment of a suicidal patient: stubborn silences as "playing dead". *Psychoanalytic Dialogues*, 20: 269–284.

References

Bion, W. R. (1957). Differentiation of the psychotic from the non-psychotic personalities. In *Second thoughts* (pp. 43–64). London: Karnac Books, 1967.

Bion, W. R. (1962). *Learning from experience*. London: Karnac Books, 1984.

Bion, W. R. (1963). *Elements of psychoanalysis*. London: Karnac Books.

Bion, W. R. (1970). *Attention and interpretation*. London: Karnac Books.

Bion, W. R. (1973). *Brazilian lectures*. London: Karnac Books, 1990.

Bion, W. R. (1979). Making the best of a bad job. In *Clinical seminars and other works*. London: Karnac Books, 1987.

Bion, W. R. (1987). *Clinical seminars and other works*. London: Karnac Books.

Damasio, A. (1999). *The feeling of what happens*. New York: Harcourt Brace.

Ferrari, A. B. (2004). *From the eclipse of the body to the dawn of thought*. London: Free Association Books.

Freud, S. (1900). The interpretation of dreams. *Standard Edition*, 4–5.

Freud, S. (1911). Formulations on the two principles of mental functioning. *Standard Edition*, 12.

Ginzburg A., & Lombardi R. (Eds.). (2007). *L'emozione come esperienza infinita*. Milan: Angeli.

Grotstein, J. (2007). *A beam of intense darkness*. London: Karnac Books.

Klein, M. (1957). *Envy and gratitude*. London: Tavistock.

Lombardi, R. (2003). Mental models and language registers in the psychoanalysis of psychosis. An overview of a thirteen-year analysis. *International Journal of Psychoanalysis*, 84: 843–863.

Lombardi, R. (2007). Sull'essere: dispiegamento della simmetrizzazione vita-morte. In A. Ginzburg & R. Lombardi (Eds.), *L'emozione come esperienza infinita*. Milan: Angeli.

Matte Blanco, I. (1975). *The unconscious as infinite sets.* London: Karnac Books.

Matte Blanco, I. (1988). *Thinking, feeling and being.* London: Routledge.

Seligman, S. (2007). Technique as a case-specific problem: reply to commentaries. *Psychoanalytic Dialogues*, 17(3): 375–384.

Tustin, F. (1981). *Autistic states in children.* London: Routledge.

Winnicott, D.W. (1960). Ego distortion in terms of the true and false self. In *The maturational processes and the facilitating environment.* London: Hogarth.

9

DEATH, TIME AND PSYCHOSIS[1]

Asymmetrical relations serve the function of barriers which permit the dif-
ferentiation between various concepts within the mind.
—Matte Blanco (1975, p.131)

In this chapter I hypothesize that *awareness of death* and *consciousness of time* play a decisive role in the analytic process and in the
mental growth of analysands with serious thought defects. Time
and death are structurally interconnected because they both refer
back to the perception of limits and the emerging from a formless
infinity. If treating psychosis is now, with the recent widening scope
of analytic practice, no longer an avoidable problem, we should
not forget that the working-through of time and death can play
an important role in the more common borderline and neurotic
conditions as well.

This assertion of mine does not directly imply anything about the
origin of psychosis, since it is a multi-factorial syndrome comprising
complex components of a biological as well as psychological nature,
which I do not mean to discuss here. The fascination that psychosis
exerts for psychoanalysis lies primarily in its mysterious side, or rather
in our awareness that what we do not know about it is infinitely
greater than what we know: a field worth exploring, without getting
discouraged by the limited and provisional nature of our knowledge.
In this context, the use of the word *psychosis* refers to the psychoanalytic perspective from which psychosis implies the predominance
of the instinctual forces of the id and the consequent conflict with
reality (Freud 1924a, 1924b), as well as to the common phenomenological implications of this internal imbalance that are encountered in

clinical psychiatry (mental confusion, delusions, hallucinations, loss of a sense of reality, etc.).

This work considers how these perceptions can serve to forge a more harmonious balance in the relationship between psychotic and non-psychotic areas (Katan 1954; Bion 1957/1967), becoming like powerful expressions of the reality principle (Freud 1911), as well as the first representatives of a limit placed on the oceanic and undifferentiated feeling characteristic of psychotic functioning[2] (Freud 1930). Such levels of mental functioning do not correspond to the more well-known and extensively explored Oedipal areas, but involve the opening up of new horizons of psychoanalysis which should be investigated with particular conceptual tools, in accordance with Loewald's prescient assertion, 'a great deal about early and archaic mentation can be learned from it' (1978, p. 506). The deepest levels involve a primal conflict between order and disorder (Prigogine & Stengers 1988), differentiation and nondifferentiation (Mahler & Furer 1968; Loewald 1978; Searles 1962; Kernberg 2003), and especially the finite and infinity (Bion 1970; Matte Blanco 1975). When it confronts the psychotic areas that have been infiltrated by denial of death and time, the analytic couple is called upon to confront an experience of confusion with no marked boundaries. In contexts of this sort the analyst must summon to his/ her aid a specific form of *reverie* (Bion 1962) aimed at elaborating very primitive annihilation anxieties (Winnicott 1974).[3]

If we use the concept of *logical class*, borrowed from set theory, for the mental functioning of the seriously disturbed patient (Matte Blanco 1975), we can consider the concepts of death and time in terms of their ability to represent the whole class of limit and hence in terms of their tractional effect on mental functioning: indeed, without limits there can exist neither being nor thought, as the philosopher Parmenides demonstrated, nor a consistent logical principle of non-contradiction such as Aristotle developed some time later. In this perspective of mental growth from the undifferentiated to the differentiated, acquiring the categories of death and time would decisively stimulate the growth of spatio-temporal organization, including the distinction between internal and external, and between past and present. The ability to differentiate opposes the tendency, in seriously disturbed patients, to use paleological thinking (von Domarus 1944; Arieti 1955), and thus facilitates the growth of normal processes of discrimination and of orderly asymmetrical logic (Matte Blanco 1975). The mental processes of discrimination support the activity of a mind which is endowed with specific functions of attention, perception, notation and memory, as well as the containment of motor discharge (Freud 1911; Bion 1962); at the same time, confronting limits fosters emotional growth and working through the depressive position (Klein 1935/1977).

The psychoanalyst who attempts to treat narcissistic psychoses, which are notoriously resistant to external influence, is fruitfully challenged to learn how to listen for and encourage the sane and creative components of the difficult patient and also how to help the patient listen to and trust his/herself. Death is, after birth, the most important event in human life. Some difficult patients, who are incapable of feeling alive and of distinguishing between life and death, can become aware of their existence thanks to the discovery of death as the expression of a burgeoning capacity to engage in reality testing (cf. Lombardi 2007a). The appearance of the perception of death and its related anxiety can be 'an "indicator" of having attained a rudimentary structuralization of self representation' (Spitz 1959), since the patient, perhaps for the first time, can become able to recognize 'that he had a self to lose' (Stolorow 1979, p. 205). But the problem of death and the fear of dying have nevertheless been somewhat neglected by psychoanalysis, and are instead generally treated as a neurotic anxiety, or subsumed under the so-called death instinct. The notions of subjectivity and internal life which psychoanalysis has revalued and promoted cannot be divorced from an acquired awareness of the limited nature of our individual human destiny.

My perspective here seems of a different orientation from the conceptualization of the death instinct (Freud 1920). While Freud – and, after him, the Kleinian school in particular – emphasize the instinctual aspect connected to hatred and destructiveness, I would myself like to stress the role played by the perceptual element connected to recognition of reality (cf. Lombardi 2010a). This does not imply the rejection of the destructive implications emphasized by Freud (1920), but rather a shift of focus from the theory of instincts to the *clinico-pragmatic problems created by the need to achieve mental growth in the difficult patient*: a perspective which seems to jibe, as we shall see, with some intuitive asides that appear in certain of Freud's works (1913, 1914, 1915b), in which he underscores the developmental and organizing roles of the perception of death.

The themes of death and time, in addition to being relevant to the psychoanalytic treatment of psychosis and serious cases generally, would seem to be indissolubly linked to the growth of subjectivity. The stimulus derived from the awareness of death and of the passage of time spans the whole of ancient Greek culture, from Homer (cf. the *Iliad*, VI, 146–149) to the tragedians, such as Aeschylus (*Prometheus Bound*), Sophocles (*Antigone*) and Euripides (*Alcestis*), and is intimately entwined with the foundation of philosophy (Plato, trans. 1969, p. 81). From then on, this correlation between the awareness of death and mental growth has variously affected the history of thought and psychoanalytic thinking (cf., e.g. Hegel 1807/1977; Freud 1915b, 1916; Rilke 1923; Heidegger 1927/1996; Becker 1973; Meyer 1973; De Masi 2004; Akhtar 2009), and so may warrant further study for this reason as well. In the course of this chapter I shall present a clinical case of psychosis which was treated psychoanalytically with four sessions a week for 12 years.

Fantasies of immortality and the awareness of death

Freud's works present us with dual and contradictory ways of considering death: on the one hand he tends to place it in the background, in contrast to the pre-eminent unconscious and its functioning, while on the other hand he fully supports the recognition of death as an important spur to mental growth. This contradiction seems to reflect the complexity of Freud's thinking and the multiplicity of viewpoints he employs, so that the same theme can reveal different implications according to the perspective he chooses in any given context. Starting from the viewpoint of the functioning of the unconscious, Freud notes, 'Hence the psycho-analytic school could venture on the assertion that at bottom no one believes in his own death, or to put the same thing in another way, that in the unconscious every one of us is convinced of his own immortality' (1915b, p. 289). Or, once again, 'What we call our "unconscious" – the deepest strata of our mind, made up of instinctual impulses – knows nothing that is negative, and no negation; in it contradictories coincide. For that reason it does not know its own death' (Ibid., p. 296). This viewpoint, according to which the thought of death is an intellectualization belonging more properly to philosophical speculation, seems nicely summed up in André Green's interpretation of Freud's thinking about death, according to which less courage is required to recognize one's own mortality than to recognize the limitations on consciousness that the existence of the unconscious establishes (1983, p. 256). Green shows us a side of

Freud which is *too* taken up by the intellectual defences which could get in the way of an emotionally consistent consideration of death and *too* eager to defend his discoveries about the Oedipus complex. A consequence of this approach is the fact that likening the fear of death to castration anxiety has led to an attitude towards death, on the part of some psychoanalysts, that minimizes its importance as a source of anxiety, as observed by Bonasia (1988) and Lasky (1990).

It should, however, be emphasized that Freud, in various passages, leaves the Oedipal straits behind him, sailing instead on the open seas of ontological implications. Freud wonders in *Thoughts for the Times on War and Death*, 'Would it not be better to give death the place in reality and in our thoughts which is its due?' (1915b, p. 299). This conscious contemplation of death, he then continues, 'hardly seems an advance to higher achievement, but rather in some respects a backward step – a regression; but it has the advantage of taking the truth more into account, and of making life more tolerable for us once again' (Ibid.). This reflection led him to transform the ancient adage '*si vis pacem, para bellum*' ('If you desire peace, prepare for war') into '*si vis vitam, para mortem*' ('If you desire life, prepare for death'). Thus Freud left little room for doubt that he considered the development of an awareness of death to be a critical element both for mental growth and for being able to experience life itself!

Freud's interest in exploring the subject of death emerges also in the brief but densely packed essay *The Theme of the Three Caskets* (1913), in which he examines a rich assortment of literary and mythological material – from *King Lear, Cinderella* and Apuleius' *Cupid and Psyche* to the Greek myths of the three Moirae and of Paris and Aphrodite – starting with the puzzle in *The Merchant of Venice* whereby Portia is obliged by her father's will to accept the suitor who chooses the right casket, the one of the three that contains her portrait. The right casket is not, however, the gold or the silver one, but the third, which is made of lead. The element common to this varied literary and mythological constellation is then apparently, according to Freud, that the lead casket corresponds to choosing one's own death, Mother Earth who takes us back into her womb. These myths would thus seem to Freud to express Man's awareness 'that he too is a part of nature and therefore subject to the immutable law of death' (p. 299).

In his work *On Narcissism* (1914), Freud identifies death as the weak link in the narcissistic mental structure: it is almost as if he were suggesting the possible clinical use of the perception of death as the way to foster progress towards mental growth in this kind of personality, which is otherwise notoriously resistant to object-cathexis and to external influence. In *Beyond the Pleasure Principle* (1920), Freud formulates the concept of the *death instinct*, which has subsequently been the subject of intense debate amongst supporting and attacking authors and schools.

Time and mental functioning

In addition to emphasizing the extraneousness of the idea of *death* to the unconscious, Freud equally emphasizes that the awareness of *time* is foreign to the unconscious. Time and death seem closely connected, in that it is the existence of time that applies limits to human existence, hence making it mortal. If, on the one hand, Freud (1932) states that there is nothing in the id that corresponds to the idea of time, on the other he finds the origin of the idea of time in the discontinuity of the functioning of the perception–consciousness, or *Pcpt.-Cs.* (Freud 1924a): a fact which seems particularly important if we correlate the atrophy of this idea in psychotic patients with their difficulty in activating their Pcpt.-Cs. Freud (1917) also finds a link between time and mourning, an experience for which the dimension of time is indispensable.[4]

A key work for Freud's appreciation of the importance of time is his essay *On Transience*, in which he states that the value of the latter 'is scarcity value in time. Limitation in the possibility of an enjoyment raises the value of the enjoyment' (1916, p. 305). But Man must come to terms with his 'need of immortality' and his 'revolt against mourning' in the face of the ephemeral nature of beauty. Even though time is conceptually linked to limits, transience and death, Freud underscores its decisive connection to life.

While the idea of death is, according to Freud, foreign to the unconscious, Melanie Klein (1952) maintains that the fear of annihilation exists in the unconscious and is the basis of anxiety: this fear is closely linked to the action of hatred, so that identification with the good breast is a basic point of organization for the primitive ego. For Klein, one's capacity for facing death depends on the state of one's internal world. A state of fragmentation and solitude, according to her, is experienced very early in life, and resurfaces repeatedly thereafter: with the looming of separations or the end of life, paranoid and depressive anxieties acquire greater force and good objects are in danger of being perceived as destroyed. Segal (1958) has analyzed in detail the death–related anxieties of an elderly patient, showing what psychoanalytic working–through can accomplish in these situations, while Jaques (1965) has explored the working–through of death in the context of the so-called mid–life crisis, when facing both the idea of the inevitability of death and the existence of destructive impulses: failing to work through this transition leads towards narcissism, greed and various kinds of destructive acting out. Bion (1966), on the other hand, interprets the theme of death anxiety, independently of object-loss, within the broader subject of the affective reaction to change. He emphasizes the conservative tendency of the primitive mind and the hatred of change that leads the patient to react catastrophically when faced with anything new. Destabilization takes place when the violence evoked by change cannot be 'contained' – which is in keeping with Bion's theory of the 'container/contained' interaction (Bion 1963). Even when, under the most favourable conditions, the breakdown is analytically controlled, there are advantages – according to Bion – to taking into account a theory of change based on the model of an explosion with expanding pressure–waves (Bion 1965).

One author who has particularly stressed the theme of death in relation to the containment of psychotic anxiety is Searles (1965), for whom no source of anxiety seems more powerful than the fact that *life is, by its very nature, limited,* to the point where, according to him, schizophrenia can be considered the desperate attempt to deny this aspect of the human condition.

Time, death and body–mind relation

The perspective of the body–mind relation (Aron & Anderson 2003; Liebermann 2000; Schilder 1950; Winnicott 1953/1958) in psychoanalytic research has recently become increasingly timely. I consider this vantage point complementary to the more established one of object relations, since a basic situation of conflict between body and mind can act as the central conflict in primitive mental states; consequently the therapeutic action of psychoanalysis aims principally at reducing the initially unbridgeable gap between these two intrasubjective components (Ferrari 2004; Lombardi 2002, 2005, 2007b, 2008, 2009a, 2009c, 2010b, 2011). The body–mind perspective enables us to glimpse the operation of the deepest areas of mental functioning and to focus on ontological themes such as those connected with life and death: according to this perspective, *death* is to be considered an attribute that pertains specifically to the *body*, whereas *the perception of death* lies, as a mental act, within the province of the *mind*.

When there is a serious internal conflict with dissociation between *body and mind*, these two systems *tend to be completely isolated from each other*, to the point where a specific working-through on the body-mind area becomes necessary if one is to establish a connection between them (see, e.g. Lombardi 2005, 2007b, 2009a). I have observed that one of the main functions of dissociation between body and mind is to *make the person in question impermeable to the anxieties activated by elements of reality*, such as those related to the passage of *time* and the existence of *death* (Kernberg 2008; Meissner 2007; Lombardi 2003b). In line with these observations I would hypothesize that the perception of death, with the anxiety this perception occasions for the ego, can thus have the important integrative function of introducing the first form of interaction or dialogue between body and mind, as well as playing an important intermediary role in consolidating a relationship between the two intrasubjective systems.

While the mind is subject to *atemporality*, which Freud (1900) describes as characteristic of unconscious functioning, *the body forces the mind* to face *linear time*, through recognizing, for example, such key events as birth and death, as well as important changes like adolescence and senescence, with their attendant physical manifestations. Thus psychoanalytic working-through that focuses on the body-mind relationship can play an important facilitating role in approaching and acquiring such an essential tool for thought as *time* (Kant 1781).

Unfortunately, limitations of space and the principally clinical focus of this chapter prevent me from discussing such extremely interesting contributions on the subject of time as those of Arlow, Loewald and Hanly, among others. I hope, nonetheless, that I have sketched in the intellectual background sufficiently to justify passing on to the clinical presentation.

A clinical case history

Caveat

I cannot proceed to the clinical section without a caveat: the reader must be aware of the inevitable problems that arise in attempting to summarize such a complex condition as is represented by a clinical case of psychosis, explored in its deepest and most contradictory implications; this complexity is not rendered less troublesome by the fact that this analysis was not conducted in English, and that translation unavoidably erects a kind of barrier. This clinical study is also conditioned by the Bionian approach that characterized the analysis, so that a limited degree of affinity the reader may feel with the attempt to observe in the absence of memory and desire (Bion 1970) can act as a further limitation. At the same time I feel that the advantages for psychoanalytic research that derive from the exploration of mysterious areas such as the most primitive levels of the mind may justify the request for a certain leniency on the part of the reader.

Rosa

Rosa was 25 when her parents brought her to see me for the first time, with a view to starting analysis. Of average height, with raven hair and marked features, she was good-looking despite some excess weight and a distinctly distrustful expression. About two years earlier she had had a severe psychotic crisis, with a long hospitalization. This episode was followed months later by a second period in the hospital after a suicide attempt (she had overdosed on prescription drugs). After these two hospitalizations, Rosa had sunk into a state of passivity and withdrawal, shut up at home just 'vegetating' and hardly communicating with anyone. Both her mother and her father had had many children and been widowed before marrying each other: Rosa was the second and last child of this second marriage. Her parents, retired and by now quite elderly, quickly adapted to this new situation, which provided the incidental benefit of not having to be separated from their youngest child. They had been urged to seek psychoanalytic help by the patient's elder sister, the only person who seemed aware of the extreme seriousness of the situation.

Some reconstructive aspects

In my general contextualization of the case, I shall have to introduce a historically inexact expedient by considering data that turned out to be significant, but that in fact emerged bit by bit over the course of time. In other words, only after many years of analysis did these data reveal their considerable weight, thanks to the containment that took place during the analytic narration of events, which were internally historicized by the patient only once they had been experienced and worked through in the *here and now* of the analytic relationship. My reluctance to hound the patient with reconstructive concerns was the result primarily of her quite long-lasting inability to orient herself in a historic dimension of her own, which was also the reason for my decision not to force intellectual activity of a reconstructive nature, so that we could instead foster the working through of the deepest levels, where disorganization and fragmentation prevail. In my experience, the significant past of seriously disturbed patients emerges unpredictably in the course of analysis, like fragments of shipwrecks emerging from the depths of the ocean. Thus one needs an analyst with a negative capability (Bion 1970), who can wait for the historical dimension to take shape asystematically and bit by bit, pulled along by the anomalous wave of events that have never been worked through. Finally, we should not lose sight of the fact that a reconstructive viewpoint cannot in itself exhaust the problem of psychosis: it can, however, if used within certain limits, be very helpful in shedding light on various actual elements that have characterized a patient's development. Moreover, a patient's communications about his/her past are often complex and polysemous and – in the presence of defects of thinking (Bion 1962) – can be used by the analyst first of all as mental models (Bion 1962; Lombardi 2003a) from which to draw indications about the patient's current mental functioning.

Rosa's father was strict and notably obsessive; as he aged his vision weakened until he became virtually blind, which seemed very much in keeping with his strong tendency towards denial. Her mother was weak and rigid at the same time: she suffered from serious diabetes which, during the years of Rosa's analysis, revealed psychosomatic implications. For example, it happened on one occasion that a grave diabetic imbalance was resolved, quite mysteriously, only after a brief mental imbalance of Rosa's, as if the emotions of hatred that Rosa confusedly expressed had allowed her mother, through projective identification, to regain contact with her own internal emotions and to establish a more stable psychosomatic equilibrium.

An alexithymic tendency (Sifneos 1973; Taylor 1987) or an inclination toward so-called *pensée opératoire* (Marty 1980), with its related tendency toward denial and the somatization of conflicts, thus seemed characteristic of both parents. Rosa herself had, when she was young, had a duodenal ulcer, which would get worse when the season changed. This somatic symptom disappeared entirely in the course of her analysis, which seems to support the theory that her repeated psychotic explosions had allowed her to work through conflicts which would otherwise have remained trapped in a pre-mental area.

Rosa's early relationship with her mother had an abnormally prolonged symbiotic phase: her mother tried to wean her when she was about two, but just at that time the family moved to a different city, so breast-feeding returned in full force until she was three. Since her teething did not prevent her mother from continuing to nurse her, it is quite likely that Rosa's later tendency to make little use of her teeth for chewing her food dates from the time of her prolonged breast-feeding. When Rosa was 20 she was diagnosed as having a very faulty occlusion, due to the lack of normal dental attrition from chewing. This failure to use her teeth, when seen together with her apparently tranquil temperament before her crisis, seemed, I found, to coincide with her lack of familiarity with the whole area of aggressive emotions. Feelings of hatred, on the other hand, characterized her analytic experience quite concretely and explosively.

Rosa's delayed weaning appeared to fit right into the climate of marked denial – as a sort of family policy – of endings and of mourning, fostered particularly through contact with a maternal personality very like what has been described as the 'dead mother' (Green 1986). From what she narrated in the central period of her analysis it emerged that the spouses of her parents' first marriages were never named, although they continued to be present, like unidentified shadows, in photographs that would occasionally turn up at home. A contributing factor to this disinclination to face the reality of death, loss and mourning was the death by drowning, just a few months before Rosa's birth, of one of her father's sons at the age of 17. This traumatic event burst into her analysis during one of her acute phases: only after this apparition of her dead brother in our sessions – as we shall see further along in this clinical account – did it become possible for Rosa to work through the mourning for this brother and consequently to include in the reconstruction of her history even a part of it that took place before she was born.

During her adolescence there emerged a strong tendency towards isolation and an unstable relationship with her peers. She also began to show a pathological Oedipal attachment to her father – in which he himself was distinctly complicitous with his youngest daughter – as a result of which Rosa worked in his office, gradually inheriting all his duties, until the business closed. At the time of her first delusional outburst Rosa had only just changed jobs. The psychotic explosion took place in the midst of a complex work situation: thanks to her role as book-keeper, Rosa had discovered a falsification of the balance-sheet as the result of a theft effected by one of the managers. On the very day when she would have been called on to testify before the board of directors, she had her first crisis, which required her hospitalization.

Quite far along in her analysis it became clear that Rosa herself had devised a psychotic system in which a key role in her internal phantasies and theories was played by theft of a very particular kind, 'the theft of time'. After this acute phase which allowed us to work through that 'theft', it became possible to reconstruct the condition of her first psychotic outburst, i.e. that the discovery of a thief in the company had coincided with the breach of Rosa's internal dissociative barrier, as a result of which her healthy and honest core had catastrophically crashed into more primordial and distorted aspects of her personality.

These data may perhaps help the reader to follow the clinical account that follows, and may also provide a logical thread for a part of the fragmented material from the explosive phases which I shall be presenting. It should be borne in mind that there is a fundamental difference between the neutral data one can collect from a good medical history in the initial phase of a psychosis and the perspective one can gain after going through various acute episodes dominated by violence and confusion. Consciousness in the so-called pre-catastrophic state is, in fact, emotionally neutral, impersonally theoretical and without implications of actual change for the patient. Post-catastrophic consciousness brings with it – after living through the catastrophe that has brought about the consciousness – a decisive change, such as liberation from, or a distinct reduction of, the psychosis.

We should also not lose sight of the invariant component (Bion 1965) looming behind the particular characteristics of this case, which spurred me to present the case here in relation to the impact on the development of the personality derived from the working through of death and time – a circumstance that had important implications for mental functioning, as I have confirmed in other cases which I have had the chance to observe.

The first years of analysis

When we began a four-session-a-week analysis, Rosa seemed emotionally absent and distrustful. She spoke of her hospitalization with difficulty, and maintained that she had suffered from an organic epileptic syndrome. When I sought to clarify this confusion, explaining the psychological nature of her illness as compared to the organico-neurological nature of epilepsy, it emerged that the patient had trouble distinguishing mental phenomena from organic occurrences – as a result of which she experienced the two kinds of phenomena practically as if they were the same thing. We worked for three months, but after an initially uneasy relationship, Rosa retreated into total silence for about a month before the Christmas break, and did not respond to my attempts to reach her. After the holidays Rosa had her family inform me of her decision not to continue. She reappeared about a year and a half later: in the meantime she had gone to a colleague for treatment. This period seemed to have served her as an occasion to develop and become aware of her own wishes, with the result that she asked me to start up her analysis again. She said she was terrified by the intensive rhythm of the four-session week and persisted in asking to begin with two sessions, working up gradually to four. I consented, but in our very first session she had a sudden psychotic outburst with confusion, motor agitation and delusional thought disturbance; hence I decided to pass on at once to four sessions so as to be able to work through the acute phase psychoanalytically, as I have described doing in other such cases (Lombardi 2003a, 2005, 2007b). Her analysis continued with this frequency for its entire duration, which was 12 years, with the additional support of a team of two colleagues: a psychiatrist who oversaw her pharmacological treatment and a consultant psychoanalyst for the family. The psychiatrist diagnosed a schizophreniform disorder and followed the current medico–psychiatric praxis in her pharmacological treatment.[5] The assistance given by the psychiatrist and the coordination and containment provided by my colleague who looked after the family were decisive elements in avoiding further hospitalizations during the resurfacing of acute symptoms, thus protecting the continuity and regularity of her analysis. Most notably, the development that took place during the last years of her analysis made a gradual reduction of her medicines possible, to the point where, having shown a stable clinical condition while trying out a significant period without the

protection of her pills, she was able to suspend her psychopharmaco-
logical treatment altogether.

In the course of this analysis Rosa presented four periods, lasting
several months each, of psychotic destabilization, during which there
emerged important elements of the working through, consolidated
in subsequent sessions in non-turbulent phases. It took, moreover,
almost four years from the start of her analysis for Rosa to resolve
the profound dissociation which caused her to deny the existence of
the psychotic periods and to fail to recognize as her own the psychic
elements that emerged during these crises.

One can perhaps imagine the exertion, the enormous emotional
cost, the personal risk and the discipline involved in exercising a *reverie* function (Bion 1962) as Rosa's development proceeded. In the
course of the analytic process the analyst in fact 'becomes' (Bion
1970) the patient, discovering in him/herself broader implications of
his/her own psychotic zone: an exploration begun during the analyst's own analysis. Prolonged contact with a patient's catastrophic and
chaotic state is very trying for the analyst, and can determine important personal choices.

For me the most immediately perceptible aspect of the analytic
relationship during the first few years of Rosa's analysis was having to face an inundating hatred that tested the limits of my powers of containment, particularly in her moments of negativism and
autistic alienation. Hatred in the countertransference – as Winnicott
(1947/1958) called it – generally took the form of violent homicidal fantasies about my patient, which emerged in part as a reaction
to the almost unbearable sense of paralysis and total inertia that she
communicated to me. The way I felt gave me some indication of the
unconscious and unthinkable homicidal hatred, particularly towards
herself, that held her in its grip. This mental experience of mine was
not, initially, clearly reflected by any similar feeling in the analysand:
hatred was not among the conscious elements she reported, nor did
she respond to my attempts to lead up to this feeling, either in an
absolute sense, by her mentally recognizing hatred, or in relation to
the transference relationship with me. On the other hand, Rosa, during our sessions in the first years of her analysis, often experienced
transitory states of extreme physical discomfort (such as nausea, retch-
ing, chest pain, stomach ache, etc.), with *no* corresponding *representation* connected with her emotions, despite my repeated attempts to
stimulate verbalization and recognition: it was as if the emotional

world had foundered on concrete somatic levels. Even when these somatic symptoms seemed connected with her experience of separation from analysis, my attempts to interpret them in this light were of no particular help and even threatened upon occasion to be counterproductive. Only with further years of analysis did it become possible to engage in the 'unfolding' of these proto-emotions which had taken on such distinctly physical characteristics and had had to remain concrete (Ferrari 2004).

Some aspects of the third psychotic breakdown

I shall be dealing here for the most part with what emerged in the course of the fourth psychotic crisis during her analysis, which evinced more clearly mental elements with more developed and recognizable representative equivalents. The principal themes had been foreshadowed during her third crisis, so I shall discuss it briefly first.

This significant third crisis, which took place between the fourth and fifth years of her analysis, began with her disquieting statement, 'I've gone back to loving myself again!' I was greatly struck by this declaration because it seemed to suggest the idea of a *constructive potential* of psychosis, which was, however, at odds with the danger represented by ego submersion due to panic and thought fragmentation. In a subsequent session Rosa suddenly interrupted her confused utterances, turned towards me and said, 'I have a pistol in my pocket.' For a moment I was prey to a terror of being shot dead, but I asked her, calmly, what pistol she was talking about. She answered, 'Truth'.[6]

The correlations between *love and a psychotic crisis*, and *a pistol and the 'truth'*, which Rosa expressed at the start of this psychotic episode, seemed to me to refer to the positive value of the experience of *catastrophic change* (Bion 1970) which the analysand had experienced in the course of her acute episode and thus, more generally, to highlight the association between explosive emotions and the emergence of new insights that are essential to mental growth.

She expressed one of her insights, for example, as follows: 'Every day I cry; I look death in the face every day and I cry. [screaming] This is what you wanted from me when I came in here. Right?' With this communication she was attributing to me her expectation that analysis would lead her to approach her fears of dying and the schizo-paranoid anxieties linked to her depression (Klein 1935/1977).

234

The devastating violence and emotional chaos that Rosa brought to her sessions in these phases of her analysis transmitted an indescribable sense of laceration, to the point where the fear of death (which seemed an immediate danger) affected her no more than me, as a human being.

This third crisis seemed to close with the distinctly positive outcome of greater contact with life, which, in external reality, meant forming a stable and dependable emotional relationship with a young man, and work relations in which she was respected and esteemed. Rosa described this change in her characteristically original way:

PATIENT: First there was everything, but there was no Rosa. Now Rosa is there. First red was green for me, green was red. Not now! Red is red and green is green. See: this is what I've learned. I've learned that if I weigh 68 kilos [150 pounds] I can't say I don't weigh that much. Things are what they are and that's it! This is what I've learned. The world is simple: everybody wants to make it complicated, but it's simple.

In this direct and unadorned way Rosa asserted her achievement of contact with 'reality' (Freud 1911) and with 'truth' (Bion 1970), which she had accomplished by means of a first gradual approach to herself, her emotions and anxieties, thanks to our work up to then in analysis. The growth of the non-psychotic part of her personality (Bion 1957/1967) she had consequently brought about could now make possible a further confrontation with the deepest aspects of her psychosis, which would involve the working through of death and her recognition of the value of time, affects and life itself.

The fourth psychotic crisis during analysis: the grey men and the theft of time

A further psychotic explosion spanning the sixth and seventh years of analysis – the *fourth acute crisis* since we started – seemed like a possible new occasion for advancing change and mental growth by dealing with catastrophe.

We'll start by looking at a few passages from the session in which, for the first time, Rosa mentioned the *grey men*. Only later did this theme become comprehensible, but I think it's illuminating to see the context in which it first appeared. In this session Rosa was moving restlessly about the room, transmitting a strong psychotic anxiety which I myself, at certain points, felt physically, in the form of having trouble breathing. Time seemed to stretch out infinitely and the session seemed endless, as did the anxiety I was prey to. Rosa's speech alternated between confused, incomprehensible ravings and, occasionally, a recognizable statement. In one of these latter moments she said:

PATIENT: What is all this about grey men? [Pause] Now there are no more grey men: I don't let anyone steal my time from me any more. I eat, I smoke, I pee: [yelling] I'm alive.

I couldn't understand what Rosa was trying to tell me with her reference to the grey men. I asked her for an explanation, but there was no answer to my request. What I managed to understand was that the analysand was laying claim to a desire to be alive, with a life that was defined in terms of physical experience (eating, peeing, smoking), which was in contrast to her anxiety about time being stolen from her. The *appropriation of her own body* (Lombardi 2005, 2007b, 2008, 2009a) and the functions associated with it proceeded in conjunction with the *appropriation of her own time* ('I don't let anyone steal my time from me any more'). Shortly thereafter, Rosa, still wandering about the room, continued:

PATIENT: I'm pissed off, Doctor, and I can't take being pissed off like this. [She screams senseless words.] Now *I* am me: I'm sad, I'm happy, but I'm still me. I'll show you my photograph ... [She produces a photo in which she is smiling.] You were handsomer when I first came to you.

ANALYST: [I am astonished by her perception of the continuity of our relationship, together with her participatory recognition of the passage of time.] Now you also make room for hatred, for being pissed off, instead of idealizing. I too can cease to be idealized and just be, for you, a real and separate person for whom you can feel hatred.

PT: Exactly, now I'm alone, I'm separate from you. It's a great thing, being alone: I can live my own life, with my own house. I need a center of gravity: ears, eyes, nose, touch, taste. This is my center of gravity.

AN: [From the passage of time Rosa had gone on to a recognition of space and how it separates, so I commented:] If you respect your emotions you can retrieve your body, your sense organs: a chance to think instead of exploding outwards.

After she had established her appropriation of *bodily space* and of *time*, it was the experience of *emotions* such as hatred, sadness and joy that allowed Rosa to establish *her own identity*. By establishing herself in space-time and in her emotions, Rosa was able to realize a relation based on *being differentiated from me*. She started with a first mirroring of herself, by recognizing herself in her photograph, then she found a reflection of herself in my appearance, by placing me and herself in space-time and noting in me the effect of passing years on one's body ('You were handsomer when I first came to you'). I had, in fact, changed from what I had been six years earlier: I was bigger, fleshier, and in this physical change in me the patient registered an equivalent to the years that had gone by. In this way Rosa included me in her working through of the passing of time, before returning to herself and to being alone in the presence of someone else (Winnicott 1958/1965), and finding her 'center of gravity' in the functioning of her sense organs (Freud 1911; Bion 1962). Thus in this sequence the patient resisted the activity of the psychotic realm and of lies (what she called 'the theft of time') through *her progressive retrieval of her body, her emotions and her sense organs* as organizers of her mental functioning, in a dynamic oscillation between recognition of herself and of the other.

But let's look at another session, some weeks thereafter, in which Rosa brought me photos of her new house and described details of it to me, commenting that it was what she had constructed with her work and her suffering. Her explosive tendency was less extreme, but the whole session was still permeated by an intense anxiety that was very hard to bear.

PATIENT: [She suddenly holds her wrist up to my face and exclaims:] See how beautiful this watch is? Look at it, there's a four-leaf clover!

ANALYST: What meaning do you attach to that?

PT: Read *Momo* by Michael Ende! [Suddenly changing the subject:] They've cut down the medlar. And you know what I've planted in its place? A lemon tree. A lemon has a bite to it.

AN: There's 'a bite to it' for you too, and you feel pain, in accepting time and change. But thanks to this pain you can open up to time: to time that moves ahead just as the hands of a watch move ahead. This enables you to live, to open up to the four-leaf clover of life. [I note that breaks, or interruptions, disappear, making way for continuity, when she can stand feelings that are 'biting' and off-putting like a lemon. I find her interest in her watch and in time altogether very positive.]

Despite a slight irritation at Rosa's intrusive gesture and her exaggerated and excited tone of voice, I felt deeply moved by her showing me her watch and reporting that she had planted a new tree, which I saw as very creative and positive. And indeed this sequence began with an explicit reference to time, objectified in the watch (see also Bonaparte 1940; Lombardi 2003b), which met with Rosa's approbation as something positive and fortunate, just as finding a four-leaf clover is commonly perceived as a harbinger of good luck. Thus the analysand was signalling to me that she was ready to make room for the idea of *time* and even to approve of it. It was at this point that she referred to the book by Ende, followed by a reference to loss ('They've cut down the medlar'), and by an openness to change, which seemed to bring with it a tolerance for frustration (the biting lemon).

It was thus that I first heard of *Momo* by Michael Ende. When I later came to read it, I discovered to my great surprise that the theme of the *grey men* came from this book and that Rosa had simply borrowed it. Her use of a literary element evinced a relation to culture as an important *transitional area* (Winnicott 1971) for organizing communication and an exchange of experiences. This confirmed my feeling that Rosa's new confusional explosions, although dominated by an anxiety which I found close to intolerable, was of a less pathological nature than her psychotic agitation and bizarre speech might have led one to believe. Hence Rosa's psychotic explosion was, I felt, to be seen as part of a continuum between the extremes of chaos and disintegration and relatively integrated ordinary emotional experience, rather than as a deterioration characterized by pathological thinking.

Despite being classified as a children's book, *Momo* is a complex metaphoric presentation of the emotional and human impoverishment of people who are entirely taken up by the concrete world and profit, and who neglect the human capacity for listening and sharing, which is represented in the book by Momo, a little girl who succeeds in foiling the plan of the grey men (grey because they lack emotional colour) to take over the world. So Rosa used the character of Momo – the little child who, with the help of a few friends, fights the power of the grey men – as a sort of model for her internal conflict, in which *the values of emotionality and regard for time, loss and mourning, as well as the ability to have human relationships, struggled against anonymity disguised as efficiency and emotional coldness*: Momo[7] was a model with which Rosa felt she could identify.

We can now consider another session, in which Momo made a further appearance. It was just after the break for summer vacation.

PATIENT: I dreamed about my father's head with a blade driven into it. The blade was driven in on the ground. This is the nightmare I never had the courage to tell you about. Yesterday I ate a dish of pasta and clams, with sauce. You couldn't see the clams. [Then, after a pause] I'm hungry. I could eat a nice dish of pasta with hot sauce. [In Italian this is called *all'arrabbiata*, made 'the angry way'.] With hot peppers. My mother is allergic to hot peppers, but I like them.

ANALYST: You recognize your hatred: the hatred you feel for me, as well as your hatred for your father. And this hatred, instead of bringing on an allergy, can nourish your mind and help it to grow, as you separate yourself from your parents and from me.

PT: Do you know *Momo* by Michael Ende? Read it. He's a philosopher, as far as I'm concerned he's a philosopher. There are these grey men. I was reading it on the subway and I couldn't stop crying. I cried the whole time.

AN: You take nourishment from pain: from the pain of time which passes. That's why you're no longer like the grey men, as you were when you tried to do away with your feelings and also with reality, which you didn't like.

PT: [At this point Rosa reports that she has been to see a gynaecologist, a fact which is connected to her sexual activity as an adult woman, a persona she had utterly disowned during the first period of her analysis. Then she

adds:] I met you when you were young. I can see when
I look at you that years have passed. I remember, in your
old office I used to smell an door of steaks cooking. [She
cries throughout the entire session.]

Rosa's mode of expression was extremely troubled, conveying a
great charge of anxiety. I found her physical presence in the session
particularly invasive because of her tendency to move restlessly about
the room, as if she were physically occupying all the available space.
Her communications were also more fragmented than I can indicate
here, with the result that it cost me considerable mental effort to
put them together. Her father with a blade driven into his head in
her dream seems in part to suggest her hatred for her father and its
modulations in the transference. At the same time, on a deeper plane,
the dream seems to depict Rosa's psychotic-level homogeneous
and indivisible mind, which was just beginning to be permeated by
asymmetrical elements of logical differentiation and spatio-temporal
organization (Matte Blanco 1988), and to make a first attempt at *symbolic order* (Lacan 1953–54).[8]

When Rosa stated that she was not allergic to hot peppers she
demonstrated her increased ability to metabolize hatred – an ability
she had acquired in six years of analysis – so that nourishing herself
with hatred (the *pasta with hot peppers*, in *angry sauce*) enabled her to
organize some form of triangulation in relation to her father and
mother. The reference to the subway gives us an image of a Rosa who
can accept solitude and find her way in the world. At this point Rosa
referred explicitly to the psychoanalytic relationship, in a context in
which we can clearly see both the nourishing element that she associated with the analytic rapport ('the door of steaks cooking'), and
the acquisition of a historico-temporal perspective in which to place
our rapport ('I can see when I look at you that years have passed').

When she refers to *Momo*, we see at work the *basic communicational
style* of a psychotic analysand, who does not – as a neurotic analysand
might – describe the most important themes of the book at length,
but instead offers the analyst her own elaborations, expecting him
then to do his share from his own perspective. If the neurotic can
be said to respect a shared reality to a greater extent, and to be more
concerned about the response and understanding of the other-than-
oneself – as a result of which, not by chance, the neurotic needs
dreams (Freud 1900) in order to approach the deepest and totally

egotistical levels of his mental functioning – the psychotic, instead, can use his communications in a dream-like way primarily to give voice to his inner world (Bion 1962). To paraphrase the painter Paul Klee (1968), we might say that the psychotic does not reproduce the visible world, but she makes it visible by means of an internal creative movement: in this sense the psychotic's communication tends to be guided chiefly by the need to organize what is spurring her must urgently from within – and, for the listener, this often involves finding her communications puzzling. In a clinical context in which words have a specific weight, the way Rosa speaks of the author of the book ('He's a philosopher') seems to suggest that something 'philosophic', such as *consciousness of self* or the capacity for reflection on her own life, was starting up in the analysand herself. It was not by chance that *Knowing Oneself* was a starting point of Greek philosophy.

The eye at the bottom of the sea

I shall now consider the material that emerged in the course of a subsequent period, in which there was an intensification of Rosa's emotional violence during our sessions, with screaming, crying and violent acts such as banging on the walls of my office with her fists. During this period, death-related themes frequently resurfaced: it was as if being freed from the ascendancy of the *grey men* had heightened Rosa's ability to contact emotions and had shown her the way to a deeper working through. She alternated between moments of being stretched out on the couch and others in which she wandered agitatedly about the office or went to the bathroom to rinse her hands and face, and she participated only fitfully in dialogue. I, meanwhile, shared her fragmented states and great pain, and sought to introduce mental bulwarks against her chaos by leading her speech towards some form of dialogue; I analyzed her tendency towards psychotic denial when it was clearly apparent; at other times I stressed the value of her perceptions.

A sudden aggravation of the conflict was evident on her return after a weekend break. That Monday, I opened the door to find Rosa with a glazed and wild-eyed look, while I glimpsed in the background the worried expression of her husband, who had accompanied her to my office. Rosa stepped in with a cautious tread, as if she were walking through a thick fog, transmitting a feeling of profound agitation. I had to restrain my surprise as quickly as possible, so as to

241

devote my resources to following her internal movements. As soon as she had stretched out on the couch she said:

PATIENT: The first dead person I saw was called Mario. [Pause] I lost an eye.

ANALYST: Seeing death makes you suffer, but you can use your eyes to see it instead of blinding yourself. Otherwise you suffer twice as much.

PT: I feel very sick, I have to spit it out. I'm about to throw up.

I had no idea who Mario was, but this was hardly the first time I had found myself faced with Rosa's mysterious communications. Just a few sessions later I realized that he was Rosa's half-brother who had drowned shortly before she was born and whom she had never mentioned to me.

As I attempted to establish some sort of meaningful relation between the elements that emerged in the verbal material, I noticed that there was a correlation between the perception of death ('the first dead person I saw') and the immediate defence by means of denial ('I lost an eye'). Her mental movements took place with extreme rapidity in an area on the border between the conscious and the unconscious characterized by concreteness. I thought that the blinding might reinforce her psychotic tendency towards denial, so I verbalized the anxiety connected with suffering ('Seeing death makes you suffer'), emphasizing the value of 'seeing' as an organizing factor that could contain anxiety.

I observed that her answer to my intervention showed some inclination to work through her pain, or rather to 'spit it out'; however, at the same time I felt my head spinning and my stomach turning, as if *I* were about to vomit, despite all my efforts to restrain myself, so that I had to start breathing slowly and deeply to contain my physical discomfort. This made it clear how intense the projective identification at work in the session was, but it seemed essential to the analysand's containing and transforming her contact with unthinkable anxiety. The atmosphere was dramatic. I took a deep breath and said:

ANALYST: Even if you vomit it up, your pain will continue to exist. If instead you manage to tolerate it, you can assimilate it a little bit at a time.

242

PATIENT: Mary Poppins is on her way. [She starts to sing.] With a spoonful of sugar, all the medicine goes down, the medicine goes down . . .

AN: [I supposed that I was the Mary Poppins figure, the nursery governess who would add a little 'sugar' to make the bitterness of pain more palatable, so I said:] Being here with me can help you to assimilate your pain.

PT: So, am I supposed to be the dry-nurse then?

AN: [I observed that Rosa was using the first person as a pointed reference to herself, as if she wanted to emphasize *her own ability* to nurse herself through her pain, as opposed to *my* ability. So I tried to shift the standpoint of my previous comment, placing Rosa in the foreground.] By accepting your pain, you are taking care of yourself just as a mother takes care of her baby.

PT: [At this point Rosa began to cry, and slowly started to calm down. Then she said:] About this you're right. [Both the easing of her emotional tension and her symbolic reply about being the dry-nurse seemed to confirm the shift in standpoint away from me, with a positive emphasis on her internal maternal ability, rather than on my external analytic intervention. She then went on:] I aborted Serena. I aborted her so many times.

AN: [I sensed that she was in great distress; I imagined that she had experienced her emotional explosions as abortions and her agitation as proof of her hopelessness at mothering. Hence I assumed that this 'Serena' referred to an emotional state, rather than to a person, as if she, in keeping with her idealized and perfectionistic criterion, would have perforce to be 'serene' in order to be acceptable to herself as a mother. So I said:] By allowing room for pain you do lose your 'serene' state; however, this is not an abortion, but is instead a constructive way of recognizing your real feelings of laceration, feelings that are like children whom you can bring up.

With my interventions I was trying to unfold (see Matte Blanco, 1975, on the unfolding of the unrepressed unconscious[9]) the massive symmetry that was preventing Rosa from expressing herself in a recognizably logical and consistent manner.

243

After this sequence Rosa got up from the couch, picked up the tissues that were wet with her tears, placed them on the flower stand next to the flowers and started singing songs I was unable to identify. It occurred to me that Rosa was equating her tears with the flowers and recognizing the value of her pain, so that her emotions, which she had previously seen as aborted infants, were now transformed into flowers that blossomed in her mind. I suggested as much, but I could not make out her response, because she spoke very quietly and confusedly. Her singing her songs was quite touching, in part because there was no remaining sign of her initial violence: indeed she had taken on a more accepting, almost affectionate attitude towards herself. Thanks to her burgeoning maternal faculty, catalyzed by analytic *reverie*, Rosa succeeded in *activating a mind's eye*, which could tolerate the perception and fear of death.

Seeing death with binocular vision

In the following session Rosa was still agitated and confused. She started by taking up the subject of death again.

PATIENT: In my life I've met far too many dead people. My mother sees only grey, I see red, green, yellow, orange . . . [then, after some confused speech:] I was looking for Giorgio's eye, but it was at the bottom of the sea.

The *mother who sees grey* seemed connected to both the *lost eye* and the theme of the *grey men*: a model of an internal mother intended as the personification of a psychotic internal object which denied both death and life. Against this level of *grey psychosis*, Rosa set up a willingness to activate the non-psychotic area (Bion 1957/1967), which she had learned about doing in the course of our analytic experience together, as she opened up to real perceptions and to the colours of feelings and of life ('I see red, green, yellow, orange').

In terms of external reality, Giorgio was a friend of Rosa's with a glass eye who had died in a motorcycle accident. Rosa's previous interpretation of Giorgio's end was that he had died in this accident because of his partial blindness, whereas if he had been able to see with both eyes he would have survived. In this context Giorgio's eye functioned as a mental model (Bion 1962; Lombardi 2003a) representing the conflict between denial and perception in the presence of the emerging discovery of death ('In my life I've met far too many dead people').The eye *at the bottom of the sea* thus seemed to represent Rosa's eye which could *see death,* and yet bear the disruptive pain attendant upon this perception.Whereas Rosa's psychotic blindness in the face of actual death had in the past produced a mental paralysis (psychic death) with the risk of suicide (death acted out), now, by contrast, Rosa seemed to be acquiring 'binocular' vision (Bion 1965), in which her emotional eye, which she had salvaged from the bottom of the sea, enabled her to bear her catastrophic emotions in the face of death and thus to have access to her actual life.

A most important particular of this acute phase was Rosa's consistent ability to note my presence and my input, and in an affectionate and grateful way which had never previously appeared: a significant element of perceptual capacity and 'binocular' vision in relation to *otherness*. It was indicative, for example, that, just at the end of the session I have presented, Rosa said, 'I thank you, Doctor, for putting up with me yet again this time,' and, in a subsequent session, 'You are my friend, a friend in my solitude, a friend I had never found before.'

In this phase of Rosa's analysis, her ability to remain connected to a perception of death and to a maternal acceptance of the essential experience of pain played an essential part in the construction of her identity, whereas rejecting death had led to her rejecting herself and losing her identity. Precisely this *conflict between acceptance and rejection of herself* in relation to the extent of her willingness to accept the fear of death became clear in a subsequent phase of our work together, as exemplified by the following statement:

PATIENT: Bastard, I'm a bastard because I don't recognize myself. [Then, turning and speaking directly to me:] *Spoon River.* Doctor, do you know *Spoon River?* It's the story of lots of tombstones in a small-town cemetery. On my tombstone we'll write, 'She wasn't really a fool, but she was a little bastard.'

Once again she employed her literary allusion – this time to Edgar Lee Masters – in a most original way, so that what the Italian author Cesare Pavese wrote of the American poet is true of her too, i.e. that 'death – the end of life' becomes a symbol which is 'nailed onto the soul for all time', and hence a symbol of life and identity.

After this fourth acute dramatic episode, Rosa did not present any further acute crises, apart from one transitory confusional period on the brink of the end of her analysis. After 12 years of intense analytic work, she finished her analysis having essentially recovered her vital potential, and in subsequent years she was able to use her own resources to deal with difficult situations, such as the death of her father and her mother, and she got in touch with me to tell me about these important changes and thank me for everything I had done for her.

Discussion and conclusion

Grey time, still ageing, teaches all things.
(Aeschylus, *Prometheus Bound*, l. 981)

In the cultural world, more often than we at times realize, we touch on subjects connected with a creative awareness of death. Even as I started to write these lines, for example, I was struck by the interest in and relevance to this subject of two important exhibitions. The first is the one-man show that MoMa in New York dedicated in 2009 to the great Belgian artist James Ensor: as you walked in you saw an enormous wall with a reproduction of the artist's *calling-card*, a sketch of four figures bearing on their shoulders *a coffin*, on which, in script, we read his name, as if he were indicating his awareness of his own mortality as the driving force behind his own creativity and subjectivity. At the same time, the Asian Museum in San Francisco was devoting an important show to the samurai, and it was my visit there that revealed to me the dual aspect of connoisseur and warrior that characterizes the samurai spirit. For their rigorous and inflexible ethos it seems to have been decisive to regard the passing scene *as if one were seeing it from the perspective of one's own death*. An awareness of death was to be the constant companion of the samurai throughout his life: living with death was also essential as a military discipline, in that consciously taking death for granted allowed the samurai to face the fray without jeopardizing the relaxed physical tone that was indispensable for controlling his own body in battle.[10] Curiously enough, I noticed, what I had brought along to read on my coast-to-coast flight was Philip Roth's latest novel, which is all about a man's never-ending battle with his own mortality (cf. also Levine 2008).

In keeping with the lines of the English poet Wilfred Owen (1984), 'Oh, Death was never enemy of ours! We laughed at him, we leagued with him, old chum,' we might assert that welcoming the awareness of death as a stimulus to life, conflict tolerance and creativity should allow us to consider Rosa's analysis as something more than the treatment of a disabling illness. Without by any means denying its attendant medico-psychiatric implications, the psychoanalyst who deals with clinical psychosis should recognize its signal quality of being an experience which is not without a certain creative component.

While Rosa's emotional explosiveness could in part be considered the expression of a constitutional or biological component of hers which laid her open to a specific containment deficit (Grotstein 2001), she seemed, psychoanalytically speaking, to approach what authors like Tustin (1981/1992) have described as an expression of the integration of autistic pockets, with the consequent outbreak of psychotic confusional states. Bria (1981), who stresses the positive developmental implications of emotional turbulence, draws a parallel between the effects of psychotic catastrophe and the benefits that the flooding of the Nile in ancient Egypt provided in terms of the harvest. Unquestionably, every acute episode led to the emergence of important insights, as well as important concrete changes in the patient's life.

In this analysand, the experience of emotions exceeded her internal containment resources: in accordance with Bion (1970), we might say that the *contained* seemed stronger than the *container*, so that the dawning of her emotions inexorably brought about an explosion in the container itself. Rosa's saying 'I've gone back to loving myself again,' just when she was beginning to show signs of collapse, is hardly surprising. Having lost its omnipotent control, her fragile ego was drawing closer to anxieties that are essential to mental growth (Freud 1926; Klein 1935/1977), despite the fact that the price was a temporary destabilization of her internal equilibrium.

The abyss of the 'deepest levels' (Matte Blanco 1988; Lombardi 2009b) that looms large in a mind still lacking the spatio-temporal functions of containment may account for Rosa's condition's not responding to traditional analytic tools such as abstractly expressed interpretations; instead, insights were generated as a result of her experience of internal contact with sensations and inchoate proto-emotions.

For my part, I found the idea of Rosa's *going back to loving herself*, when she came into the office in a confusional state, to be consistent and significant: it was no accident that during the first long years of this analysis I always found her acute phases of destabilization more significant and more helpful than the apparently 'normal' phases. Recently, Williams (2010) has maintained that periods of psychotic confusion can foster the disincorporation of an unconscious 'invasive object' which is impeding the establishment of a sense of identity. Rosa's early relationship with her parents, (for example the *mother who sees only grey*), seems to have involved non-containing internalizations – as a result of which her whole internal world was jeopardized.

Analytic *reverie* allowed Rosa to engage in the growth of her personality in the context of the analytic process, bringing into play the primitive levels that precede the formation of the psyche-soma: thus, first the repeated episodes of physical malaise and then her chaotic agitation revealed *the involvement of the body as the generator of new experience.* The body is where sensations and emotions are first experienced in their disorganized pre- and proto-symbolic form, before one can attempt representation and abstraction. Hence Rosa's psychoanalytic experience seems a good example of what I have elsewhere described as the 'body—affect—thought' progression (Lombardi 2009c): a progression which is essential, considering that in serious states of body-mind dissociation *there is no chance of repairing the dissociation except by establishing a new thinking apparatus based on the asymbolic and presymbolic germinative levels, which are bodily in nature.*

Rosa's clinical development led her to start constructing a mental space which allowed her to recognize the otherness of her analyst, as various of her statements reveal. So when Rosa recognized the passage of time in the bodily signs of my ageing, she was also speaking about her parallel, newly acquired ability to recognize her own real body, with its attendant activities of growing and ageing. In this way the body begins to be characterized by a sense of limits and can consequently be integrated into the realm of thinkability: this gives rise to a dialogue between one's body and one's mind (cf. Lombardi 2003c, 2008), which is, in my view, the starting-point of the subjective dimension. Similarly, when Rosa states, 'You are my friend, a friend in my solitude, a friend I had never found before,' she is referring also to her burgeoning capacity to see in herself a friend to be respected and tolerated, rather than an enemy to be destroyed.

Searles (1965) stresses the importance of helping the schizophrenic patient to differentiate the real perception of death from his complex and disorienting delusion. Starting from an initial vegetative and asymbolic condition, in which there was no orientation towards thought or awareness of limits, Rosa had to face her mortality so as to be able to start *thinking*. From her acceptance of this limit to life, Rosa might be able to derive *mental spectacles*, which could *place limits within her originally undifferentiated internal system*.

My task as an analyst was particularly arduous because I was continually called upon to *differentiate*, in the verbal material, *between defensive* and *perceptual orientations*: for example, I had to avoid being thrown off by her outward violence and my inevitable anxious reaction, which might lead me to consider it *destructive*, whilst it might well, instead, actually be *constructive*.

In the delusional denial of death she brought to a session, her *dead* brother was felt to be *living*, and Rosa herself was simultaneously *alive and dead*. However, this explosive moment was, at the same time, the occasion for opening the way to a working-through in which the analyst became the bearer of the non-psychotic orientation towards recognizing her brother's death and working through the mourning, thus creating the conditions for learning to *distinguish death from life* and achieve access to a real emotional life. Working out a distinction between the *atemporality of death* and the *temporality inherent in mourning and emotions* made a decisive contribution to Rosa's ability to perceive and internally acquire linear time.

The theme of the grey men and Momo gave a representative shape to the conflict between affect denial and control, on the one side, and genuinely affective and relational elements on the other. The theft of time continually perpetrated by the grey men seems like a negative depiction (Bion's *minus K*) of the loss inherent in our relationship with time: whereas time inevitably brings us face to face with loss, Rosa's psychotic theory inverted loss, transforming it into acquisition, theft.

At this point the material contains some interesting sequences, such as 'I'm alone, I'm separate from you. It's a great thing, being alone. I need a center of gravity: ears, eyes, nose, touch, taste. This is my center of gravity.' Freud (1911) stresses the importance of activating a *consciousness attached to the sense organs* as the source of mental functioning: a hypothesis that became the cornerstone of Bion's (1962) theories about learning from experience. By accepting the responsibility of activating her sense organs, Rosa was creating the conditions for an autonomous development of the ego, which could liberate her from her psychotic bondage.

The theme of the eye 'at the bottom of the sea' seems to contain a condensation reminiscent of so-called schizophrenic *organ-speech* (Freud 1915a): the symbolic function of the mind is treated as equivalent to the physical organ that represents it (the eye). Rosa is actively approaching the shapeless sea of infinite emotions in order to immerse herself in it and retrieve her eye-mind, which can allow her to emerge from the abyss of the 'dark and formless infinite' (Bion 1967) and can provide access to an ability to think in the presence of emotions (Bion 1962). Rosa's 'eye of thought' is forged – like Nothung, Siegfried's mythical sword in the *Wagnerian Nibelung* saga – in the incandescent furnace of chaos, in contact with the oceanic realm of emotions.

Rosa's statements about *Spoon River* and her future tombstone, starting with 'I'm a bastard because I don't recognize myself,' are emblematic of the correlation between *acceptance of death* and *acceptance of self*, revealing once again a tragic conflict: there is no self-acceptance without facing our ineluctable end.

> To put meaning in one's life may end in madness,
> But life without meaning is the torture
> Of restlessness and vague desire –
> It is a boat longing for the sea and yet afraid [...]
> Yet all the while I hungered for meaning in my life
> And now I know that we must lift the sail
> And catch the winds of destiny
> Wherever they drive the boat.
> ('George Gray', from E. L. Masters,
> *Spoon River Anthology*)

Notes

1 A first draft of this paper was presented at the 46th IPA Congress in Chicago in July 2009 for the *Regression and Psychosis* panel, chaired by Liliane Abensour (Paris), with, as Discussants, David Rosenfeld (Buenos Aires) and Anne Louise Silver (Washington, DC). Translated by Karen Christenfeld. Published as Lombardi, R. (2013). Death, time and psychosis. *Journal of the American Psychoanalytic Association*, 57: 691–726.

2 This emphasis on the needs bound up with mental functioning does not imply a regression to 'one-person psychology' or the obliteration of the analyst's experience, but is intended simply to place the effective focus

of the psychoanalytic working-through on levels where the patient's evolution can be fostered. From a sociological perspective, Chodorow has recently noted that 'attention to the psychoanalyst's experience and action has increased as the status of psychoanalysis has declined' (2010, p. 218): too much emphasis on the analyst can involve the risk of underestimating the patient's primary need to develop a mind of his or her own.

3 The fear of death becomes the condensation point of ontological annihilation anxieties that reach far down to pre-symbolic and pre-verbal levels. These anxieties can, for example, be faced by small children in their experience of falling asleep.

4 For the first time in his *oeuvre*, Freud introduces the idea of time as a psychotherapeutic factor when he asserts, 'It is also well worth notice that, although *mourning involves grave departures from the normal attitude to life*, it never occurs to us to regard it as a pathological condition and to refer it to medical treatment. We rely on its being *overcome after a certain lapse of time*' (1917, 243–244, my italics). It would seem that this is the ultimate source of what became the idea that if, in the psychotic's mind, time is paralyzed – as in the case of the Mad Hatter, whose pocket watch is stopped at a perpetual tea-time – no psychotherapeutic development is accessible.

5 Although Arieti (quoted by Silver 2005, p. 693) felt he had had the best results with patients who received no pharmacological therapy, I view medication as an essential integration and aid to the psychoanalytic treatment of psychoses.

6 In the myth of Oedipus and the Sphinx there is also a link between the search for knowledge and the threat of death.

7 I later discovered that Alberto Schon had written a brief and poetic essay (1985) about this book.

8 In his reformulation of the logic of the Unconscious, discovered by Freud (1900, 1915a), Matte Blanco (1988) distinguishes two basic *modes of being* which characterize human nature: *the indivisible mode of being* – to which the categories of space, time and differentiation are essentially alien, and which is ruled by symmetry, which, like an acid, cancels out every possible distinction between sensations, feelings, thoughts, objects, people, etc. – and the *heterogenic mode of being*, which always unfolds within the frame provided by the rules of classical logic – the ordered spatio-temporal logic which is the basis of all scientific development in the Western tradition. The exploration of psychosis brings us up against this basic situation of conflict, as a result of which the deepest areas of the patient are saturated with the *indivisible mode of being*, to the point where they involve a radical obstacle to any organized form of thinking and distinguishing. The psychoanalytic process promotes the integration

of the two modes of being, permitting the activation of communication and exchange between 'indivisible emotions' and differentiating rationality. The blade in her dream might correspond to the introduction of a first differentiation in the indivisible, with the resulting starting up of dialogue between emotion and reason even in the most regressive areas.

9 Freud was the first to recognize that the unconscious is not limited to repressed material. 'We recognize that the Ucs. does not coincide with the repressed; it is still true that all that is repressed is Ucs., but not all that is Ucs. is repressed' (1923, p.17). Matte Blanco (1975) develops this concept of Freud's in a way that particularly fosters the understanding of the depths of disorganization and chaos of the serious patient, for whom psychoanalysis makes possible, as he sees it, the 'unfolding' of a structurally unconscious dimension, or one that was initially foreign to the spatio-temporal organization of thought – thus a dimension that was originally adimensional or multi-dimensional (for the clinical implications of this concept cf., e.g. Kernberg 2003, 2009).

10 Although without the training of a samurai, the analyst confronts a similar situation when faced with a homicidal transference while analyzing a psychotic patient.

References

Akhtar, S. (2009). *The wound of mortality. Fear, denial and acceptance of death.* New York: Aronson.

Arieti, S. (1955). *Interpretation of schizophrenia.* New York: Brunner.

Aron, L., & Anderson, F. S. (Eds.). (2003). *Relational perspectives on the body.* New York: Other Press.

Becker, E. (1973). *The denial of death.* New York: Simon & Schuster.

Bion, W. R. (1957). Differentiation of psychotic from non–psychotic personalities. In *Second thoughts* (pp. 43–64). London: Karnac Books, 1967.

Bion, W. R. (1962). *Learning from experience.* London: Karnac Books, 1984.

Bion, W.R. (1963). *Elements of psychoanalysis.* London: Karnac Books.

Bion, W. R. (1965). *Transformations.* London: Karnac Books.

Bion, W.R. (1966). The catastrophic change. *Bulletin of the Psychoanalytic Society*, 5.

Bion, W. R. (1967). *Second thoughts.* London: Karnac Books, 1984.

Bion, W. R. (1970). *Attention and interpretation.* London: Karnac Books.

Bonaparte, M. (1940). Time and the unconscious. *International Journal of Psychoanalysis*, 21: 427–468.

Bonasia, E. (1988). Death instinct or fear of death? Research into the problem of death in psychoanalysis. *Rivista di Psicoanalisi*, 37: 272–314.

Bria, P. (1981). Catastrophe and transformations: 'Geometries' of the mind in Bion's transformational perspective. Considerations in terms of bi–logical epistemology. *Rivista di Psicoanalisi*, 27: 503–512.

Chodorow, N. J. (2010). Beyond the dyad: individual psychology, social world. *Journal of the American Psychoanalytic Association*, 58: 207–230.

De Masi, F. (2004). *Making death thinkable*. London: Free Association Books.

Ferrari, A. B. (2004). *From the eclipse of the body to the dawn of thought*. London: Free Association Books.

Freud, S. (1900). The interpretation of dreams. *Standard Edition*, 4–5.

Freud, S. (1911). Formulations on the two principles of mental functioning. *Standard Edition*, 12: 213–226.

Freud, S. (1913). The theme of the three caskets. *Standard Edition*, 12.

Freud, S. (1914). On narcissism. *Standard Edition*, 14.

Freud, S. (1915a). The unconscious. *Standard Edition*, 14: 159–215.

Freud, S. (1915b). Thoughts for the times on war and death. *Standard Edition*, 14.

Freud, S. (1916). On transience. *Standard Edition*, 14.

Freud, S. (1917). Mourning and melancholia. *Standard Edition*, 14.

Freud, S. (1920). Beyond the pleasure principle. *Standard Edition*, 18.

Freud, S. (1924a). A note upon the 'mystic writing pad'. *Standard Edition*, 19: 227–232.

Freud. S. (1924b). Neurosis and psychosis. *Standard Edition*, 19.

Freud, S. (1926). Inhibition, symptom and anxiety. *Standard Edition*, 20.

Freud, S. (1930). Civilization and its discontents. *Standard Edition*, 21.

Freud, S. (1932). New introductory lectures on psycho–analysis. *Standard Edition*, 22: 1–182.

Green, A. (1983). *Narcissisme de vie narcissisme de mort*. Paris: Editions de Minuit.

Green, A. (1986). *The dead mother. On private madness*. Madison, CT: International Universities Press.

Grotstein, J. S. (2001). A rationale for the psychoanalytically informed psychotherapy of schizophrenia and other psychoses: towards the concepts of 'rehabilitative psychoanalysis'. In P. Williams (Ed.), *A language for psychosis*. London: Whurr.

Hegel, F. (1807). *Phenomenology of spirit*. Oxford: Clarendon Press, 1977.

Heidegger, M. (1927). *Being and time*. (J. Stambaugh, Trans.). Albany: State University of New York Press, 1996.

Jaques, E. (1965). Death and the mid-life crisis. *International Journal of Psychoanalysis*, 46: 502–514.

Kant, E. (1781). *Critique of pure reason*. (Reprint translated by M. Weigelt, 2007, London: Penguin Books)

Katan, M. (1954). The importance of the non–psychotic part of the personality in schizophrenia. *International Journal of Psychoanalysis*, 35: 119–128.

Kernberg, O. F. (2003). The management of affect storms in the psychoanalytic psychotherapy of borderline patients. *Journal of the American Psychoanalytic Association*, 51: 517–544.

Kernberg, O. F. (2008). The destruction of time in pathological narcissism. *International Journal of Psychoanalysis*, 89: 299–312.

Kernberg, O.F. (2009). The destruction of time in in pathological narcissism. *Journal of the American Psychoanalytic Association*, 89: 299–312.

Klee, P. (1968). *The Diaries of Paul Klee* (F. Klee, Ed.). Berkeley: University of California Press.

Klein, M. (1935). A contribution to the psychogenesis of manic-depressive states. In *Love, guilt and reparation and other works 1921–1945*. New York: Delta, 1977.

Klein, M. (1952). The mutual influences in the development of ego and id. *Psychoanalytic Study of the Child*, 7: 51–53.

Lacan, J. (1953–54). *The seminars of Jacques Lacan: Book I. Freud's Papers on Technique* (J.-A. Miller, Ed., J. Forrester, Trans.). New York: Norton, 1991.

Lasky, R. (1990). Catastrophic illness in the analyst and the analyst's emotional reactions to it. *International Journal of Psychoanalysis*, 70: 455–473.

Levine, H.B. (2008). Mortal combat: the tragic vision of Philip Roth. *Journal of the American Psychoanalytic Association*, 56: 283–293.

Lieberman, J. S. (2000). *Body talk. Looking and being looked at in psychotherapy*. New York: Aronson.

Loewald, H.W. (1978). Instinct theory, object relations, and psychic-structure formation. *Journal of the American Psychoanalytic Association*, 26: 493–506.

Lombardi, R. (2002). Primitive mental states and the body. A personal view of Armando B. Ferrari's concrete original object. *International Journal of Psychoanalysis*, 83: 363–381.

Lombardi, R. (2003a). Mental models and language registers in the psychoanalysis of psychosis. An overview of a thirteen-year analysis. *International Journal of Psychoanalysis*, 84: 843–863.

Lombardi, R. (2003b). Knowledge and experience of time in primitive mental states. *International Journal of Psychoanalysis*, 84: 1531–1549.

Lombardi, R. (2003c). Catalyzing the dialogue between body and mind in a psychotic analysand. *Psychoanalytic Quarterly*, 72: 1017–1041.

Lombardi, R. (2005). On the psychoanalytic treatment of a psychotic breakdown. *Psychoanalytic Quarterly*, 74: 1069–1099.

Lombardi, R. (2007a). Sull'essere: dispiegamento della simmetrizzazione vita-morte. In A. Ginzburg & R. Lombardi (Eds.), *L'emozione come esperienza infinita*. Milan: Angeli.

Lombardi, R. (2007b). Shame in relation to the body, sex and death: a clinical exploration of the psychotic levels of shame. *Psychoanalytic Dialogues*, 17(3): 1–15.

Lombardi, R. (2008). The body in the analytic session: focusing on the body-mind link. *International Journal of Psychoanalysis*, 89: 89–110.

Lombardi, R. (2009a). Through the eye of the needle: the unfolding of the unconscious body. *Journal of the American Psychoanalytic Association*, 57: 61–94.

Lombardi, R. (2009b). Symmetric frenzy and catastrophic change: a consideration of primitive mental states in the wake of Bion and Matte Blanco. *International Journal of Psychoanalysis*, 90: 529–549.

Lombardi, R. (2009c). Body, affect, thought: reflections of the work of Matte Blanco and Ferrari. *Psychoanalytic Quarterly*, 78: 126–160.

Lombardi, R. (2010a). Flexibility of the psychoanalytic approach in the treatment of a suicidal patient: stubborn silences as 'playing dead'. *Psychoanalytic Dialogues*, 20: 269–284.

Lombardi, R. (2010b). The body emerging from the 'Neverland' of nothingness. *Psychoanalytic Quarterly*, 79: 879–909.

Lombardi, R. (2011). The body, feelings, and the unheard music of the senses. *Contemporary Psychoanalysis*, 47: 3–24.

Mahler, M., & Furer, M. (1968). *On human symbiosis and the vicissitudes of individuation*. New York: International Universities Press.

Marty, P. (1980). *Les mouvements individuelles de vie et de morts: Vol. 2. L'ordre psychosomatique*. Paris: Payot.

Matte Blanco, I. (1975). *The unconscious as infinite sets*. London: Karnac Books.

Matte Blanco, I. (1988). *Thinking, feeling and being*. London: Routledge.

Meissner, W.W. (2007). *Time, self and psychoanalysis*. New York: Aronson.

Meyer, J. E. (1973). *Tod und neurose*. Göttingen: Vandenhoeck & Ruprecht.

Owen, W. (1984). *The complete poems and fragments* (J. Stallworthy, Ed.). New York: W.W. Norton.

Plato. (1969). *Phaedo* (B. Jowett, Trans.). New York: Walter J. Black Editions.

Prigogine, I., & Stengers, I. (1988). *Entre le temps et l'éternité*. Paris: Fayard.

Rilke, R.M. (1923). *Duino elegies* (Reprint translated by S. Cohn, 1989, London: Carcanet Press).

Schilder, P. (1950). The image and appearance of the human body. New York: International Universities Press.

Schon, A. (1985). 'Momo' di Michael Ende o la leggenda del tempo rubato. *Rivista di Psicoanalisi*, 31: 405–406.

Searles, H.F. (1962). The differentiation between concrete and metaphorical thinking in the recovering schizophrenic patient. *Journal of the American Psychoanalytic Association*, 10: 22–49.

Searles, H.F. (1965). *Collected papers on schizophrenia and related subjects*. London: Hogarth Press.

Segal, H. (1958). Fear of death. Notes on the analysis of an old man. *International Journal of Psychoanalysis*, 39: 178–181.

Sifneos, P.E. (1973). The prevalence of 'alexithymic' characteristics in psychosomatic patients. *Psychotherapy and Psychosomatics*, 22: 255–262.

Silver, A. S. (2005). In the footsteps of Arieti and Fromm-Reichmann: psychodynamic treatments of psychosis in the current era. *Journal of the American Academy of Psychoanalysis and Dynamic Psychiatry*, 33: 689–704.

Spitz, R. (1959). A genetic field theory of ego formation. New York: International Universities Press.

Stolorow, R. D. (1979). Defensive and arrested developmental aspects of death anxiety, hypochondriasis and depersonalization. *International Journal of Psychoanalysis*, 60: 201–213.

Taylor, G.J. (1987). *Psychosomatic medicine and contemporary psychoanalysis*. Madison, CT: International Universities Press.

Tustin, F. (1981). *Autistic states in children*. London: Routledge, 1992.

von Domarus, E. (1944). The specific laws of logic in schizophrenia. In J.S. Kasanin (Ed.), *Language and thought in schizophrenia: collected papers* (pp. 101–114). Berkeley: University of California Press.

Williams, P. (2010). *Invasive objects. Minds under siege*. New York: Routledge.

Winnicott, D.W. (1947). Hate in the countertransference. In *Collected papers: through paediatrics to psycho-analysis*. London: Tavistock, 1958.

Winnicott, D. W. (1953). Mind and its relation to the psyche-Soma. In *Collected papers: through paediatrics to psycho-analysis*. London: Tavistock, 1958.

Winnicott, D. W. (1958). The capacity to be alone. In *The maturational processes and the facilitating environment*. London: Hogarth Press, 1965.

Winnicott, D. W. (1971). *Playing and reality*. London: Tavistock.

Winnicott, D. W. (1974). Fear of breakdown. *International Review of Psycho-Analysis*, 1: 103–107.

Index

257